SPURN LIFEBOAT STATION - THE FIRST HUNDRED YEARS

THE HISTO

LIFEBOAT STA 310

TO MAY 1911

ROY BENFELL

Published by Roy Benfell
3 Maple Grove, Garden Village,
Hull HU8 8PL

First Published 1994

Front Cover: Wreck of the Transport Ship "Tomas", by John Ward
Photo taken by David Forth and reproduced with the kind permission of Ferens Art Gallery, Hull City Museums, Art Galleries and Archives.

ISBN 0 9523467 0 2

Produced by
Burstwick Print & Publicity Services
Hull

ACKNOWLEDGMENTS

This history could not have been written without the help of a number of people.

The author wishes to thank the Wardens, Brethren and staff of Trinity House, Kingston-upon-Hull, for their kind permission to work with the original documents from the archive connected with the lifeboat station and for their constant interest and encouragement : Captain D.C.Thomas, Harbour Master, Humber, (now retired), for his kind permission to work with original documents from the archive of the Humber Conservancy Board; the staff of the Local History Department of the Hull Central Library; the staff of Humberside County Records Office, Beverley; Mr.A.Credland, Keeper of the Maritime Museum, Kingston-upon-Hull; all those people who generously loaned postcards and photographs and allowed them to be copied and used - all are honoured individually along with the photographs. Dr. T.W. Carman for his computer expertise in turning this text into a form suitable for the printer.

Where documents are quoted directly all the original punctuation and spellings have been retained.

All proceeds from the sale of this book are for the Humber Lifeboat Appeal and the RNLI.

CONTENTS

ESTABLISHING THE STATION

Spurn Head is a long, narrow peninsula made of sand and shingle, curving south-westwards into the Humber estuary from the Holderness coast. The peninsula is some three miles in length, less than twenty yards wide at its narrowest point and rises little more than twenty feet above sea level. Wave action removes material from the soft boulder clay of Holderness Plain, washes it southwards and wind action piles up the dry sand into the spit. The sand is anchored by the roots of sea-buckthorn and marram grass. Further extension southwards is limited by the position of the deep water channel of the Humber very close to the tip of the peninsula and the strong river and tidal currents.

Within the Humber estuary and just off its mouth in the North Sea are many extensive banks of sand and mud. These, along with Spurn Head itself, are constantly changing and presenting hazards to shipping in the area. This has been a busy shipping region for hundreds of years, with routes from Hull, Grimsby and Immingham crossing the north - south coastal shipping lanes and the whole picture complicated by whaling, and more recently, fishing boats and ferries.

There have been lights at or near Spurn Point - the southern tip of the peninsula - since the fifteenth century to warn shipping of the dangers, but the sand banks and storms have taken a heavy toll of vessels of all types. The waters can quickly become very confused and rough when the out-flowing river is met by an incoming tide and there is any sort of wind blowing. One such occurrence started the process of establishing a lifeboat station on Spurn.

A newspaper paragraph in 1802 suggesting the establishment of a lifeboat station at Spurn prompted Henry Greathead to write to Trinity House, Hull, in October of that year offering to build a lifeboat for Spurn, but no action was taken. On March 7th 1803 Mr.James Iveson of Hedon also wrote to Trinity House, Hull, urging the establishment of a lifeboat station at Spurn after an incident involving the loss of a ship and its crew. He referred to this tragedy again in a second letter accompanying a donation to Trinity House on November 8th 1810. Part of the letter is quoted below :-

"I therefore think it proper to explain that I am not influenced by motives of ostentation, but by a clear conviction that the Establishment of a Life-Boat at the Spurn, will be the certain means of saving the lives of many of our fellow creatures, and of preventing the recurrence of catastrophes the most distressing which the human mind can imagine. This conviction is not the fabrication of imaginary circumstances, or of analogous reasoning, but is the natural result arising from the knowledge of one simple fact, which is plain to the meanest capacities; and it was under the impression of this conviction, that I ventured some years ago to propose to the Trinity House, the Establishment of a LIFE-BOAT at the SPURN. When a ship takes the ground upon the Shoals called the Stoney Beach, an accident which frequently occurs, the tide gradually leaves her in apparent safety, and the crews, if strangers, imagine that on the return of the tide, the ship will ride off without further damage or danger. The people on shore, from constant experience, know, that on the return of the tide, the conflict between it and the current of the Humber occasions such a surf, that the ship will inevitably beat to pieces, and the crew perish. Yet the people on shore have no means of affording help to the mariners, or even of communicating to them, though within a comparatively short distance, the peril of their situation, so that the mariners might, in many cases, find safety in their own boats. Thus the mariners wait with patient confidence, and the people on shore with the most distressing anxiety, till the awful period arrives - when the ship is lost, and the people perish. Numberless instances of this sort can be recited by the inhabitants on the coast, and one in particular, not very many years ago, when a large ship was placed precisely in this situation, and after remaining from the ebb to the flood tide, went to pieces, and the crew, consisting of thirteen, all sunk to rise no more, in sight of many spectators."

Trinity House replied saying that the matter had been considered by the Board but because of the problems of isolation, lack of men to provide a crew, and cost, the matter had been dropped. However, it was now felt that these problems could be overcome and that Trinity House was prepared "to lend its aid and assistance in carrying the plan into effect."

For some unknown reason no action was taken by the Trinity House, nor any other authority until another letter was sent to the Trinity House in Hull on April 7th 1810. On that date Mr.William Iveson, the Agent of Mr.Francis Constable of Burton Constable, wrote on his behalf urging the establishment of a lifeboat station at Spurn and making generous offers of practical help towards that end. Parts of the letter are quoted :-

"Gentlemen,

The frequent distresses which happen to Navigation off the coast of Holderness, and particularly near the mouth of the Humber, and the total shipwrecks which too often ensue, have induced Mr.Constable to attempt the establishment of a Life-boat at the Spurn. Towards this end he has obtained the shell of the building lately used as a Barracks for the officer and soldiers stationed there before the Batteries were dismantled. This building Mr.Constable proposes to fit up for the residence of the master of the Boat, with a suitable apartment for receiving and lodging the sailors who may be brought on shore. Mr.Constable will also provide and fit up all necessary out-buildings for this establishment, and will also erect a new and suitable building for the Life-boat and her Carriage, as soon as he is informed of the dimensions necessary for the purpose. Mr.Constable will also engage twelve able men, to be always ready as a boat's crew, and will also provide the means of a livelihood for the master of the Boat ...."

"Mr.Constable having no immediate interest in shipping or mercantile concerns, and being influenced solely by motives of humanity, believes that the expense he thus engages to sustain, and the efforts he has made, and proposes to continue, for the maintenance of this Establishment, will be thought ample on his part. For the rest, he looks to the commercial and shipping interests at Hull. When the wealth and number of persons to be interested in this undertaking are considered, the expense of the Boat and Carriage seems to be a very trifling object ..."

"It is Mr.Constable's desire that the master of the Boat should be chosen and recommended to him by the Trinity House and that the navigation of the Boat, and every thing relating to the conduct of her, should be guided by Rules dictated by that Body."

Further letters included more detailed proposals and slightly modified some of the outlines included in the first proposal. The Barracks - a modest building - was to be converted into a tavern to be run by the master of the lifeboat. There would be accommodation for his family, provision for a dozen rescued sailors to be housed and a room where hammocks could be slung to provide sleeping space for the lifeboat crew. As well as running the tavern the master was to be allowed to sell provisions to ships, general goods and food. As it was estimated that at least five hundred ships called at Spurn each year for gravel or fishing or with visitors the master was expected to make at least one hundred pounds a year. In all matters not relating to the lifeboat the master was to be responsible to Mr. Constable, and "should his conduct become such as to be injurious to Mr. Constable's interests he must expect Mr. Constable will remove him."

Mr. Constable's offer was gratefully accepted by the Trinity House and a boat was ordered from Henry Greathead of South Shields. It was thirty feet in length, ten feet beam and three feet six inches deep amidships. It rowed ten oars and as it could be rowed in either direction without being turned it needed a man at each end "to steer her and to be ready at the opposite end to take the steer Oar when wanted." The boat was painted white on the outside as this was thought to make the boat more easily visible to people in distress and had the words "Spurn Lifeboat" in black lettering. This was true of all the Spurn boats before the station was taken over by the RNLI. The cost of the Boat was one hundred and ninety seven pounds. A carriage for the boat, with sixteen feet diameter wheels, was ordered locally from G & W Boyd of Hull at a cost of fifty pounds. A subscription list was opened in June 1810 with the Corporation of Trinity House, Hull, the Corporations of the Town of Hull and the Dock Company each giving fifty guineas and Lloyds Coffee House, London, fifty pounds, along with many other smaller donations. The combined costs of the lifeboat and carriage were easily met.

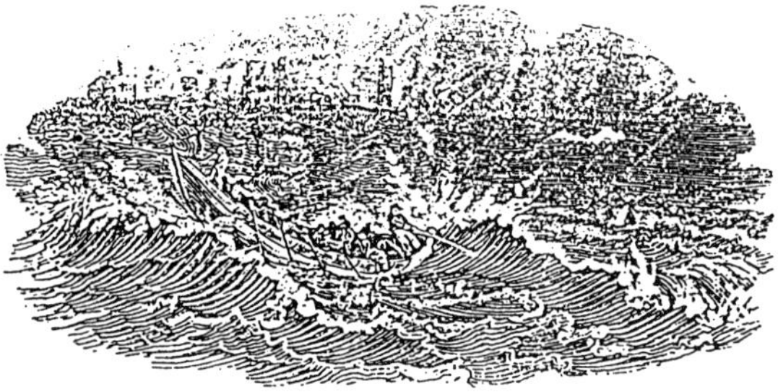

DESCRIPTION, AND INSTRUCTIONS FOR THE MANAGEMENT

OF THE

LIFE-BOAT,

Built and Invented by Henry Greathead, of South Shields;

IN THE COUNTY OF DURHAM.

THE BOATS in general of this description are painted white on the outside, this colour more immediately relieving the eye of the spectator at her rising from the hollow of the sea, than any other; the bottom of the Boat is at first varnished (which will take paint afterwards), for the more minute inspection of purchasers; the Oars she is equiped with are made of Fir of the best quality, having found by experience that a rove Ash Oar, that will dress clean and light, is too pliant amongst the breakers; and when made strong and heavy, from rowing double banked the purchase being short, sooner exhausts the rower, which makes the Fir Oar, when made stiff, more preferable.

IN the management of the Boat she requires twelve men to man her; that is five men on each side rowing double banked, with an Oar slung over an Iron Thole with a Grumet (as provided) so as to enable the rower to pull either way, and one man at each end to steer her, and to be ready at the opposite end to take the steer Oar when wanted. As from the construction of the Boat she is always in a position to be rowed either way, without turning the Boat, when man'd the person who steers her should be well acquainted with the course of the tides, in order to take every possible advantage; the best method, if the direction will admit of it, is to head the sea. The Steersman should keep his eye fixed upon the wave or breaker, and encourage the rowers to give way as the Boat rises to it, being then aided by the force of the Oars she launches over it with vast rapidity, without shipping any water. It is necessary to observe that there is often a strong reflux of sea, occasioned by the stranded wrecks, which requires both dispatch and care in the people employed that the Boat be not damaged; when the wreck is reached, if the wind blows to the land, she will come on shore without any other effort than steering.

I would strongly recommend practising the Boat, by which means, with experience, the danger will appear less from the confidence the people will have in the Boat.

Henry Greathead.—

South Shields, Oct. 13, 1802.—

☞ *This may be rendered of more utility, by being posted in some conspicuous place, for the perusal of such people as are likely to be employed in the Boat.*

North Shields: Printed by W. Barnes.

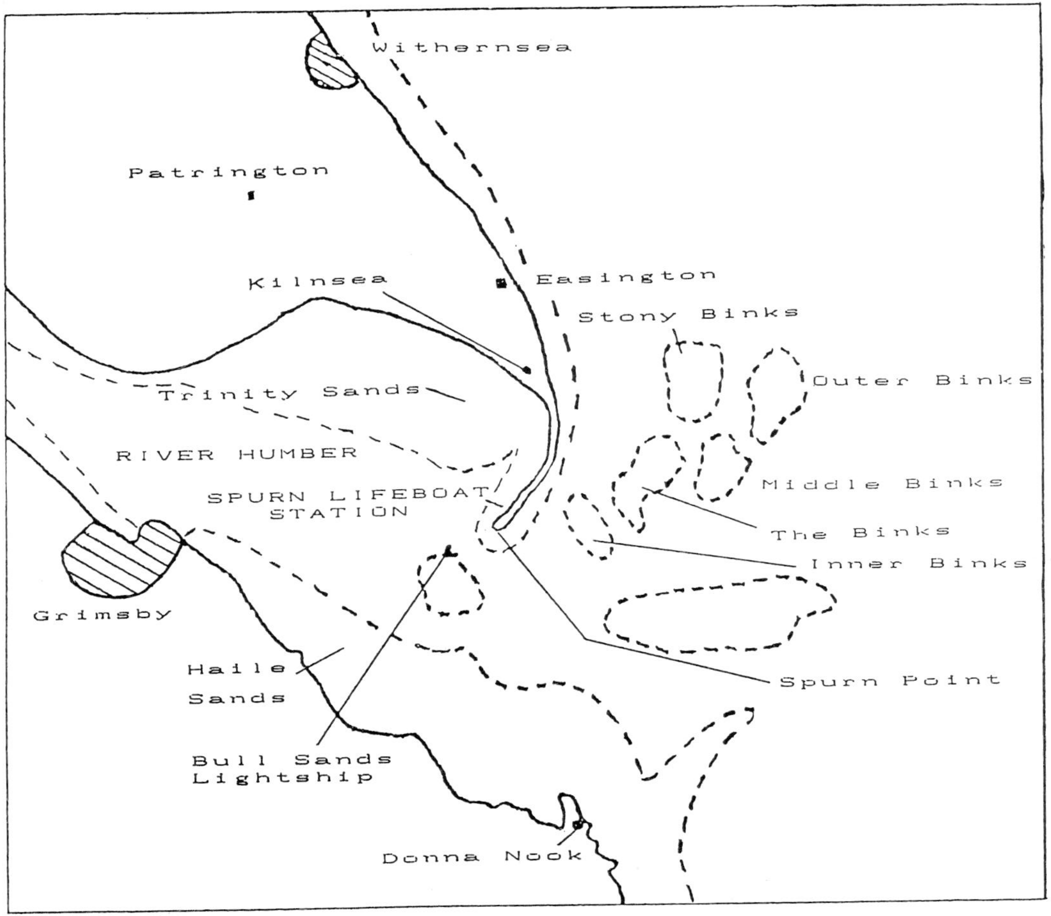

LOWER HUMBER ESTUARY

Trinity House advertised the post of Master of the Life Boat and candidates were interviewed in July and on 14th July 1810 John Coulter, Master Mariner of Kingston upon Hull, was appointed Master and Robert Richardson, Mariner of Kingston upon Hull, was appointed Mate of the Life Boat. Within a month John Coulter had vanished from the scene, never having served, and Robert Richardson was appointed Master on 25th August 1810 and was to hold the position for thirty one years. If Richardson's income from the Tavern did not reach one hundred pounds a year the deficit would be made up by Mr. Constable. A month after being appointed Richardson applied to Mr. Constable for a loan of sixty pounds, against his expected income, to be able to furnish the Tavern. Two years later the debt had not been cleared and Mr. Iveson wrote to Trinity House, saying

"when the Corporation chose and sent down a Master it might have been hoped that they would have chosen a man who had a capital sufficient to carry on the business of a publican .... but contrary to this, the Master chosen by the Trinity House was wholly without capital..."

The reply from Trinity House said, in reference to Mr. Constable's proposals

"this House did everything therein required of them and that the Master of the Life Boat having no Capital was no part of the consideration with them, his abilities to perform the service was their object, and which will govern the Board in their choice when a successor is required."

On October 2nd 1810 the Brig 'Thomas' left South Shields with the new lifeboat in tow and arrived in Hull several days later. The lifeboat was on display until the end of the month when it was taken to Spurn to be ready for service.

During September 1809 Mr. Constable had found eleven men willing to form a crew for the lifeboat and this group was added to by October 1810. When the lifeboat was stationed at Spurn the men were expected to practise in the boat and initially they were paid three shillings and sixpence for each day's practice. This system of payment did not continue for very long and it had certainly stopped by the time the first cottages were built for the crew at Spurn.

On November 14th 1810 the first crew was selected from the volunteers and on November 15th the first service was performed. Richardson sent the following report to Trinity House and to Mr. Iveson:-

"Sir I have the Honour to transmit to you an account of the proceedings of the Life Boat on Wednesday a ship called the John and Charlotte of Newcastle - Captain John Clark - came into the Humber waterlogged - 11 feet water in her hold. She would not answer her helm but run ashore on trinity sand. Myself and fourteen of the crew belonging to the Life Boat went on Wednesday morning to her assistance notwithstanding the Crew was but chosen the day before they behaved with great courage and used every exertion to get her off though without any hope of success. At length we got her off on Thursday night but was obliged to run her ashore on Clea Sand she having made nine feet of water in her hold from trinity to Clea sand notwithstanding all our efforts at the pumps. We expected her going down every moment but I am happy to say through the valiant exertions of the Life Boat Crew we got her to Grimsby on friday morning. The Crew belonging to the ship would not lend any assistance whatever notwithstanding the ship was expected to founder every moment. Captain Clark behaved extremely well to my Crew."

Richardson was obviously well satisfied with the performance of the crew during this first service.

Initially horses were kept at Spurn to be used when launching and recovering the lifeboat, but it was very quickly realised that the boat was too heavy to be dragged across the large expanse of sand and mud at all times other than high tide. The lifeboat was, therefore, kept afloat and a lighter tender which could be manhandled was kept in the boat shed and the horses were disposed of. This emphasised the problem of isolation. Although there was space for the crew to sleep at the Tavern the men lived with their families at Kilnsea and Easington some four miles away and they were not always on Spurn, even during the day. The lifeboat could not be launched until a crew had been mustered and Richardson, when possible, sent a man to gather together the crew, but this was not always possible.

In his report on the second service on 21st November 1810 when a sloop called the "Young John", from London, had lost its topmast and rudder in a storm and run ashore and was taken to Grimsby by the lifeboat, Richardson said he found it "very inconvenient not having a horse kept here constantly for the purpose of going for the men in cases of necessity for it will be impossible for a man to go fast enough on foot in extreme cases especially if the wind be in his face.

The man that went for the crew was very ill from the violent exertions he made to get the hands down. In night time it will be still worse."

A system of signals was developed where by Richardson would hoist a flag by day and burn a tar barrel at night to try to attract the attention of the people in the villages. This was an improvement but still caused long delays before the lifeboat could be launched.

The crewmen were employed loading ships with gravel and cobbles from the beaches, but at night time and when it was not possible to work, the men went home to their families. During 1811 some of the men refused to go to Spurn to keep watch

RULES and REGULATIONS

TO BE OBSERVED AT SPURN

By the Captain and Crew

OF

The Life-Boat.

TRINITY-HOUSE, KINGSTON-UPON-HULL.

THIS HOUSE having, with the Assistance of a Liberal Subscription from the Public at large, caused Cottages to be erected at SPURN, for the Accommodation of the CREW of the LIFE-BOAT, require that the said Crew shall live amicably amongst themselves, and be at all times ready and willing to afford every Assistance in their power to those Ships and Vessels which may stand in need thereof: And as a further encouragement to their residence and good conduct there, the said Crew will be allowed to live Rent Free for the first Year.

Rules and Regulations.

AS an inducement to the permanent residence of the Boat's Crew at SPURN, and for their encouragement to habits of Industry, *Francis Constable*, Esquire, the Lord of the Manor, gives them the exclusive preference of the Laborage on all Gravel and Cobble Stones, shipped or [illegible]n on board any description of Vessels whatever, at SPURN; and [illegible] *Fewson*, who is *Mr. Constable's* Coast-Bailiff for the District, which includes the SPURN, and conducts the Gravel and Cobble Business, is directed to see that the Crew of the Life-Boat have all the Work or Laborage of such Gravel and Cobbles, if they can possibly perform it; and he is not on any Account to allow any Extra or other Men to be employed thereat, unless the number of Vessels at any one time in want of Gravel and Cobbles, be greater than the Crew of the Life-Boat can dispatch.

ROBERT RICHARDSON, the present Master of the Life-Boat, (and every subsequent Master) is invested with the full Command of the Boat's Crew, whenever it is necessary to call them together, for the purpose of rendering Assistance with the Boat, or for any other cause relating to her.

The Crew of the Life-Boat is to consist of Eleven Men, (exclusive of the Captain) who shall participate in all the Benefits, Rewards, and Emoluments arising from the Services of the Boat.

The Captain and Crew of the Boat, are on all occasions to use their utmost Endeavours, in the first place, to save the Lives of the Crews of such Ships and Vessels as may unfortunately be driven on the Outer or Inner Banks, or on Shore elsewhere in the neighbourhood of SPURN; their subsequent care only is to be the preservation of the Cargoes and Ships; but in no case whatever is the Life-Boat to be made use of for the purpose of carrying out Anchors or Cables, unless the greatest necessity exists for so doing.

The Captain and Crew of the Boat are strictly enjoined not to make any Charge for their Services with the Boat, but to leave all matters of Salvage or Remuneration to the decision of the TRINITY-HOUSE.

Whenever the Boat is made use of, the Captain is to see her afterwards properly Housed and taken care of.

Any of the Crew of the Life-Boat whom the Captain may dismiss for Disobedience to his Orders relating to the said Boat, or for Misconduct therein, *Mr. Fewson* will not, on any account, permit or [illegible] to be again employed at SPURN, either as an Extra Man or in any other Capacity whatever.

The Captain of the Boat when he thinks proper to Work at Loading the Vessels with Gravel and Cobble Stones, shall share equally with the Crew, otherwise, it is directed he shall not demand any thing therefrom.

The Captain of the Boat is moreover required to be sober, watchful, and at all times ready and diligent in the performance of his Duty: he must keep a regular Journal of the Wind and Weather, the Situation of the Pilot Cutters, with their Numbers; as also any other Occurrences connected with his Office; and when required, make his Report thereof to this House.

The Captain of the Boat is also, when necessary, to direct the Crew to keep Watch in the Night; and to enforce and put in practice these Rules and Regulations, and cause a Copy thereof to be placed in each Cottage, as well as in some conspicuous part of his own House.

The Captain of the Boat is moreover, if required by *Mr. Constable*, on no account to take any Man into his Service, without a proper Certificate of the Place of his Settlement.

William Rawson, Printer of the Advertiser, Lowgate, Hull.

and the Easington men told Richardson that if there was any sea running he could take the boat out himself. Richardson requested permission to reduce the number of men in the Life Boat Company to twelve, the number required to man the boat, "as the Easington men owing to the Distance could never be had to assist the Boat when wanted."

In many of the existing reports of services up to 1819 Richardson made reference to the difficulty of mustering the crew and the delay this caused, but in April 1816 a letter was sent from Trinity House to Mr. Constable concerning the building of cottages at Spurn for the crew and their families. Mr. Constable was slightly hesitant because of the terms under which he owned the land and because of his increasing age, but he did agree to lease to Trinity House some land on Spurn on which cottages could be built. He asked for a nominal rent for the whole parcel of land of seven shillings per annum. However it was not until December 1818 that a lease was drawn up and signed. A public subscription list was opened to meet the estimated cost of eight hundred pounds - the Dock Company and the Mayor and Aldermen of Hull declined to contribute - and the cottages were built and occupied by October 1819 and a plaque was set up bearing the following words -

"AD 1819 these Cottages were Erected by Public Subscription under the Direction of the Trinity House of Kingston upon Hull on Ground Granted for that purpose by Francis Constable Esquire for the accommodation of the Crew of the Life Boat stationed here; Whose Services in the laudable endeavour to save from destruction, both the lives and property of their fellow Creatures in the hour of Peril, have been fully acknowledged by the Liberality of the Contributors hereto.

Francis Hall)
Wardens."
John Thackray)

With the crew now resident at Spurn one major problem had been overcome and launches could now be made much more quickly. The lifeboat community was now permanently established at Spurn and a pattern of life began to evolve.

Overleaf: Spurn, possibly in the 1920's, clearly showing the remains of the original lifeboat cottages to the left. *Courstesy of Miss V. Cross*

EARNING A LIVING

The main source of income for the lifeboat crew was loading ships with gravel and cobbles from the beaches. Initially they were paid four shillings and sixpence per tide's work, but this was reduced to three shillings and sixpence. For this the men had to dig the material from the beach, riddle it and load up baskets which were hauled on board, or fill wheelbarrows which were pushed up planks onto the ships. The system of payment was changed and the men were paid for the amount of material loaded. This averaged about one shilling per ton, and had to be shared between all the men working.

Sloops collecting gravel on the Binks. Early 1900's. *Courtesy of Mr.&Mrs. J. Gell*

Mr. Constable ordered that the lifeboat men should have "full preference and priority" in the loading of gravel and cobbles from the Spurn beaches, not from other areas, and that no other men should be employed unless there was more work than the lifeboat men could cope with. He also ordered that no man dismissed from the lifeboat could ever be employed again at the gravel trade. Other men - referred to by the lifeboat crew as the Countrymen or farmers - were employed at the gravel trade and they strongly resented the privileges given to the lifeboat crew and over the next forty years there were serious confrontations between the two groups. Matters were made worse by some captains asking for the Countrymen to load the ships in preference to the lifeboat crew.

Gravel working on the Binks. *Courtesy of Easington School*

On December 28th 1811 Richardson wrote to Trinity House -

"Yesterday the 27th George Nixon Master and owner of the Dove, in Mr. Woodmansey's employ laid on for a load of Gravel. He had sent for the Easington men to come to load him. The Boat Company having come down I went on the Beach and told him he should not have any Gravel without he employed my men, which he gave his consent to, but when they had done he told them he would not pay them. I went down on the Beach and demanded their Wages, which he refused to give me. He told me he should pay the Easington men as he had sent for them and William Wilson took up his gun which was loaded. He pointed at me and swore he would shoot me, which I verily believe he would have carried his threat into execution had there not been many spectators and he was backed in it by William Clapham, Robert Bird, Thomas Bird, John Ransom. I would have taken the gun from Wilson but the above men all swore they would fall on me if I touched him so that I am in Danger of my Life from them. There is three of them which always brings guns with them to Spurn, which is William Wilson, Robert Bird, Thomas Bird, which if they are suffered to do I am confident my Life will fall a sacrifice the first opportunity."

SPURN LIFE BOAT.

TRINITY-HOUSE, HULL,
24th December, 1839.

WHEREAS, on the establishment of the Life Boat at Spurn, in the year 1810, in order to induce the permanent residence of the Boat's Crew there, the late Francis Constable, Esq. deceased, the then Lord of the Manor, gave them the exclusive preference of the Labourage on all Gravel and Cobble Stones, shipped or laden on board any description of Vessels whatever at Spurn; and the Coast Bailiff appointed by Mr. Constable for the District which includes the Spurn, and who conducted the Gravel and Cobble business, was directed to see that the Crew of the Life Boat had all the Work or Labourage of such Gravel and Cobbles if they could possibly perform it, and he was not to allow any extra or other men to be employed thereat, unless the number of Vessels at any one time in want of Gravel and Cobbles was greater than the Crew of the Life Boat could despatch.

And Whereas the valuable privilege conferred on the Crew of the Life Boat, as above-mentioned, has been, and is now, continued by Sir Thomas Aston Clifford Constable, Baronet, the present Lord of the Manor.

And Whereas much insubordination and disorderly conduct has taken place between the Crew of the Life Boat and the Extra Men employed from time to time by the Agent of the Lord of the Manor, in the loading of Vessels with Gravel and Cobbles, and much dissatisfaction has prevailed amongst the Owners of such Vessels, as to the mode and manner in which they are so loaded. NOW FOR REMEDY of the inconveniences complained of, and as a means of ensuring good order and conduct on the part of the Crew of the Life Boat in future, at all times, during their employment in the business aforesaid.

THIS CORPORATION DOTH HEREBY STRICTLY ORDER AND DIRECT—

That the Crew of the said Life Boat, and every individual thereof, shall from henceforth work at and load with Gravel and Cobbles the Vessels resorting to Spurn for that purpose, in such routine and turn, and in such manner and way, and at such time and times, as the Agent of Sir Thomas Aston Clifford Constable, or any Sub-Agent by him to be appointed for the purpose, shall direct and appoint. And in case of neglect or disobedience to the proper and reasonable orders and directions of such Agent or Sub-Agent, the party or parties neglecting or disobeying such orders and directions shall, on conviction thereof to the satisfaction of this Corporation, be immediately dismissed from the service of the Life Boat, and from the Cottage or residence provided for him or them at Spurn.

By order,

WM. BUNNEY,

Mr. Constable employed a Coast Bailiff who was responsible for managing the gravel trade and maintaining the privileges given to the lifeboat crew. Mr. John Fewson was bailiff when the lifeboat station was established and he was succeeded by Mr. Child. Although Mr. Fewson controlled the trade, the lifeboat crew were under the command of Mr. Richardson and there were constant complaints from the men to Trinity House. The crew stated that the Countrymen were taking work away from them by physical force. They described gangs of thirty or forty men at a time fighting the lifeboat crew to take the work. In December 1839 Trinity House issued new instructions which placed the lifeboat crew under the direction of the Coast Bailiff as far as the gravel trade was concerned. This was an attempt to solve the problem, but it failed. The crew complained that both Mr. Fewson and Mr. Child favoured the Countrymen, as in a letter of 1839 -

"by the Life Boat Rules Mr. Child is to see that we have all the work at Gravel and Cobbles that we can do: we have complained to him but he takes no notice of us and encourages his own Men."

Every time a complaint was received by Trinity House it was passed on to Mr. Iveson before any action was taken. On one occasion Mr. Iveson wrote that the lifeboat men had no right to work at cobbles, only gravel, but Trinity House quickly referred him to Mr. Constable's instructions. On all other occasions documented, except two, Mr. Iveson found reason to excuse the Countrymen and dismiss all claims against Mr. Fewson and Mr. Child. One exception he decided was a case of equal blame and for the other he said that if the lifeboat men thought they had a case they could take the Countrymen to court.

As time went by the supply of material diminished as more was taken away than could be replaced by the sea. This in turn led to increased tension between the two groups. In 1850 Spurn was breached by the sea and the Admiralty took control and limited the removal of gravel or shingle to specific areas, following a survey. On 11th November 1850 Michael Hansley Welburn, the Master of the Lifeboat, wrote the following to Trinity House -

"This day being fine weather two vessels went out to load at Sea Side, when our Crew followed them to Kilnsea and got on board the sloop Chance Beacock. Got all the tools in readiness, putting handles to the Baskets ready to start work when the Easington workmen came down and demanded the vessel saying Mr. Child ordered that the Life Boat Men should not work any more at loading vessels as our House (Trinity House, Hull) and the admiralty had taken the power of the beach out of Sir Clifford's hands and that the Easington and Kilnsea people should not be starved out by the Life Boat's Crew's interference.

Opposite shows a OS Map of 1855 showing a breach in the peninsula

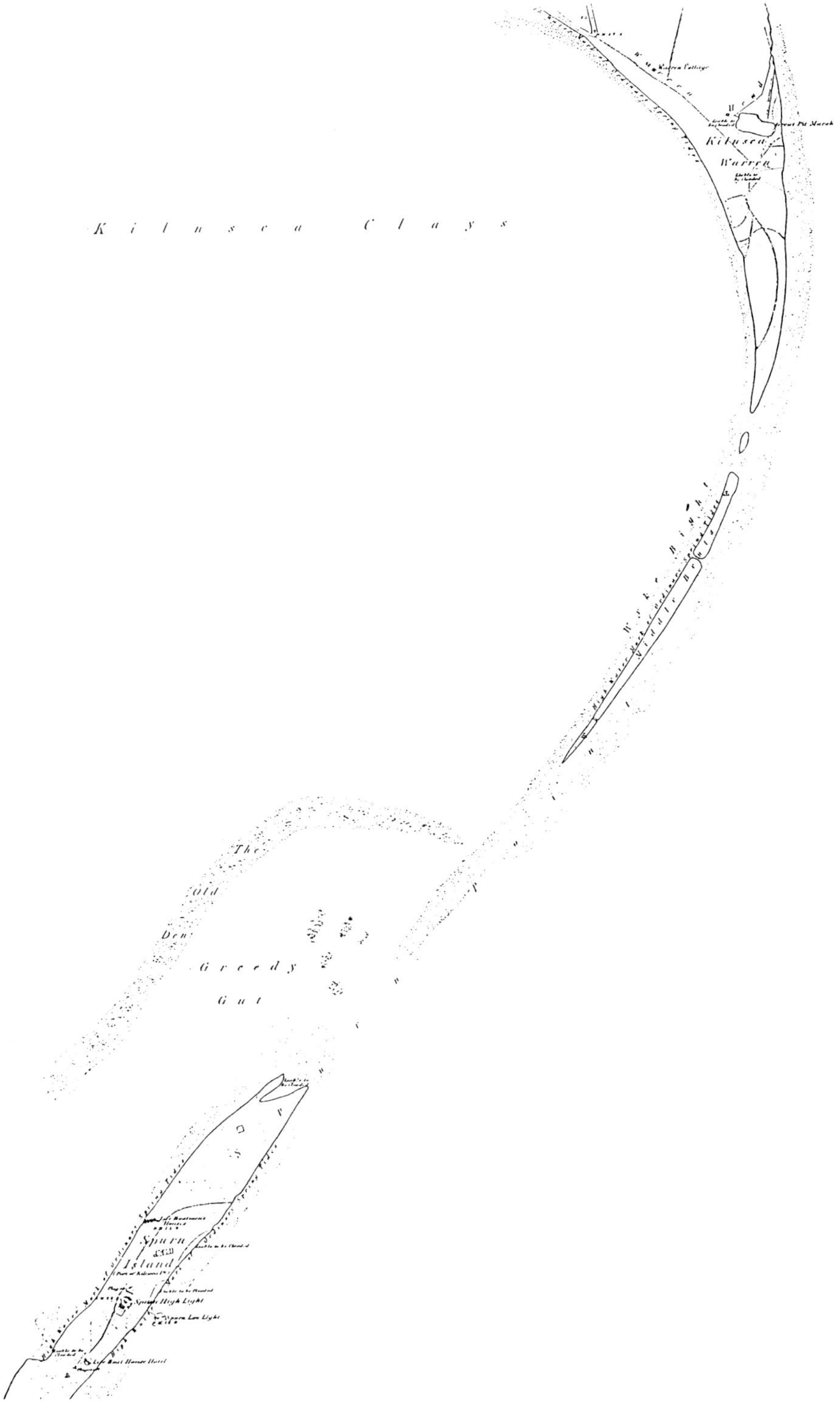

Warren Cottage
Great Pit Marsh
Kilnsea Warren
Kilnsea Clays
The Old Den
Greedy Gut
Spurn Island
Spurn High Light
Spurn Low Light
Life Boat House Hotel

Our Men went up to Mr. Child's house to know the reasons as by our printed rules, he was the man to see our people had the work to see if they could accomplish it. His reply was he should not trouble himself any more on our behalf and would not allow us to work any more. The Mate asked three times for a document from his Lord which he refused to give. Gentlemen the greatest enmity dwells in the feeling of the Country Men (and not less in Mr. Child)....Appealing for your benevolent protection. Our Mens last weeks earnings was four shillings and sixpence each."

With the decline in material so there was also a decline in earnings. There were many weeks when the men earned nothing at all from the gravel trade, nor from salvage, and life became very hard. In November 1843 a letter signed by every member of the crew and the Master was sent to Trinity House asking for relief -

"we are compelled to ask you for a little necessary relief for we have only just made a bare living all last summer and for this last five or six weeks we have not averaged above four shillings and sixpence per week so that we cannot support our families and unless we have some relief we shall be compelled to apply to our parishes."

Trinity House replied by asking for a statement of savings. Later a statement of earnings was asked for and for the twelve months this was thirty four pounds, fourteen shillings and three halfpence. Out of this one pound was needed to pay the rent for the cottage and taxes, leaving the families with about thirteen shillings and fourpence per week. No relief was given on that occasion and the Master was asked to send monthly statements of earnings.

Over the following years there were frequent appeals for relief, some signed by the whole crew, some from individuals and some from the Master. Relief was granted from time to time, but not constantly, and the amount varied, but averaged five shillings a week for husband and wife, one shilling a week for each child under fourteen years of age, and three shillings and sixpence a week for a single man. The crew complained that all goods were 15% more expensive at Spurn than in the towns and they could not afford coals, food and clothing. In December 1850 the crew members were awarded some money for salvage work on a wreck and Trinity House wanted to retain a proportion of the money in a reserve fund. Every member of the crew wrote to Trinity House asking for the full award or they would resign, and the money was paid.

The gravel trade continued to decline, the breaches in Spurn became wider and in November 1854 the Admiralty imposed a complete ban on the removal of material of any kind from the beaches of Spurn Head. An appeal was lodged with the Admiralty, but refused. Work could still continue on the Binks, but the lifeboat crew had no privileges there and earnings became even more meagre.

George Grant, the Master of the lifeboat, wrote to Trinity House on June 23rd 1855. Life had been very difficult for the crew and their families, and they were all threatening to leave Spurn, three men having already left. Grant wrote -

"I have called them all together and they have agreed to stay in their situations if you will allow them sufficient money to buy materials for the fishing business. The work that they was employed at was finished last Tuesday and there is no more prospect of any more work on the Island so that there is no other prospect but the fishing. As the fishing season is fast spending it is requisite for the men to be at work as soon as possible, so perhaps you will oblige with an early answer, as it will take some time to get the materials together. You will remember what you said when you was at Spurn respecting advancing the men the money and that is what the men is depending on."

Trinity House loaned some money to Grant for fishing gear and he was able to buy nets at Patrington, but there were no fishing boats for sale, nor could he find any men "that is agreeable to come to Spurn without there is a prospect of getting a living."

A fishing boat was found but the lifeboat men were not free to fish anywhere. They could only work where established fishermen did not fish, and more men left Spurn. On September 15th 1855 Grant wrote to Trinity House saying that only five men remained at Spurn - not enough to man the lifeboat - and continued -

"I have tried to get some fishermen and have had many promises but none of them have come so I think it will be the best for you to advertise for some."

The Brethren not only advertised for crew members, but also decided to pay each man the sum of ten pounds per annum. This was on top of a share in the fishing and salvage, and with a house at a rent of only one shilling per month it was hoped to attract more crew members.

One month later on October 16th 1855 Grant again wrote to Trinity House

"I am directed by the Life Boat Crew to acquaint you that one of them has left and the others have determined to leave as they cannot get nothing like a living. They have tried the fishery but there is no fish to catch within the limits that the smack is allowed to go and they cannot stay here to hunger..... it is impossible for thirteen shares to get anything like a living without some alteration."

By the end of October permission was given for the fishing boat to sail as far north as Flamborough Head, but not beyond it, and southwards from the mouth of the Humber as far as the light on Spurn could be seen. This must surely have presented problems had the lifeboat been required on service.

WANTED
FIVE
FISHERMEN

TO SUPPLY THE PRESENT VACANCIES IN THE

CREW OF THE LIFE BOAT

STATIONED AT SPURN POINT.

Each man will be allowed after the rate of Ten Pounds per Annum, and to have the occupation of one of the Cottages at Spurn at a rent of One Shilling per Month, and also to share in the Earnings of a Fishing Smack and Boats, which are used in collecting Buoyage, in fishing at the entrance of the Humber, and in rendering Salvage Services to Ships in distress.

Application to be made in person or by letter at the Warden's Clerk's Office, in the Trinity House, at Hull, where further Particulars may be known.

BY ORDER,

EDWARD S. WILSON,

SECRETARY.

Trinity House,
Hull, 18th Sept., 1855.

On November 27th 1855 Grant asked Trinity House to advertise for five more men. One had never been replaced, two had been dismissed for bad conduct and two had been drowned on service. Earnings continued to be minimal and relief was allowed by Trinity House. In April 1856 there were only four crew members, plus the mate and master, left at Spurn and Trinity House offered to pay the men two pounds ten shillings per month. By the end of June there was again a full crew, but it appears that about this time a decision must have been taken to reduce the crew in number from twelve to ten.

During the next few years the men were able to earn some money driving piles for groynes on the beach and for protection of the lighthouse. They also unloaded and positioned chalk stone around the lighthouse, to protect the cottages and to fill the breaches in Spurn. For unloading and positioning the chalk they were paid two shillings per tide's work.

The Board of Trade gave permission for the lifeboat crew only to begin taking gravel and cobbles from a limited area of Spurn beaches on 19th June 1868. Work could continue as usual on the Binks and elsewhere but a Royalty of one penny per ton had to be paid for any material removed from Spurn. Six days later the crew wrote to Trinity House complaining that the Countrymen were on the Spurn beaches and taking work from them. On July 6th the Board of Trade re-imposed a

Building sea defences at Spurn *Courtesy of Easington School*

complete ban on all working on any part of the Spurn beaches. During seventeen days three thousand tons of cobbles and gravel had been removed from Spurn and of that the lifeboat men had removed only four hundred tons.

In spite of this setback the next twenty years were relatively prosperous and during most months the men were able to earn at least sufficient for their families to live on. This was also a period of stability in crew membership, with few changes of personnel. In 1890, however, conditions changed.

On 25th August 1890 the crew wrote the following to Trinity House -

"We the undersigned men of the Spurn Life Boat Crew wish to ask for a raise of wages seeing that we have so much Competition in our fishing trade and that the markets are not so good as they have been in the past years and our provisions cost us about 15% more at Spurn than in other places and as you know that the salvage of ships is not half as Good as it was we the Crew of the said Life Boat ask the Brethren of the Trinity House to Grant us the sum of four pounds per month seeing that we cannot make ends meet in the winter."

Landing chalk for the chalk bank. Photograph probably taken in the 1920's, but clearly shows the methods used earlier.
Courtesy of Woodend Museum of Natural History, Scarborough, and Spurn Bird Observatory

The Board of Trade hereby signify their consent to the removal of shingle from the shore at Spurn point, coloured Red on this tracing, by the Crew of the Life Boat stationed at Spurn Point upon the terms stated in their letter of this date to the Secretary of the Trinity House Hull.

Whl. Board of Trade
June 8th 1868

C. Cecil Trevor

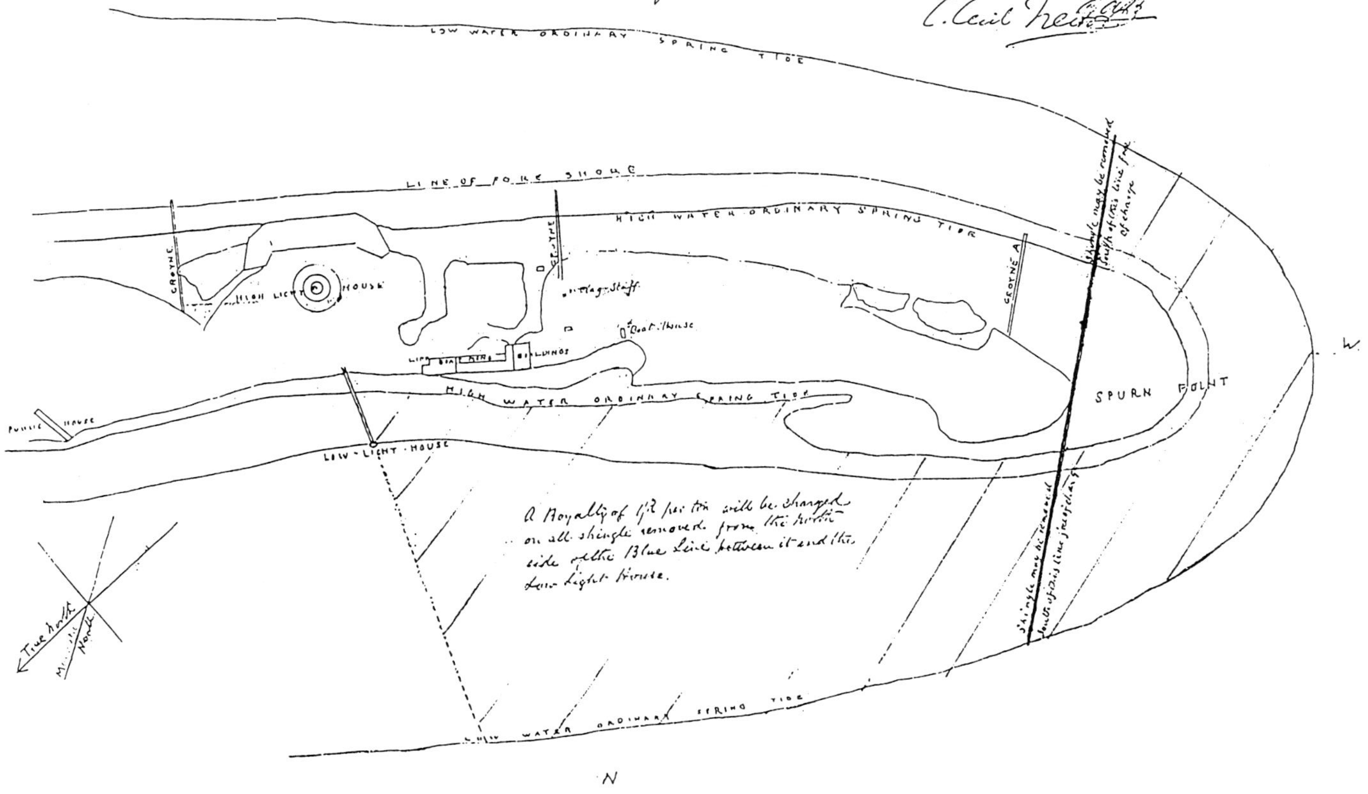

The request was refused. Despite the refusal to grant an increase the men all agreed to continue at Spurn but asked for proper provision for a school for their children. This was agreed and a school was opened in January 1891. The Master was later asked to send a list of all prize money from salvage. This was done for the ten year period from February 1882 to February 1891 and the total was eight hundred and thirteen pounds, to be shared by the whole crew.

In February 1891 storms severely damaged fishing grounds off the Norfolk coast and "many Sheringham Crab Catchers are clearing the fishing grounds near Spurn." With this loss of work and income five of the lifeboat crew left Spurn, but were quickly replaced and the work of the station continued.

The conflict with the Countrymen appeared to have come to an end as there were no more complaints in letters to Trinity House, but in October 1907 a notice from the Humber Conservancy Commissioners was sent to owners and masters of vessels in the gravel trade banning the removal of any material from Spurn or the Binks, the foreshore or bed of the Humber without first having obtained a license from the Commissioners. Offenders were threatened with proceedings and a penalty not exceeding twenty pounds.

On January 1st 1908, as a result of the Humber Conservancy Act of 1907, the responsibility for the Lifeboat Station passed from Trinity House to the Humber Conservancy Board. By that time the wages for the crew had risen to three pounds ten shillings per month and the men still earned money from fishing, salvage and gravel work. This pattern continued unchanged until the station was taken over by RNLI on 1st May 1911.

NOTICE TO MASTERS & OWNERS of Ballast Lighters, Sloops, etc.

REMOVAL OF GRAVEL AT SPURN.

The attention of the Humber Conservancy Commissioners having been called to the continued systematic abstraction of gravel, shingle, and other material at Spurn and on the Binks,

Notice is hereby given

that by Section 8, of the Humber Conservancy Act 1905, any person who at any time digs, carries away, or removes any sand, gravel, shingle, or other material from the foreshore or bed of the Humber, without first having obtained the license in writing of the Commissioners, shall for every such offence be liable to a

PENALTY NOT EXCEEDING £20.

Masters of Vessels and others concerned are hereby cautioned that the practice of removing gravel, shingle, or other material from Spurn or the Binks must be discontinued and that no gravel, shingle, or other material is in future to be taken without the license in writing of the Commissioners.

Proceedings will be taken to enforce the above penalty of £20 against any person offending.

By Order,

ANDW. M. JACKSON,

Clerk.

Hull. 5th October, 1907.

Landing oil for the lighthouse at Spurn. Work often done by members of the lifeboat crew. About 1900. *Courtesy of Mrs. D. Lawrence*

Making crab pots at Spurn. About 1900 *Courtesy of Mrs. D. Lawrence*

LIFE ON SPURN

When the station opened the Master lived at the Lifeboat Inn or Tavern, the converted barracks, situated on the seaward side of the peninsula. There were also living on Spurn the lighthouse keepers and their families. When the first cottages were built for the crew of the lifeboat the population of Spurn increased dramatically. Apart from the gravel work the Master sold liquors and provisions at the inn - called the Lifeboat Hotel on the O.S. Map - and also on the beach to the local residents and the crews of the gravel ships, fishing boats and to visitors.

Labourers at the gravel trade were given an allowance of sixpence a day by the ships' masters which had to be spent at the Lifeboat Inn. Some of the men objected and said Richardson charged too much at twopence halfpenny a pint for ale. A lighthouse keeper by the name of Nixon was allowed to sell liquors from his house and he only charged twopence a pint and the men wanted to go to him. Richardson alleged that this was poorer quality ale, a statement supported by Mr. Iveson, who advised Richardson to -

"sell the cheaper stuff as the labourers at Spurn are no judge of quality and their heads and stomachs can bear anything."

This was not borne out in June 1839 when John Ezart complained to Trinity House that Richardson had sold him some rum in a dirty bottle and this had caused illness for which he needed medical attention and made him unfit for work for some days.

The decline of the gravel trade led to a decline in trade at the inn and on October 1st 1846 Robert Brown, the then Master, wrote to Trinity House -

"I therefore determined to ask your leave to erect a Tenement for the accommodation of visitors, a considerable number of whom have been down, and across the Humber from Cleathorpes, during the late summer, but for whom we have no accommodation."

He went on to say that he had obtained permission from Sir Clifford Constable to use some land, and his request was granted.

Two years later, in September 1848, Brown wrote quite a different letter to the Wardens of Trinity House -

"...on my application for the renewal of my licenses at the Annual Licenses day at Patrington on Thursday the Reverend Christian Sykes, Chief Magistrate, told me that my Licenses was only to sell in the House and that if I did sell on the beach he should prosecute me. I therefore thought it necessary that I should lay this before you as the whole of my livelihood depends on the privilege of supplying vessels on the beach while loading Gravel and Cobbles."

Five days later Brown resigned his position as Master because the loss of beach trading made it quite impossible for him to make a living.

During the next three years the problem was the dilapidated state of the cottages and inn, which was not improved by a violent thunder and hail storm in June 1851 during which one hundred and five panes of glass were broken by hailstones described as four or five ounces in weight and five inches and more in diameter.

An increasing concern was encroachment by the sea, which was rapidly washing away the sand in front of the inn. In January 1855 Mr. Foale, a surveyor, warned that -

"..the Master's House either in whole or part will be swept away unless effective measures be taken to prevent it."

He repeated the warning a year later and in August 1856 in the monthly report is the simple statement -

"..very large tides this week and this morning about half of the Captain's house washed down."

This marked the end of the arrangement whereby the lifeboat Master ran the tavern. Following the collapse of the building he moved temporarily into one of the crew cottages which was empty and when the new houses were built he occupied one of those. By this time the crew members were paid by Trinity House and perhaps it was decided that there was no longer a need for the Master to have extra provision.

In September 1856 George Harrison of Blanket Row Brewery wrote to Trinity House asking for some arrangement respecting the old inn, as he was owed more than two hundred pounds advanced to Grant, the master, for valuation of fixtures and fittings and stores, expecting that they would pass from Master to Master. It was now impossible to recover these things or the money and he asked for an opportunity of making something to help cover the loss by selling goods whilst work was going on at Spurn. In August 1867 there was a Notice of Bankruptcy hearing in Hull regarding George Harrison, Brewer.

The second Lifeboat Inn at Spurn, made from the remains of the original lifeboat cottages. Mr. James Hopper was the innkeeper. *Courtesy Mr. K. Greyson*

Another veiw of the second Lifeboat Inn at Spurn. *Courtesy of Mr. Mrs. J Gell*

Following the building of the new houses for the crew it appears that at least some part of the old cottages was refurbished and made into a second Lifeboat Inn or Tavern. John Quinton was followed by Fewson Hopper and James Hopper as tenants and the inn continued to serve the local people, the visitors and the men who came over to Spurn from Grimsby on a regular weekly trip for an evening at the inn.

When in 1816 Trinity House wrote to Mr. Francis Constable asking him to lease some land for cottages for the lifeboat crew he replied through his agent that as he himself was "past sixty three years" he did not wish to be involved in any building on Spurn, but he was prepared to allow Trinity House to build the cottages. The maximum term of the lease must be twenty one years because of the conditions under which Mr. Constable held the land, and so the lease would have to be renewed from time to time. When the lease was finally drawn up in December 1818 a parcel of land on the western side of Spurn was allotted to Trinity House for -

"..the yearly rent or sum of seven shillings of lawful British money at the feast of St. Michael the Archangel in every year" during the full term of twenty one years. There were various conditions listed, including Constable family access to the land, ownership of fishes Royal, metals, fossils and minerals. All rents must be paid on time and Trinity House could not lease or let any part of the land to anyone else without licence from Mr. Constable.

The second lease in 1842 contained the same conditions, but the rent had risen to five pounds per annum. There was also a new clause saying that Trinity House -

"shall and will upon the complaint in writing of the said Thomas Aston Clifford Constable his heirs or assigns dismiss from their service and employ any Master or Commander of the said Life Boat within one Calendar Month from the delivery of such complaint, and him eject from and out of the said tenement or dwelling house."

Following such a dismissal Trinity House could not appoint a new Master without the written approval of Mr. Constable.

The plans for new houses gave rise to a third lease in 1858 with the same conditions and it was followed by a series of one year leases until 1908.

Little is known about the first cottages. They were made of brick, had slate roofs, and floors made of square bricks. There were coal-burning fireplaces, often stoked up with fuel collected from the beach. There was no supply of fresh water on Spurn and the people had to collect rain water, have water sent down in casks by boat from Hull or sail to Grimsby to fill up containers. The houses were constantly battered by the weather and frequently flooded by high tides. On 5th February 1845 a high tide -

"..filled our Houses half way up the Ovens, wet the beds, wasted our fresh water with the flasks floating away, broke away part of the fencing and washed away our coals and left the Houses in a very wretched state for we expected every wave to burst the doors in ... our Wives and Infants having to be upstairs about four hours without any fire on account of the chimney smoking so bad and when they came down the House floors was near an inch thick with mud."

Trinity House ordered a survey of the houses to be carried out after this flood and the report said that the houses would be flooded to a depth of a foot or more in the future, but that there was no actual danger. Later records report water knee deep and "three feet high in the cottages" during severe gales. The strong winds frequently damaged chimneys and tore off roofing slates, hailstones shattered glass, and woodwork rotted, so that repairs were constantly necessary. In May 1855 a survey was completed for major renovation and protection work, but because of the estimated cost of three hundred pounds consideration was adjourned.

In January 1857 plans were drawn up for a terrace of ten new houses, with the Master's house at one end and the Mate's at the other and the crewmen in between, at an estimated cost of twelve hundred pounds. In April of that year the Grimsby firm of Ellis and Johnson signed the contract to build the houses for one thousand three hundred and fifty pounds and the work was completed in February 1858. These houses stood until 1975 when the crew of that time moved into the present RNLI houses.

Rising tide, Spurn. Shows lifeboat houses built in 1885 and the school to the right and the remains of the original cottages in the distance. *Courtesy of Mr. K. Grayson*

Pleasure boats at Spurn, early 1900's. *Courtesy of Mr. Mrs. R. Robinson*

Holiday postcard, early 1900's. The paddle steamers are the SS Solway and SS Humber.
Courtesy of Mrs. D. Lawrence

The new houses were subject to the same attack by the weather and tides as the old cottages and were in constant need of repair. In June 1863 four lighter loads of chalk stone were positioned to protect the cottages. The pay for unloading a lighter carrying up to eighty tons of stone was two pounds, to be shared between all the men working. Piling and planking backed by three hundred tons of chalk stone was put in place in 1875 but the sea continued to cause damage. The houses were painted at least every other year and Mr. Pattinson swept the chimneys every three months from the 1860's at least up to 1911. The cost of sweeping all the chimneys in the first quarter of 1911 was one pound.

The houses still had no supply of fresh water and rainwater was still collected and casks filled in Grimsby. In June 1900 a child died of diphtheria and the Medical Officer of Health ordered an inspection. The report condemned the water supply system in the following words -

"I find that the inhabitants are dependent on rain water for all purposes. This is collected in tanks and handed out at intervals to the men. They then store it in barrels which have been tarred; this is most insanitary and the water is black and bad."

Trinity House was ordered to install a new and better water system and this was completed two months later.

The lifeboat families were not now the only people living on Spurn. There were the families of the lighthouse keepers, the inn keeper, Coast Guards, Lloyds Signal Station and later a teacher. At its highest the population rose to more than one hundred and thirty and from 1819 when the first cottages were built there were always seventy people or more. One lady died having lived forty five years on Spurn.

The women tried to earn a little money by catering for visitors. Besides the gravel and fishing boats, paddle steamers brought day trippers from Hull and Grimsby, there were works outings, Sunday School celebrations, Church groups and many others. On the 10th July 1865 a party of three hundred visitors was expected, a works outing by paddle steamer from New Holland. On July 8th a small group set sail for Grimsby to buy supplies to cater for the party. The good, clear weather gave way to a sudden thunder storm and John Marshall, a lifeboat man, dropped dead in the boat. At first it was thought he had been struck by lightning, but it was later decided he had died of fright. He left a widow and four children, the oldest being eight years old.

Life was not always peaceful amongst the residents of Spurn. Apart from the disputes with the Countrymen there were squabbles between families with some people earning unpleasant reputations. One Master complained he always had more trouble with the women than the men, although there were disputes between Master

Gravel sloops and day visitors on the Binks, 1905. *Courtesy of Mr. J Kirkwood*

and crew and one Master was accused of cowardice by four of his crew, who also blamed him for loss of life amongst the crew of a wrecked ship. An inquiry cleared the Master of the charges and the four men were dismissed. In spite of the difficulties the people worked together most of the time and the lifeboat service was maintained.

In November 1839 the lifeboat crew pointed out to the Wardens at Trinity House that there was "no place of worship nor a school for our children within seven miles of Spurn." This was an exaggeration as it is only some four miles to Kilnsea and Easington. The first reference to the possibility of conducting services at Spurn was in October 1846 when the Rev. George Inman, Vicar of Kilnsea, wrote to Trinity House saying that the hamlet of Spurn lay within the parish and four miles from Kilnsea. The population of Spurn was now seventy two and the people wanted religious instruction and worship. As he now had a curate at Easington, it would be possible to conduct two full services every three weeks, together with regular administration of the Sacraments, Baptism and attendance on the sick. In winter the duty could be done only every other Sunday. He also suggested the possibility of establishing a Dame School at Spurn to instruct the children. The vicar listed all the families by name and occupation, separated males and females, divided the children into age groups and said how many people were ready for instruction and the Sacraments.

Because of the distance to be travelled to carry out these duties the Rev. Inman would need a two-wheeled carriage and horse and the curate would need a horse, and he hoped Trinity House would provide these. A pencil note at the foot of the letter reads "no funds available."

The Primitive Methodists did begin to conduct services at Spurn in the mid 1850's and continued to hold them every week at least until May 1911 except on a very few occasions when the weather and sea made the journey impossible. Church of England services began about 1869. Both churches applied to Trinity House for grants to cover some of the cost of transport to Spurn and although the amount varied for the Church of England in the early years it settled at seven pounds ten shillings per annum and the Primitive Methodists received the same amount for their Horse Hire Fund. The Primitive Methodists frequently sent copies of their quarterly preaching plan for the Patrington Circuit to Trinity House. In March 1896 the letter of appeal for the grant accompanying the preaching plan points out that they had regularly taken services at Spurn for more than forty years and that the travelling distance just to serve Spurn during that quarter was three hundred and fifty five miles.

Either in 1881 or 1882 the Church of England people in some way offended the lifeboat families, who refused to attend any more of their services. In January 1883 the curate at Easington, Mr. Willoughby, wrote to Mr. Winson, the Master of the lifeboat, what was described as

"a very conciliatory note and intended to soothe any unpleasant feelings there might be on the part of the Boatmen."

This effort was not successful as the extract from Mr. Winson's reply clearly shows -

"..as regards the Service being held in the Light House I have nothing to do with it where you hold your service.... If the Honourable Gentlemen of the Trinity House feel disposed to pay you for doing nothing, the same as during the last three months simply preaching to one or two Light Keepers I cannot help that. I cannot compel our people to go to the Light House after the way they have been turned out, neither do I think that any of them will go there to hear you so you can please yourself where you go to."

Following this disagreement the Anglican services were stopped and the grant discontinued. In correspondence with Trinity House Mr. Winson repeatedly said that the lifeboat families preferred the Methodist form of service and there was a time when two members of the crew were themselves local preachers. The Archbishop of York visited Spurn on the 13th June 1893 and the Church of England

PATRINGTON CIRCUIT.

Primitive Methodist Preachers' Plan, 1892.

"O LORD REVIVE THY WORK."

PREACHERS' NAMES AND RESIDENCES.

1 J. G. SMITH, Patrington
2 J. W. CHAPPELL, Withernsea
3 J. Smales, Fitling
4 W. Smith, Sup., Elsternwick
5 I. Woodhouse, Sup, Elsternwick
6 G. Jackson, Withernsea
7 M. Dent, Burton Pidsea
8 R. W. Dry, Withernsea
9 W. Woodhouse, Withernsea
10 E. Freeman, Rimswell
11 M. Sergeant, Welwick
12 W. Usher, Keyingham
13 J. Sergeant, Halsham
14 C. Waller, Elsternwick
15 J. C. Johnson, Burstwick
16 G. Bell, Elsternwick
17 B. Screeton, Patrington
18 J. Frankland, Patrington
19 J. Colley, Patrington
20 H. Screeton, Patrington
21 M. Robson, Patrington
22 J. Jackson, Ottringham
23 T. Mason, Withernsea
24 W. Chessman, Patrington
25 J. Limon, Withernsea
26 T. Gedney, Halsham
27 R. Westmoreland, Keyingham
28 T. Nicholson, Holmpton
29 W. H. Johnson, Withernsea
30 M. Tarbotton, Keyingham
31 C. W. Medforth, Keyingham
32 W. Hodgson, Ottringham
33 R. Moore, Hilston
34 J. R. Bishop, Withernsea
35 W. H. Woodhouse, Withernsea
36 W. H. Carr, Withernsea
37 R. Ward, Holmpton
38 P. Taylor, Roos
39 G. K. Smith, Patrington
40
41 T. Kitchen, Burstwick
42 J. W. Blashill, Patrington
43 J. W. Herd, Patrington
44 J. Eastwood, Ottringham
45 J. Coates, Withernsea
46 R. Emmerson, Humbleton

EXHORTERS.

47 H. Sergeant, Halsham
48 E. Briggs, Halsham
49 J. Hodgson, Withernsea

AUXILIARIES.

50 J. Ablett, Stoneferry
51 J. Wilkinson, 14, Worship-St.,
52 T. R. Sizer, [illegible]-St., Hull
53 W. Longman, 11, Silvester-St.
54 J. Robinson, Hull
55 J. Moody, Sutton
56 J. R. Woods, Patrington
57 H. B. Hall, Flambro'
58 J. Goodinson, Hull
59 Rev. G. Bennett.

REFERENCES.

A..Teachers' Yearly Meeting
CF..Circuit Fund Collection
CA..Chapel Anniversary
CM..Camp Meetings
E..Evangelist
F..Conference Fund Collection
G..Collection for Lighting
GF..General Chapel Fund Coll.
H..Harvest Thanksgiving
L..Lovefeast
M..Missionary Meeting
MS..Missionary Sermons
P..Prayer Meeting; or Provide
Q..Quarterly Collection
S..Sacrament
SS..Sunday School Anniversary
T..Tickets to be renewed
W..Widows & Orphans Fund Coll
Y..Trustees' Yearly Meeting
[illegible]..Circuit Committee
LM..Leaders' Meeting
RM..Revival Meeting
SC..Special Collection
HH..Local Preachers' Horse Hire
GG..Great Gathering
FF..Filey Fishermen
SO..School Opening

PLACES.

Each place is earnestly desired to raise the following amount in order to meet the quarterly out go.

Society Stewards and Secretaries.	Amount	PLACES.	Time.	April 3	April 10	April 17	April 24	May 1	May 8	May 15	May 22	May 29	June 5	June 12	June 19	June 26
C. Towler and J. Frankland Secretary.	£7 2s. 1d.	PATRINGTON														
		School Address......	11										1ss			
			2	29Q	42	2	59MS	38	1sc	14	51sc	2	1ss	15	9sc	2
			6	29Q	21	2s	59MS	38	1sc	14	51sc	2	1ss	15	9sc	2
		Mon. Band of Hope	7													
		Thursday Preaching	7½	17	1	18	MM	12	1T	20	2	21	1	24	2	42
		Friday, Class.........	7½	1	1	1	1	1	1	1	1	1	1	1	1	1
		Sat. Band Meeting	7½	18	19	20	21	1	42	43	1	18	19	20	42	43
H. Seymour. W. Usher, Sec.	3/17/6	KEYINGHAM......	10½	38	2ss	30	1MS	7		2Q		18sc	CM	48		49
			6	38	2ss	27	1MS	7	35	22Q	20	18sc	9L	31	12sc	23
		Wednesday	7½	1		2		1T		2		1s		2		1
B. Coy. J. Staniforth, Sec.	1/8/5	EASINGTON	2		1Q		29MS		11sc		19sc		38sc		2ss	
			6	6	1Q	18	29MS	49	11sc	36	19sc	21	38sc	22	2ss	29
		Tuesday	7		1		2		1T		2		1s		2	
E. Freeman A. Fotty, Secretary.	1/13/1	RIMSWELL	2	1Q		15		48	2sc	7	1s	25	55ss	47		1sc
			6		6		13sc		8sc		29		55ss		33	
		Tuesday	7		2		10		2T		1		2		1	
Mrs. F. Clark. P. Taylor, Secretary.	2/6/6	ROOS	2		9HH	57CA	14		19Q		15sc		2sc	1CM	34	
			6	22	9HH	57CA	14	33	19Q	44	15sc	46	41sc	1L	10	16
		Wednesday	7	2		1		38T		1s		2		1		2
R. Wells. G. Fisher. Secretary.	4/1/0	BURSTWICK	2	55Q	18	1CA	26	19SM	35	2sc	27	58	7sc	41	14	ss
			6	55Q	18	1CA	26	19SM	36	2sc	12	58	7sc	16	14	ss
		Tuesday	7½	1		2		PT		2		1s		2		1
R. Smith.	1/16/2	HOLLYM	6	42Q	43	17SM	49	21sc	29	23	38CA	8	6sc	19	32	44L
		Thursday	7		2		P		2T		1s		2		1	
J. Ellis J. Foster.	3/7/2	HALSHAM	2	49Q		25SM		9sc		1sc		14sc		30	CA	58
			6	23Q	38	15SM	10	9sc	13	1sc	6	14sc	2	27	CA	58
		Thursday	7	2		1		PT		1s		2		1		2
J. Caley. M. Fenwick Secretary.	2/3/11	ELSTERNWICK	2		33Q		34		27sc		26sc		29		38	
			6	2	33Q	46	35	16	27sc	21	26sc	1s	29	3sc	38	36sc
		Tuesday ...	7	2		1		PT		1s		2		1		2
G. Woodhouse. G. Kitching, Secretary.	2/11/9	WELWICK	2	18Q		29	59MS	6		15	2ss	9		26sc		38sc
			6	18Q	34	29	20MS	6	25sc	15	2ss	9	11	28sc	17	38sc
		Wednesday	7		1s		2		1T		2		1		2	
H. Dibnah. E. C. Johnson, Secretary.	3/4/7	HUMBLETON ...	2	2Q		26sc		CA		21sc		1sc		14sc	CM	9sc
			6	48Q	47	26sc	24	CA	33	20sc	16	3sc	46	14sc	7L	9sc
		Monday	7	2		1		PT		1s		2		1		2
G. Jackson. R. W. Dry. Secretary.	£9 12s. 4d.	WITHERNSEA......	10½	1Q	20	15sc	9	44	2sc	34	1s	38sc	53	2ss	51	1sc
		Pier Head	3											2ss		
			6	1Q	19	23sc	9	44	2sc	7	1sc	38sc	53	2ss	51	1sc
		Wednesday	7		2		23		2T		1		2		1	
		Fri. Class Meeting ..	6¾	2	2	2	2	2	2	2	2	2	2	2	2	2
		Fri. Mutual I. Socty	7½	2	2	2	2	2	2	2	2	2	2	2	2	2
		Sat. Band Meeting	7	6	9	23	25	2	29	34	35	36	2	9	23	25
J. Alvin. J. Parrott Secretary.	2/1/4	PATRINGTON	10½		11	2Q	41		1sc		42	2sc	P		ss	2CM
		HAVEN	6	43				24		17				20	ss	L
		Thursday	7	1		2		1T		2		1		2		1
J. Liversidge, T. Winson. Secretary.	1/8/5	SPURN HEAD ...	2	35	24Q	19	2sc	31	23sc	9	18sc	42	33sc	44	29sc	55
			6	28	24	24	2sc	23	21	25	24	24	15	16	21	21
T. Nicholson. H. Gell, Secretary.	2/1/4	HOLMPTON	2		23Q		8		42		25		49		18	
			6	34		21		43sc		28sc		35sc		11sc		6
		Monday	7		2		28		2T		1s		P		1	
J. Gray. S. Charlton. Secretary.	10/0	KILNSEA	6	35	24Q	19	36sc	34	49sc	9	18sc	42	33sc	44	29sc	55
		Monday	7		1		2		1T		2s		P		2	
J. Eastwood.		OTTRINGHAM	2		38Q		1sc		21sc		7		23sc		13	

Seat Letting in all the Chapels.

Patrington	March 4th..........	June 4th	September 4th......	December 4th ......
Keyingham	February 3rd	May 3rd	August 3rd	November 3rd ......
Easington..........	February 3rd	May 3rd	August 3rd	November 3rd ......
Roos	March 8th	June 8th	September 8th......	December 8th ......
Burstwick	March 18th	June 18th..........	September 18th	December 18th......
Hollym	March 3rd..........	June 3rd	September 3rd......	December 3rd ......
Halsham	January 1st	April 1st	July 1st............	October 1st ......
Elsternwick	March 9th..........	June 9th	September 9th......	December 9th ......
Welwick	January 18th........	April 18th..........	July 18th	October 18th ......
Humbleton	February 8th	May 8th	August 8th	November 8th ......
Withernsea	January 20th	April 20th..........	July 20th	October 20th ......
Patrington Haven ...	January 10th.......	April 10th..........	July 10th	October 10th......
Kilnsea	January 1st	April 1st	July 1st	October 1st ......
Rimswell	January 1st	April 1st..........	July 1st..........	October 1st.......

CAMP MEETINGS.

KEYINGHAM, June 5th, ... Nos. 36, 35, 34 and 9

ROOS, June 12th, ... Nos. 42, 21, 18 and 1

HUMBLETON, June 19th, ... Nos. 44, 26, 22 and 7

HOLLYM, June 26th, ... Nos. 44, 34, 32 and 22

PATRINGTON HAVEN, June 26th, ... to be arranged for

NOTICES.

"Let all things be done decently and in order."

1. PREACHERS.—Every Local Preacher or Exhorter must mark his Appointments on the Plan, and punctually attend them; but if he should be prevented from doing so, by affliction or otherwise, *he must* get them supplied from among his brethren whose names are on the Plan. When he fails to provide for his appointment, he must forward his reason to the Quarterly Meeting in time for the business of the Preachers' Meeting, which meeting shall determine whether the offender shall be admonished, sunk in number, or have his name removed from the plan.

2. LEADERS.—Every Leader must read the Society Rules in his Class once a Quarter, call over the names of his Members at each Class Meeting, collect the weekly contributions, and have his accounts ready for the Quarterly Meeting.

3. SOCIETY STEWARDS.—Each Society Steward must see that all Special Services, Lovefeasts, &c., are duly announced by a written notice, provide the requisite elements for Lovefeasts and the Lord's Supper, cause to be announced the previous Sunday's Offerings, and forward the Report, and all Monies belonging to the Circuit Fund, to the Quarterly Meeting by 12-30. He must see that all the Collections are duly made according to the appointments on the Plan.

4. BAPTISMS.—The officiating Minister must register each Baptism, and give a Certificate of the same to the Parents, for which 1s. shall be paid. Both Parents are requested to be present at the ceremony.

5. MARRIAGES.—Patrington and Withernsea Chapels are Licensed for the Solemnization of Marriages. Twenty-one day's notice must be given to the Registrar, and three day's notice to the Minister.

6. The CIRCUIT QUARTERLY MEETING will be held at WITHERNSEA, Monday, June 6th, to commence at 1 o'clock.

7. CIRCUIT COMMITTEE and SUB-MISSIONARY COMMITTEE is composed of all the accredited Local Preachers, and R. Wells, G. Woodhouse, J. Ellis, & H. Johnson. J. G. Smith, Treasurer; J. W. Chappell, Secretary.

8. STATION SUNDAY SCHOOL UNION COMMITTEE is composed of the following persons:—B. Screeton, E. Chessman, A. Guy, C. Waller, R. W. Dry, W. Usher, R. Westmoreland, B. Coy, G. Woodhouse, M. Harrison, R. Moor, G. Fisher, J. Ellis, S. Charlton, C. Jeckylls, J. Alvin, R. Wells, and J. W. Chappell, Sec. To meet at Withernsea, June 6th at 1 p.m.

9. BOOK STEWARD.—J. G. SMITH.

10. CIRCUIT STEWARDS.—W. Woodhouse and J. Limon.

11. WEEKLY OFFERINGS.—Boxes are placed in the Chapels for the Offerings of Members and Friends who wish to weekly and systematically support the cause of God.

LOCAL PREACHERS' HORSE HIRE.

Every Preacher who travels six miles out and six miles in from the place where he resides, shall receive 1s. 6d. per day. All claims on this Fund to be made the week before the Quarterly Meeting.

This Rule does not apply to Auxiliaries.

The Sunday Schools will be visited by one of the Ministers during the Quarter, if possible.

MISSIONARY MEETINGS will be held:

EASINGTON, ... Monday, April 25th
WELWICK, ... Tuesday, April 26th
KEYINGHAM, ... Wednesday, April 27th
PATRINGTON, ... Thursday, April 28th

Deputation: Rev. G. Bennett, (of Hull)

ADJOURNED QUARTERLY MEETING will be held at PATRINGTON, on Friday, May 6th, at [illegible] o'clock.

ASH & KING, PRINTERS, HIGH-STREET, HULL.

School House ~ Spurn Point.

HARVEST
HOME
BROWNS

services were restored, along with the travel grant. In January 1907 Trinity House asked for information concerning the services. The Anglicans held services fortnightly, alternating morning and evening. The vicar or curate conducted the services three times a year and a lay reader twice a month. When the service was in the morning the attendance was one or two adults and twenty children and in the evening six adults and twelve children. The Primitive Methodists held services every Sunday afternoon, plus mission services in the winter. The attendance was twelve adults and twenty children.

All the services were held in the lighthouse before the disagreement, but after January 1891 they were held in the newly built school. The uneasy relationship between the two groups continued at least until May 1911.

On August 13th 1867 Mrs. Winson, wife of a crew member who later became Master, began the first school by teaching the children of Spurn in her own home. She did this work for several years until it was taken over by Miss Hopper, sister of a crew member. In September 1890 Thomas Winson, now Master of the lifeboat, wrote to Trinity House about -

"one grievance that the men feel very much, and that is the schooling of their children...

I beg to say that under the present system the children are not taught at all, no pains whatever taken with them...

Miss Hopper's time to a great extent is taken up with Telegraphing and very often has to look out for ships coming in. In fact a great deal of her time is occupied in going between the Watch House and the Schoolroom every day consequently the children never get taught much.

I beg, Honoured Sir, to suggest with your kind permission, that the Telegraph Instrument be removed into the Lloyds office and that my Wife take the management of the School again."

The Board of Trinity House agreed that this should take place and appointed Mrs. Winson as the official teacher at a salary of twenty five shillings a quarter. Miss Hopper formally resigned in December 1890.

Opposite: Spurn Head Harvest Festival. Rare Photograph taken inside the school. Early 1900's *Courtesy of Mr.&Mrs. R. Robinson*

General Election, 1906.

HOLDERNESS DIVISION.

MR. WILBERFORCE

THE LIBERAL CANDIDATE,

will address the

Electors of SPURN,

at 3 p.m.,

On Saturday, Jan. 6th,

in the

Schoolroom.

Dr. COATES and other Speakers

will be present.

Printed and published by Mark Taylor, 18 Chapel Lane, Lowgate, Hull.

During 1890 Trinity House had agreed to build a school on Spurn and this was completed on January 10th 1891 but was not opened for children until January 19th as it was thought "best to let the Paint get thoroughly dry before commencing." It was a one-roomed building some twenty six feet by twenty feet, with its own small yard.

In 1893 the school became a local authority Public Elementary School with a certificated teacher and the number of children in attendance varied between about fifteen and twenty. In May 1892 there were thirteen girls and seven boys, with an age range from four to thirteen years. The position of the school teacher was far from easy living amongst such a close community. Apart from storm damage which at times caused the school to be closed, the children were kept away by parents to gather coal from the beaches or perform similar tasks. There was also interference from parents. In February 1896 the school master complained about interference from one of the lifeboat crew, John Spauls. One of the boys was being kept behind after school as a punishment and Spauls told the boy and others that he should have destroyed the books and other things. There were fears that the school master would leave if interfered with in this way, and as this was not the only complaint against him Spauls was dismissed, which meant not only the loss of his place in the crew, but also his cottage on Spurn.

The school building was used for church services, for Sunday School and other activities. At election time candidates for the local area held meetings in the schoolroom and the place appears to have become something of a community centre.

The school closed in December 1945.

Isolation and difficulty of communication with Spurn was a problem recognised before the lifeboat station was established, but some improvements were made over the years. In September 1839 a mechanical telegraph was built - this was the eastern end of a chain of stations linking back to Hull and was used to relay shipping information. This was replaced by an electric telegraph on January 25 th 1871 and a telephone was installed in the Master's house in October 1893. Spurn also had its own post office from 1868 until probably 1920.

From time to time the monotony of life at Spurn was broken by a variety of incidents, some pleasant, some not so pleasant. In August 1862 a lifeboat station was established at Withernsea and the Spurn crew were eager to go the ceremony, but Trinity House refused to grant permission and the men had to stay at home ready for a call.

A report was sent to Trinity House in December 1868 that a man dressed as a coastguard was going round Paull and other villages begging for money for a new pair of wheels for a boat carriage for Spurn. Major Pricket had given him one pound ten shillings and Mr. Wray had donated one pound, as had others, before it was realised that the man was a fraud. The people at Spurn were not involved in any way in the escapade. A happier incident occurred in August 1873 when a young boy landed on the beach in a small boat, having been adrift for two days. He had survived the ordeal and recovered.

Without doubt one of the highlights in the lives of many of the people at Spurn at the time must have been the visit of His Royal Highness the Duke of Edinburgh on August 15th 1881. A letter was sent from Trinity House to Mr. Winson, the Master of the lifeboat, on August 11th telling him that -

"the Warden has been privately informed that the Duke of Edinburgh will arrive in Hull on Saturday evening in the Lively and on Monday morning inspect the North Shore Coastguard, and afterwards embark at Spurn Point on board the Lively...

The Warden fully relies upon your paying every attention to His Royal Highness that you possibly can, and placing at His disposal if necessary yourself and crew should the arrangements be carried out and the embarkation does take place at Spurn."

Following the visit this beautifully presented letter was sent to Trinity House by the Master, who received a congratulatory reply for all the arrangements he had made.

On the morning of 15th July 1883 Mr. Winson was on the beach and saw a small boat in the Humber about two miles from Spurn, being blown erratically by the wind, with the person in the boat not being able to control it. His report continues -

"As she got nearer to the Beach I could see that only a Boy was in charge. I hailed the Boy and directed him to keep the Boat before the sea. As the small Boat got in the breakers of the Beach I went into the water and pulled her ashore. I then observed another Boy in the bottom of the Boat apparently dead from exposure. I at once took him up to my house and with the assistance of my crew I am pleased to inform you we succeeded in bringing him round, but not before we had had four hours continual application of hot blankets, hot bath, hot bottles of water, continual rubbing with hot flannels and with difficulty got a little Brandy down his throat. About six and a half hours after the Boy became conscious. I Telegraphed to the Parents, likewise for a Doctor, but the Doctor did not get here until the danger was over. I am pleased to say the Boy is much better this morning but very weak yet and will not be able to be removed for some time. The Boys Mother has been down: The Doctor says had the Boy been five minutes longer in the Boat he would have been dead.

Spurn about 1903, Showing lifeboat cottages and school to left and raised look-out post on right. *Courtesy of Mr.&Mrs. J. Gell*

I beg to say one Boy is 13 years of age and the other 14 years, belong to Hull, one is named Hansen of Queen Square, Blanket Row , the other is Holt from near the same place. They both left Hull about noon on Sunday and driving about the river all night. The Boat is very small, only about 10 feet long."

A happy outcome to an adventurous escapade which could easily have been tragic.

About three quarters of a mile to the south of Kilnsea old church, on the second of June 1885 a "coffin" was found. It was quite black and very much decayed and was found between low water neap tide and low water spring tide lines where the sea bed was clay. The outside length was between five and six feet, but inside length was only a little over four feet. When first found it was said that all the bones of a skeleton were intact and that the body had been placed in "a cramping position." There was no lid but the coffin had been packed with stiff marley clay and was found with the head towards the north. By the time Mr. Winson, the Master, saw it only a human thigh bone remained, which he took to be of a "medium sized man." There appears to have been no further investigation carried out.

Spurn Point. 16th August 1881

To the Honourable Gentlemen of the Trinity House.

Gentlemen,

I beg to inform you of the visit of H. R. H. The Duke of Edinburgh to Spurn Point yesterday, on receiving orders from the Honourable Gentlemen of the Trinity House to place myself the Lifeboat Crew, and the boats under my charge at H. R. H. Service, I at once had the boats painted - Cushions made to fit the seats and the Stern sheets carpeted, yesterday I had a roadway of planks laid down over the wet sand for His Highness to walk into the boat. but previous to His Highness's arrival at Spurn yesterday I received orders from Capt Grey of the Coast Guard, to go to Kilnsea on horseback to Pilot His Highness's Carriage to Spurn, as it is a very difficult road for a stranger - I met H. R. H at Kilnsea at half past one o'clock and after Lunching at the Coast Guard Station I piloted His Highness's Carriage safely to Spurn. After waiting at Spurn half an hour for the "Lively" to make her appearance we rowed His Highness and attendants safely on board - on arriving on board the "Lively" His Highness requested me to take him out fishing after sending our boat ashore I accompanied His Highness in the Steam Pinnace; we stayed out fishing until eight o'clock. I am pleased to say we were very successful we caught a very nice lot of soles likewise flat fish and shrimps. His Highness was very pleased indeed and would like to come again next month - I beg to say I made every preparation I could to the best of my ability, hoping this will meet with your approval -

I beg to remain,

Gentlemen,

Your obedient servant

Thomas Winson

Master of the Lifeboat -

Spurn,

On a pleasanter note, at the end of July 1886 the crew received an invitation to dine at Londesborough Park on Friday 13th August on the occasion of the Coming of Age of Lord Londesborough's son. Trinity House gave permission for the entire crew to attend the "Great Festivities", which they did, then spent the night in Hull before returning to Spurn the following day "having all enjoyed the Great Treat very much."

A letter from Mr. Winson to the Board of Trinity House on 15th April 1892 was

"to inform you that yesterday morning a large whale landed on the Old Den inside Spurn after cruising about the entrance to North Channel some time. The whale is 76 feet long, 24 feet girth. Its mouth is 15 feet 6 inches long and its tail across is 15 feet 6 inches... I Telegraphed for a Tug from Grimsby to tow the whale away which they succeeded in doing last night high tide and landed on the Beach at Cleethorpes with the intention of exhibiting. Today we went up with the Tug and assisted to moor the whale on the Beach.

I think the fish is a Greenland Whale. We killed it by stopping the blow hole up with sea weed mud and gravel."

A smaller 25 feet long whale washed up on the beach dead in December 1910 was simply cut up and buried.

One hundred years ago it must have been much easier than now for boys to sail off in boats, as on August 15th 1892 there was another instance of some boys being saved at Spurn. A half-decked shrimp boat, the Saucy Jack, from Grimsby ran aground on the Binks and there were seven boys in her, their ages ranging from twelve to seventeen. As it was near low water they were able to wade ashore to the beach to be looked after by the lifeboat crew. The Master comments that it was a great wonder they were not all drowned as they had been out all night and had some narrow escapes. They had collided with a smack and lost the anchor and chain, broken the bowsprit and damaged the stem of the shrimper. Fortunately once more there was a happy ending to the adventure.

The Mayor of Grimsby, Mr. George Doughty, wrote to Trinity House asking permission for the Spurn lifeboat to take part in the lifeboat display off Cleethorpes on 15th September 1894. There were to be lifeboat races and other matters of interest to the public. Permission was granted provided the crew returned with the boat as soon as possible after the display to be ready for any call.

These incidents, and others like them, must have helped to ease a hard life at Spurn.

ROBERT RICHARDSON 25th AUGUST 1810 - 31st DECEMBER 1841

Robert Richardson, Mariner, of Kingston upon Hull, was appointed Master of the Lifeboat at Spurn when John Coulter left the position at the beginning of August 1810. Coulter had been appointed in July, but within three weeks had left without ever serving and the reason for his departure is not known. Richardson was to live in and run the inn or tavern created from the modified barrack building left behind by the army and he was expected to make an income of at least one hundred pounds a year.

Following his appointment he was sent to Spurn to make ready for the arrival of the lifeboat after it had been on display in Hull, and to meet the Lifeboat Company or group of volunteers or men chosen by Mr. Francis Constable to make up the crew. Instructions from Trinity House were given to the Mate and crew

"to assist the Master as well in selecting for her a safe and convenient place until the House and Carriage is prepared, as in making themselves acquainted with the Service by practising at the Oars at every opportunity."

The boat arrived at the end of October having been on display for almost three weeks and the men spent a lot of time "practising at the oars." The first crew was selected from the Lifeboat Company on the 14th November and the first service was on the following day. The John and Charlotte of Newcastle, coal - loaded, got into difficulties at the mouth of the Humber and was taking in water. The lifeboat was launched but the service was spread over three days before the ship was taken safely to Grimsby.

A week later Richardson wrote to Mr. William Iveson, Agent for Mr. Constable,

"It is with pleasure I send the pleasing intelligence of the second time of the Life Boat being the happy means of preserving a vessel and her Crew. On Wednesday the twenty first a sloop came on shore upon the Binks about seven in the morning, the wind blew strong east south east. It was so thick we could not see the vessel but heard Distinctly the Dreadful Cries of the men on board." The crew was mustered from Kilnsea and Easington and the lifeboat launched to assist the vessel which

"had lost her topmast, likewise her rudder and stove her boat to pieces. We steered for her with the Life Boat and got her to Grimsby. She is called the Young John, William Barker Master, from London, belonging to Scarborough."

During the early part of 1811 Trinity House wrote to Bridlington, North Shields, Newcastle on Tyne and Leith where lifeboats were already operating, seeking help and advice on establishing, funding and operating a lifeboat station. Some of the suggestions received were put into practice. From the end of 1810 to at least 1850 the documentary record is very patchy and incomplete and many services must have taken place for which no evidence can now be found. One of the very few reports for 1811 tells of a single - handed rescue by Richardson, illustrating again the problem of the crew living at Kilnsea and Easington at this time.

"I have likewise to inform you that I have been the happy instrument of saving seven lives. On the morning of October 4th a Brig belonging to Sunderland, Coal - loaded, broke from her moorings and got ashore upon the Stone Banks. I had not a man to watch consequently had no one to send for hands. The wind blowing very hard SSE. As I had no one to assist me I ventured in a small boat of my own and am proud to say was the happy means of saving their lives But had nearly lost my own in the attempt as my boat was upset and I was thrown out of her with great violence but thanks be to God got safe to shore."

A letter written to the Warden and Brethren of Trinity House on 15th February 1814 by William Garland, Captain of the Amity, of Lynn, is one of the rare occasions on which gratitude and thanks were expressed to the lifeboat crew, even though in this incident the lifeboat was never launched.

"Having been unfortunate in losing my vessel - viz Amity of Lynn - on the 29th ult. in a violent gale from the eastward - very thick with snow - between the Spurn and Kelsea I take the Liberty of addressing you who are the Patrons and Managers of one of the most humane institutions in the Kingdom - I mean that of the Life Boat at the Spurn, as I am fully convinced had no such boat been there - my crew and self would all have perished - as will appear from the following narrative -

The Ship was forced on shore the first quarter ebb - sea making a broach over the Ship at the time which was about half past 1 pm - at half past 2pm the vessel Drift so as to admit of us putting on shore but from the weather being so very thick with snow we were not able to know where we was - having wandered up and down on the strand abreast of the Ship until half past 4pm, not daring to lose sight of the Vessel, almost exhausted from the severity of the weather, we got on board again intending to take the chance of saving ourselves by Battening all the hatchways down and remaining by the Vessel - But here the Almighty disposer of all events seems to have heard our prayers, as between 6 and 7pm a man, viz Thos. Jacobs who had the watch - he being one of the Life Boat's Crew - was passing along the strand from Kelsea to Spurn - saw the Ship, he came along side and intreated me and the crew to quit the Vessel or when the aflood made we should all be lost and this evidently would have been the case as not a vestige of the cabin was remaining in its place next morning.

The afore mentioned good humane man conducted us to the Life Boat house -

but with the greatest difficulty being obliged at times to carry an aged man (who had been the Cook) who otherwise must have perished ere he reached it, as we were nearly set past ourselves in the Snow - and had we much further to have gone it would have been impossible from the state we were in - As when we reached the house of those Hospitable People - viz Richardson to whom every praise is due their attention and care of myself and crew will never be obliterated from my memory - They undressed us like Children and put on us flannel Drapes - gave us nourishment and put us to bed - I mention the man of the Watch and those of the Life Boat house in particular that you Gentlemen by whose support the said establishment is kept up may act as in your judgement thinks proper."

Pilot Cutters were always on duty sailing about the mouth of the Humber, but were not always as helpful as could be expected. On the morning of 6th October 1815 the crew of the lifeboat, in response to signals of distress, went to the assistance of the ship Rawcliffe near the Patrington Channel, bound from Honduras to Hull. The ship had been aground on the Stony Binks, was dismasted and had twelve feet of water in the hold. Already on board were the Master and crew, together with the Master and Mate of the sloop James Walker who were claiming salvage. The lifeboat crew were asked to pump out the ship and clear the wreckage when another sloop came alongside offering help, which was accepted. Later two Pilot Cutters, Numbers 4 and 5, came to the ship and the services of a pilot were requested. This request was flatly refused unless the two Pilot Cutters were allowed to help. This was considered unnecessary, but the Pilots were adamant and the Master of the Rawcliffe was forced to accept the unwanted assistance. Presumably this attitude was taken because of the possible money involved in salvage or bounty.

The captains of ships were not always very helpful, again because of the possibility of paying out money. On November 25th 1815 the ship Bell, Captain Meek, from St. Petersburg, went aground on the Stony Binks and hoisted a light for assistance. The lifeboat crew was mustered, the boat launched and they went alongside to assist. The captain refused all assistance, but said at the same time he would have reported the lifeboat crew had they not launched. In a statement on January 11th 1816 Captain Meek claimed he fired a blue light for a pilot and at no time needed the lifeboat. A direct contradiction to the report from Richardson.

On the morning of January 20th 1816 the Brig Gambier went aground on the Binks and fired five signal guns for assistance. It took about two hours to muster the lifeboat crew and row out to the vessel, but approaching the Gambier they met the Master and crew in their own boat rowing for the shore. Richardson asked the Master to transfer to the lifeboat but he refused and sent the Mate and a boy. A lifeboat man went into the long boat to see the crew safely ashore. Richardson was the first man to board the Gambier and was therefore able to claim salvage after he and his crew had saved the vessel. Captain Thomas Smith, Master of the Gambier, had been worried about the lifeboat crew doing this and the Mate claimed Richardson had been first on board as a result of trickery. The total value of the Gambier and its cargo was nine thousand six hundred and five pounds seven shillings and threepence, but how much was paid to the lifeboat crew for salvage, if anything, is not known, but it was one of the rules governing the station at Spurn that agreements over salvage claims could only be reached by the Brethren of Trinity House and not by the Master or crew of the lifeboat.

The building of the cottages on Spurn for the crew and their families made it much easier for the lifeboat to be launched quickly when required and there was a sudden and dramatic increase in the population on Spurn as the families moved in during the early part of 1819.

Having the crew living on Spurn and able to give a faster service had no effect on some of the ships' Masters and they continued to refuse assistance, sometimes with tragic results.

At 7.0pm on Sunday 21st February 1819 the alarm was given of a vessel grounded on the Binks; it was blowing hard from the east north east. The lifeboat was afloat and quickly launched, but on reaching the vessel, the Industry of Yarmouth, the Captain "told us to shuff off as he did not want any assistance." After some discussion the lifeboat moved away from the vessel and "rowed about for nearly an hour and went alongside again." The captain still persisted in refusing assistance and that the vessel would come off when the tide flooded. Richardson warned that this would not happen, but was again told to "shuff off." Richardson shook hands with the Captain and said perhaps the lifeboat would be wanted when it was too late, to which the Captain replied "I shall stand to the consequences myself." The lifeboat stood by until 9.0pm when it returned to Spurn and remained afloat. Half an hour later a light was hoisted on the ship and the lifeboat launched immediately. The crew rowed hard towards the ship but she disappeared when the lifeboat was still some three hundred yards away.

"I heard some one cry out for God's sake help but being so very dark and the sea so heavy I could see nor hear no more of it. We could not get ashore again until seven o' clock next morning owing to the wind and sea being so heavy. We found her next morning on her broadside."

Some twelve hours later she drifted into deep water and sank.

In April 1819 a complaint was received at Trinity House from the lifeboat crew who alleged that Richardson was demanding an equal share of the money earned from the gravel trade without actually working himself. There had been a similar complaint a year earlier and it had been made clear that neither Richardson nor

No. 1

I *Do hereby agree with* ROBERT RICHARDSON, *the Master of the Life-Boat at* Spurn, *that the consideration or remuneration for such Services or Assistance, as Himself, his Crew, and the said Life-Boat, or any of them may perform, afford or render to me or to my Ship or Cargo, shall be left to the decision and determination of the Guild or Brotherhood of Masters and Pilots Seamen of the* Trinity-House *of* Kingston-upon-Hull, *and such Sum or Sums of Money as they may award or adjudge to be paid for such Services or Assistance, I do hereby promise and agree to pay accordingly.*

Witness my Hand, this J. Anderson *day of* October 23rd *in the Year* 1819

Witness - Thos. Lowery

No.

I *Do hereby agree with* ROBERT RICHARDSON, *the Master of the Life-Boat at* Spurn, *that the consideration or remuneration for such Services or Assistance, as Himself, his Crew, and the said Life-Boat, or any of them may perform, afford or render to me or to my Ship or Cargo, shall be left to the decision and determination of the Guild or Brotherhood of Masters and Pilots Seamen of the* Trinity-House *of* Kingston-upon-Hull, *and such Sum or Sums of Money as they may award or adjudge to be paid for such Services or Assistance, I do hereby promise and agree to pay accordingly.*

Witness my Hand, this [illegible] *day of* [illegible] 29 *in the Year* 18[illegible]

Witness John Hartman

anyone else should receive money without working. On this occasion the complaint also included the alleged problem of Richardson employing a man to look after the lighthouse and then giving him the same privileges as the lifeboat crew to work gravel. A deputation from Trinity House was to go down to Spurn to sort out the problem.

During August of 1819 an Agent to Lloyds complained that the charges for assistance were too high, although they were levied by Trinity House, based on the reports from Spurn. This led to a system of printed slips, to be signed by the Master of the ship assisted and witnessed, agreeing to pay such sums as may be levied by Trinity House.

The Minerva, coal - loaded from Newcastle to Rochester, got into difficulties on the Binks at 2.0am on January 21st 1820 and hoisted two lights at the masthead. There was an easterly gale at the time. The lifeboat was launched immediately and

"we got to the point end when a very heavy snow storm came on and continued till half past three. We rowed in the direction we had first seen the lights although we kept on the edge of the Banks. It afterwards appeared that we had gone past her. The flood began to make, the snow storm abated and then saw the ship's lights and made for them, the gale increasing. Got within two hundred yards when the sea making so heavy and the wind got to East by South, a gale still increasing. We was not able to reach the ship or pull the boat ahead. I'll do my crew the credit to say that they used their utmost efforts to reach the ship but without effect. I then down anchor and showed them a light which they joyously answered, which I repeated three times, which they did the same. They all gave a dreadful shout for help, they then firing two muskets or small guns seemed to hurry about the decks and set fire to a tar cask, which had they done at the first we might possibly been so near able to discern as the light it made was considerable larger than both the Spurn lights put together. I made a signal with a lantern with the hope they would take to the boat and make for us, as it was utterly impossible for us to get to them. I have every reason to think that her boats was carried away. She kept a light till five o' clock when it totally disappeared from the sea making so heavy over her. The cries of the Unhappy Sufferers were dreadful. We had the disastrous sight to see the ship upset and the unfortunate crew perish, without being able to render them the least assistance. She laid down about seven o' clock in a few moments. The last cries of the Unfortunate Crew were distressing beyond description. She immediately broke up and we was immediately surrounded with the wreck of the ship, but had not the good fortune to fall in with any of the crew."

A graphic account of a disaster when the forces of the wind and sea proved stronger than the "utmost efforts" of the lifeboat crew.

There was a much happier outcome to a service in June 1821 when the Thomas,

Transport No. 40, went aground on the Binks and was wrecked. Once again Richardson's report to Trinity House brings the incident to life.

"On Friday morning (the 8th inst) about half past one o' clock am the wind being ENE a strong breeze - I saw a vessel on the Binks, but saw no signal of distress. Immediately mustered the crew of the Life Boat, launched her and went to the vessel, she proved to be the Thomas of London, a Transport No. 40 bound for Hull, with 26 Troops and an officer (Major Tovey) on board - The Master of the ship asked me what I would take an anchor out for - I told him I could not make no bargains of that nature, the preservation of their lives was my object - as the ship was in a very dangerous situation, and could not possibly get off - I then offered to take all the people into the Life Boat and carry them to shore, and said if I afterwards found carrying an anchor out would be of any service I would endeavour to do it - I then took the Troops with Major Tovey into the Boat by means of a sling from the Main Yard - The Agent (Lieut. Pritchard) said the Troops might go but he felt himself bound to stay by the ship with the crew, as the Pilot had told them there was no danger - I then, it being about four o' clock, put the Troops and Major Tovey on board the Bee Revenue Cutter which was cruising near and remained with the Boat at the edge of the breakers - The crew of the ship were at this time pumping until eleven o' clock when the ship filled with water - The crew then hoisted a Signal of Distress at the Peak End and took to the Main and Mizzen Rigging - As soon as I observed the signal I immediately tried to get to the ship and with great difficulty got to the larboard bow and hailed them to let go the Stopper and Shank Painter and let go the anchor lest it should stove the Life Boat- I then let go the Life Boat's anchor the sea being very heavy - All the ship's boats had previously been washed away but we succeeded in getting the whole of the crew 26 in number with two women and a child much exhausted into the Life Boat about twelve o' clock - The Captain of the ship, Lieu. Pritchard, the Carpenter, and the two women were much bruised and hurt - I am sorry to say one woman was unfortunately drowned and that the Lieut. Pritchard nearly lost his life in endeavouring to save her - there were six or seven of the crew overboard at the same time but all were saved - When I got a little way from the ship a man was perceived in the Mizzen Rigging - I immediately put the crew on board the Pilot Boat No. 6 and returned to the ship and succeeded in bringing the man off whom I put on board the Bee Revenue Cutter - During the time I was employed in taking out the crew from the ship the sea was breaking over her tops and I expected every moment her masts coming over her sides which had they done the Life Boat and crew together with the ships crew must have perished as no other boat could then approach the ship - I then returned on shore, myself and crew much exhausted having been in the boat nearly eleven hours - the wind still ENE.

I am likewise sorry to say the Life Boat was much injured and stoved.

(Signed) R.Richardson. "

A letter from the Navy Office dated 9th August 1821 announced that the Commissioners of the Navy had allowed "Ten Guineas to the Master and two guineas to each of the crew of the Life Boat" in recognition of the service to the Thomas.

The Brig 'Better Luck Still' of North Shields, Captain Robert Mills, grounded near the southern end of Spurn on an ebb tide at 5. 0 am. The lifeboat was launched and reached the brig at 6.0 am, took out an anchor and the crew helped to strike and stow the sails.

Despite great efforts the ship could not be towed off and some of the crew stayed on board the brig to help and the lifeboat returned on the following day. In his report to Trinity House on December 7th 1821 Richardson then described the first serious injury received by any of the crew members. In the act of heaving off the brig

"myself getting out on the anchor to reach an axe to cut the cable, the Life Boat being fended off by a Boat Hook the sea heaving the Boat catched the end of the Boat Hook and darted the whole length of the Boat Hook into the thick part of my thigh. Being severely wounded was obliged to be brought on shore by three of my own crew."

Despite this injury Richardson was on board, in charge, the next time the lifeboat was launched.

Wreck of the Transport Ship "Thomas", by John Ward.
Reproduced by kind permission of the Ferens Art Gallery, Hull City Museums, Art Galleries and Archives Hull.

Life Boat, at Spurn.

The Public is respectfully informed, that during the tremendous Gale of the third Day of *December* last, the Life Boat stationed at Spurn Point for the Preservation of the Crews of such Ships and Vessels as may unfortunately happen to be wrecked there, and in the Vicinity, drove from her Moorings, and was so much damaged and broken, as to render her a complete Wreck and totally unserviceable.

The Corporation of the Trinity House, who have had the Care and Direction of this Life Boat since its first Establishment in the Year 1810, have from time to time, solicited the pecuniary Aid of the Public, and have also contributed largely from their own Funds, towards its Support, and to enable them by building Cottages at Spurn, to provide for the permanent Residence there of the Master and Crew, in order to secure their prompt and immediate Assistance in the Hour of Danger.

The Funds thus raised were prior to the recent Loss of the Life Boat, completely exhausted. And as the re-placing of the Life Boat at Spurn, at this perilous Season of the Year, has become as well a Measure of Humanity, as of Necessity; it is hoped the Appeal now made to the Public, and especially to the Merchants, Ship Owners, Underwriters, and others interested in the Maritime and Commercial Interests of the Port, for further Support and Assistance towards attaining this desirable Object, will not be made in vain.

It will be satisfactory to the Public to be informed, that the Establishment of the Life Boat at Spurn, has fulfilled the most sanguine Expectations with regard to its Utility; having been the means of saving the Lives and restoring to their Families and the Country nearly two hundred Fellow Creatures, and of preserving at a trifling Expense much valuable Property, which must otherwise have been totally lost; thus proving in the fullest manner the Importance of the above highly beneficial Establishment, and the absolute Necessity of its being kept up and supported.

Trinity House,
Kingston-upon-Hull,
2nd January, 1824.

SUBSCRIBERS.

	£.	s.	d.
The Corporation of the Trinity House, of Hull.	100	0	0
[illegible]	50		
Capt. [illegible]	1		
Earl Mulgrave	25		
[illegible]	2		

(over)

On October 11th 1823 an un-named brig was caught in a heavy gale from SSE and was driven stern first onto the Middle Bank where she capsized. Richardson tried to muster the lifeboat crew, but found only the mate and three men. All the others had gone to Kilnsea. The brig sank completely within a quarter of an hour and all hands were lost. Richardson said that had the crew been present and the lifeboat launched it would have been impossible to reach the brig before she sank.

The lifeboat was kept afloat so that it could be launched at any state of the tide, but from time to time it was swept away from its moorings during storm conditions. Mostly it was found, little damaged, and returned for service. During a gale on 3rd December 1823 the lifeboat overturned at its moorings and sank and was badly damaged, making it necessary to have a new boat built. A public subscription list was opened and there were many small donations as well as a few for fifty pounds or twenty five pounds. An appeal was sent to the Hull Corporation and the following reply was received at Trinity House from the Town Clerk

"RESOLVED that the sum of Fifty Pounds be subscribed by this Corporation towards the establishing of a New Life Boat at the same place, upon Condition that for the future the Life Boat be under the superintendence and management of a Committee, to consist of an equal number of members of this Corporation, the Corporation of the Trinity House, and the Ship Owners Society at this Port, and that the Boat be used only for the purpose of saving the lives of persons on board Vessels wrecked or in distress, and not for preserving Cargoes."

This conditional offer was politely declined.

A new boat was ordered from Thomas Mason of Hull, at a cost of one hundred and seventy pounds and it was delivered in the early summer of 1824. The dimensions were as follows "extreme length thirty feet two inches, extreme width ten feet, extreme depth three feet seven inches." It rowed ten oars and could be steered from either end and was made mostly of English oak.

By October 1838 the boat had been modified by replacing copper air boxes with boxes made of Baltic Redwood, copper cylinders used to drain the boat were replaced by cylinders made from elm. Cork fitted under the gunwales to act as a fender was removed as it was found to hold a lot of water and sand. The boat was fitted with a rudder, mast and sail which were "found of the greatest utility." The mast was twenty two feet long and eighteen inches thick. Following these changes

"should the boat at any time ship a sea she frees herself through the Cylinders in the short space of one and a half minutes without the aid of Bailing. This Boat is considered much superior in principal to the one formerly stationed at Spurn, and which was built by Mr. Henry Greathead of Shields."

This second lifeboat at Spurn must have been lighter than the first one as it was kept in the boat shed from time to time and not always afloat.

As for the old boat, Mason wrote to Trinity House on 15th May 1824 saying

"the most suitable service the old Life Boat can be put to I find she will answer for a Shrimp Boat for the Humber, but the owners of such like Vessels being miserably poor I shall not be able to give more than Five Pounds for her."

Richardson made a statement to Trinity House on 13th September, 1824, concerning the behaviour of two of his crew, Henry Spendlove and William Watson. They "insulted me most grossly, swearing at me and challenging me to fight and disobeying my orders in every respect." Richardson alleges they would not load vessels with gravel correctly, would not get into the Life Boat without assurances that they would be paid and that Watson was frequently intoxicated. Some ten days later Spendlove had the morning watch and failed to report a brig, the Alexander, from Shields, in difficulty on the Banks and when the alarm was raised by Richardson's son, Spendlove refused to go into the lifeboat. The two men were dismissed, but through October complaints were sent to Trinity House about Richardson and his wife and their behaviour towards the crew and rescued sailors. Several captains of ships, regular visitors to Spurn and Major Tovey who was rescued from the Thomas, all wrote in defence of Mr. and Mrs. Richardson and the complaints were dismissed.

The report sent by Richardson on 14th September 1830 to Trinity House contains the earliest reference to any kind of steam assistance to the lifeboat, and reads as follows -

"I have to inform you that on Sunday morning the 12 inst the Keeper of the High Light gave the alarm that a Brig was on shore on the Middle Bank with the Lights open about a Handspike length to the Northwards; the Boat being in the House I immediately called all Hands and launched her and proceeded to her, the wind blowing very strong from the SSW at about 9.0 am came alongside the Brig. I went on board and found her to be the Ann of Shields, Captain Shallett Hewson, who from ignorance of the set of the Tide had unwittingly run her ashore - I and the Boats Crew immediately rendered her all the Assistance we could by setting her sails and clearing away - The Prince Frederick Steamer very kindly lent us assistance in towing the Life Boat out, we having had the misfortune on account of it blowing so hard, to carry away our Mast and Sail or we should have been alongside the Brig sooner, had that Accident not occurred - about 12pm we got her off and on account of her not steering she about five minutes after went on the Inner Bank and swung with her head to the southward and freed about three feet - the Steamer took a Hawser from her to endeavour to tow her off, she hauled her off about half a length and the rope broke and she could not stop any longer when the ebb tide made she came off about three o' clock we set all sail on her and reached her out and brought her up abreast of Kilnsea - at 10pm - got her under way and worked her into Clea-ness the Grimsby Packet came to us and stopped by - I then sent the Life Boat to the Spurn - next day we got her under way and the Steamer towed her up to Hull where we arrived about half past two pm."

A letter of thanks was sent by a captain or crew on only a very few occasions, having been rescued by the lifeboat crew. One such letter was written in November 1830.

"November 3rd 9am in attempting to sail into the Humber unfortunately was Drove on the Outer Binks in two minutes after the vessel came to the ground she upset fortunately all of us got upon the Bottom. We cut away all the Weather Rigging expecting her to righten but she sunk in the sand and all of us was washed off and fortunately we all got hold of the corner of the main top and all clung to each other expecting every second to be in eternity. In about half an hour our Hearts was uplifted by the sight of the Life Boat close to us but owing to the Rapidity of the Tide after all exertions of the Boat they were about two or three hours Rowing before they got to us and picked us all safe off the wreck, ten in number. We whose Names is inscribed here under Return our sincere thanks to the Commander and Crew of the Life Boat for their Bold endeavours in saving ten of us from a Watery Grave. In ten minutes more would have been our last. We humbly Return thanks to the Commander of the Life Boat for his humanity towards us with Clothing and all other Necessaries of life.

The Brig Leeds of Newcastle, 207 Tons, John Jameson and Ralph Carnaby owners, from the port of Newcastle Coal Loaded for London.

James Muirhead	Master
Thomas Main	Mate
James Ridley	Carpenter
John Munroe	Cook
George H. Matthieson	Seaman
James Cleghorn	Seaman
George Addams	Apprentice
George Cummings	Apprentice
James Frampton	Apprentice
Robert Goodall	Apprentice

NB Most of the Crew were half naked having thrown off part of their clothes with intention to attempt to swim to the Life Boat."

A heavy gale in February 1835 broke the lifeboat moorings as she lay afloat. As the boat drifted she was battered by the storm, her air boxes filled with water and she sank. It was only with great difficulty that she was recovered, beached, drained and then taken to Hull for repairs. During the storm a schooner ran aground on Trinity Sand. The Mate was knocked overboard and drowned but the lifeboat crew was unable to assist in any way."

A reminder of the rigours of the situation at Spurn comes in the letter of resignation in April 1837 of Willaim Coupland, a crew member for two years. He left the service because "my Constitution not being able any longer to do the work connected with my living here I shall be compelled to seek some other Employment which I am able to do."

John Harrison, the Mate, died in September 1837 after an illness lasting six months, and was buried at Easington. He had served in the lifeboat for eighteen years. There was no pension scheme to help his widow and she also had to leave the cottage at Spurn and find somewhere else to live.

The Shipping Gazette, on the 8th March 1838, carried an article which was critical of the Spurn lifeboat crew and three Humber Pilot Cutters numbers 4, 5 and 6, following the loss of three colliers during a severe gale. In his report Richardson wrote that the three brigs were in imminent danger at 1pm on 24th February and he immediately mustered the crew of the lifeboat. One brig, the Edgar, grounded on the Middle Bank and the crew reached shore safely in their own boat. Because of the state of the wind, sea and tide it was impossible then to launch the lifeboat and they hoisted a flag on the beach hoping the other two brigs would run ashore; but they did not. During the afternoon and evening the conditions worsened and it was impossible to see anything at all. At half past ten it became clearer and a light was seen. With the help of the crew from the Edgar the lifeboat was launched, but in trying to cross the Banks a tremendous sea hit her, broke six of her oars and drove her onto the Banks. The rudder iron broke and she became unmanageable. All the time the sea was breaking over the boat and crew and the men became completely exhausted. They were compelled to let the boat drive before the wind and with great difficulty reached the shore at about four am and saved their lives. The two brigs and their crews were lost. John Winter, Robert Smith and Joseph Brown, the masters of the three Pilot Cutters, wrote to Trinity House in defence of the lifeboat crew in impossible conditions.

Mr. A.G. Carte, Ordnance Store Keeper of the Citadel in Hull, wrote to Trinity House in October 1841 following a tragedy when four crew members of the Whitby lifeboat lost their lives on service, urging the Wardens and Brethren to provide the crew of the Spurn boat with Life Belts designed and made by himself. He pointed out that other crews in the north used them and never went on board the lifeboat without them and he hoped this would be the practice at Spurn. "Twelve Belts with the strongest straps I can obtain" were sent to Spurn on the 20th November 1841 with directions for their use and a repeat of the warning never to go out in the lifeboat without wearing them. These belts were the first safety measures ever provided at Spurn and they cost twelve shillings each.

During the first week of November 1841 Richardson received a letter from Trinity House telling him he was to be retired at the end of the year on grounds of age. On the 9th of November Richardson wrote asking for one more year so that he could clear all debts with his brewer, otherwise he would be forced to sell his possessions to pay off his debts. He claimed he was still capable of good service in the boat, but at the same time said he needed younger crewmen as some were becoming inefficient through age. His plea was turned down and the position of Master was advertised. Ten men applied for the post, including three members of the crew, and Joseph Davey was appointed to take up his new position on January 1st 1842.

There were many other services carried out by the lifeboat and crew besides the ones referred to here. These were mostly to vessels which had gone aground on some part of the Binks or on the banks in the Humber. Lives were saved, ships were pulled clear and pumped dry. Very often the lifeboat stood by the vessels in distress for many hours, waiting for the tide to lift them clear of the sands. These services often lasted ten, twelve or more hours, with no protection for the crew, no food or hot drinks and many times with the men on board the casualty wanting nothing to do with the lifeboat or its crew. Life was hard, the service very demanding, but the men were always there when required.

During December 1841 Richardson went through the process of checking the inventory of articles at Spurn, both for the inn and the lifeboat. He also sent all documents and copies of Rules to Trinity House along with a list of "all I can recollect of lives I have been the humble instrument in saving during my long service at this station."

Richardson's list is not complete, even when compared with existing documents, and it must be remembered that the documentary record is itself far from complete. There are several years for which no evidence of any kind can be found, and some of Richardson's claims cannot be verified because of this. If, however, Richardson's list is combined with existing records he and his crew were responsible for saving the entire crew of a ship on at least three occasions, without any numbers being quoted, as well as the lives of at least three hundred and forty four people. Whatever Richardson's shortcomings as a businessman and publican he did set a standard of service and devotion to duty for others to follow. His pride is reflected in the last sentence of his final letter to Trinity House after thirty one years as Master, when he wrote

“The Life Boat has never been afloat without me in her throughout my long service, and I have to thank God that I never lost a Life of one of my Crew.”

A proud record indeed.

JOSEPH DAVEY 1st JANUARY 1842 - 13th FEBRUARY 1843

Joseph Davey was appointed to the position of Master of the Life Boat at Spurn in early December 1841, to take up his appointment on January 1st 1842. He was twenty eight years of age, a married man with no children.

Davey visited Spurn during the last three weeks of December, inspected the buildings and noted where repairs were needed, checked the inventory and also ascertained the ages of all the crew members. Before the end of the month he sent letters of dismissal to six of the men, and to a seventh shortly afterwards. Some of the crew had served since 1819, but two of them were under forty years of age. All these men sent "Humble Petitions" to Trinity House, some of them supported by Richardson, asking for reasons for their dismissal and for some financial consideration in their difficult time. All the men lost their houses as well as their work and some had large families of young children to provide for. The older ones knew it would be extremely difficult, if not impossible, to find other work and feared they would "be obliged to lay ourselves on the Kilnsea parish and be removed by the union for we all have large families then we shall be sold up and ruined." Trinity House offered no support to these families.

This was not a very promising beginning to Davey's term as Master.

The first two letters from Davey to Trinity House in the first week of January 1842 were seeking clarification about items of furniture and fittings at the inn for which Richardson was seeking payment. Davey asserted the items were more numerous and the sum involved much greater than he had been led to believe before he accepted the appointment. He also asked for a new supply of rockets, lines and six pound cartridges rather than four pounders, as he thought they would carry the line straighter and a greater distance and could be trusted.

There is very little correspondence from Davey to be found in the records at Trinity House, but of the nine letters sent between February 14th and September 22nd 1842 two contain requests for stores and paints for the lifeboat, six are concerned with deteriorating relationships between Davey and the crew, and men either leaving or being dismissed and one contains similar references as well as a brief report of a service with the lifeboat.

Davey clearly did not command the respect, loyalty or confidence of the crewmen. Men were discharged for taking leave without permission, swearing at the Master, and one, William Richardson, on grounds of age as he was sixty three years old and the younger men thought he could no longer do a fair share of the work on the beaches. Having been dismissed he refused to leave his cottage even though another man had arrived at Spurn complete with furniture to occupy the same house. Davey appealed to Trinity House for help, but there are no documents to reveal the solution to the problem. One man left to find a better job and Davey feared others would follow. He re-employed one of the crew he had dismissed in December, to fill one of the gaps.

Just to add to Davey's problems he claimed that many false stories about him were being spread in Hull, which made life very uncomfortable for him at Spurn. He was convinced he had "so many enemies about" that he could not trust anyone to deliver a letter without opening it and perhaps destroying it and he thought this was the reason for lack of response from Trinity House to his appeals for help.

Mrs. Davey did not settle or like living in the house at Spurn and Davey asked for a surveyor to be sent down "to see what state it is in for I will assure you gentlemen that my wife got cold the first week we was in the House so that if there is nothing done at the House it is almost impossible to live in it for when it blows it is almost fit to blow one out of the House."

The letter written on April 10th 1842 includes a report on a service to the sloop Rose, of Hull, which had "sunk on the Sandhail" - sands on the south side of the Humber, south east from Grimsby. Davey thought he saw three men in a small boat astern of the Rose and that in view of the conditions, with a heavy gale from the north east, it would not be possible to launch a lifeboat from the south bank. He therefore launched the Spurn boat. When they reached the casualty the three men had managed to get ashore and no other assistance was possible. All the crew members were soaked and the conditions made it impossible to return to Spurn that day. "Mr. Hind, the Lloyds Agent, sent us up to the Public House at North Sumercoates to get our clothes dried and get some refreshment, and I have had a letter from Mr. Moon to-day for the expenses and the amount is one pound sixteen shillings for Meat Allowance and Lodging." The lifeboat returned to Spurn the following day.

The only other service for which there is any record took place on January 10th 1843. The sloop Rose, of Boston, twenty three tons, was riding in the Hawk Roads, parted from her cables and ran onto the beach. The master and Mate took to the rigging and were taken off at 6.0am on the following morning when conditions had eased. The lifeboat and crew, along with two pilots, were employed in recovering two anchors and ninety five fathoms of chain and heaving the vessel off the beach. For this service Captain Taylor of the Rose was asked to sign an agreement, witnessed by Thomas Cotick, to pay Davey twelve pounds. This was in direct breach of the rules which stated that only Trinity House could reach agreements about payments for any kind of service by the lifeboat. Captain Taylor also stated that he never saw any copies of the Rules and Regulations anywhere at Spurn, nor had he been asked to sign a document, which Davey should have presented, leaving all matters of arbitration concerning assistance to the Board of Trinity House.

Joseph Davey was dismissed from the Spurn lifeboat station on February 13th 1843.

The post of Master of the Life Boat was advertised and twenty nine men applied. By the end of February Robert Brown had been appointed.

It is not known exactly when Joseph Davey left Spurn. It is possible that he left immediately he had been dismissed and that William Laycock, Mate, took over as acting Master. It is also possible Davey left at the end of the month or waited until Brown arrived at Spurn. A letter by Davey on 25th March 1843 asking Trinity House to pay him for work he had done at the inn begins by saying "I have left Spurn and have given up to Captain Brown the whole of the materials connected with the Life Boat and Tender at Spurn in a quiet and peaceable manner."

Richard Jackson, Master of the schooner Elizabeth, of Hartlepool, wrote to Trinity House on February 28th 1843. He stated that at 2.0am on Sunday morning, 19th February, his ship, coal loaded for Yarmouth, ran onto the Stony Binks in thick and stormy weather. The ship remained there for four hours, beating hard, during which time the crew constantly had pitch kettles, tar barrels or candles burning at the masthead. They tried to launch their own boat with three men in it, but it was smashed by the sea and the three men lost. In all this time they received no assistance from the lifeboat or anyone else at Spurn. The Elizabeth eventually floated off, got into the Humber, took a pilot on board and reached Hull. In April Robert Brown was asked to investigate the matter and found that the lifeboat had launched at 3.0am but conditions prevented the crew from reaching the schooner. The anchor was dropped and the lifeboat rode until they saw the vessel float off and take a pilot on board at 6.0am. As William Laycock remained in the crew after Brown's appointment and is not named in this report it is probable that Davey was still in charge of the lifeboat on this service.

This investigation brought to an end a very unhappy period in the history of the lifeboat station at Spurn.

ROBERT BROWN MARCH 1843 - 31st OCTOBER 1848

Robert Brown was one of a large number of applicants for the post of Master of the Life Boat at Spurn. He was described as a sober and industrious man and he had served one year as Mate and three years as Master for the company which employed him at the time of his application. He had served the company satisfactorily in several capacities and was a steady, careful and sober man and confidently recommended for the position at Spurn. He took up his appointment sometime in March 1843.

The documentary record of Brown's term of office at Spurn is very fragmentary, but it was a time of great hardship for himself and the lifeboat crew. The gravel trade declined progressively, as did the crew's earnings, and there were repeated appeals to Trinity House for relief. Brown's trade at the inn also declined and he could not make a living and these difficulties probably caused the unrest amongst the crew and the number of changes which took place.

The first service is recorded in a letter of May 19th 1843. A vessel was aground on the Middle Bank at two o' clock in the morning. The lifeboat was launched, but the strong wind and flooding tide prevented the crew from reaching her. The lifeboat stood by waiting for slack water, and two Pilot Boats, Numbers 2 and 3, took off the crew from the ship. When the lifeboat was able to reach the vessel they saved the ropes and sails, but found all the decks started and her stern post and she became a total wreck. Four members of the lifeboat crew were very late to the boat for that service and one of them continued to neglect his duties and Brown asked for permission to discharge him. Trinity House replied that although the Board did not want changes to be made if at all possible, but wanted stability, permission was granted in this case.

In July and September of that year the lifeboat was launched and stood by vessels grounded on the Binks until they floated off. On the second occasion the lifeboat was standing by from 8.30pm until 2.30am.

The Express, laden with potatoes from Gainsborough to London, went aground on the Inner Binks at 11.0pm on February 22nd 1844 and hoisted a light for assistance. The lifeboat was launched immediately but had to stand by her until 6.0am when the lifeboatmen were able to board her. They found all the crew lashed to the rigging. The lifeboatmen assisted the Express into the Humber and afterwards laid her on the beach at 8.0am.

There was more crew trouble on March 1st 1844 when two gravel vessels were blown ashore. The lifeboat crew were asked to discharge them, which they did, but two of the men then refused to assist in pumping the vessels into the Humber and

Brown wanted to discharge the men. One of the two, Thomas Megginson, strongly denied the charge and claimed that he had been at Spurn for twenty five years and had never been in any trouble. The two were dismissed, but Megginson was later re-employed.

On September 9th 1844 all the crew signed a letter which was sent to Trinity House asking for financial assistance. The crew pointed out that there was no gravel to work and therefore the men could not earn a living. They had remained at Spurn all summer expecting to earn something, but they were now deeply in debt to Mr. Brown and could not stay any longer unless there was "Maintenance from the House" and they intended to travel to Hull to meet the Board of Trinity House on the following Saturday. This was followed by a letter from Brown on September 21st asking for assistance as his earnings were far short of what he had been led to expect. The Constable family had not been financially involved in the lifeboat station since at least 1839 and there was no-one to make up the master's income to one hundred pounds if his earnings fell short of that figure. He also pointed out that all the crew members owed him money and had no means of paying him and he considered this situation responsible for the troubles amongst the crew

"I likewise beg with much regret to represent to your Worshipful Board the great degree of insubordination at present prevalent amongst the Crew of the Life Boat the Result in my opinion of the small Amount of their earnings consequent upon the want of Employment this cause of complaint has now arrived at such an extent as to interfere materially with the efficient performance of the duties of the Station."

On that occasion the Board decided not to grant any relief.

The brig Squirrel, of Whitby, Captain Moorsom, was on the beach in February 1845 and some of the lifeboat crew were engaged to free it and get her off. This they did, but the Captain then refused to pay the agreed sum of seven pounds. When the crew appealed to Trinity House for help the Board decided that as this was only a matter of labour and not a lifeboat incident no order could be made to the Captain.

The following letter was written on 24th August 1845

"We the undersigned do with Reluctance appeal to your Honourable Board to take into consideration the Deficiency of the accommodation of shipwrecked seamen which we six ships Crews experienced on Tuesday Night after being Drenched for hours on Board our Ships we seamen being fortunate to save our lives that Night when we got on shore found nine Bedcabins but no covering to comfort our shaking Bodies we the seamen do Petition to you for the sake of others as well as ourselves that do come ashore the ships being full of water as ours was for a dry shirt to be in readiness and covering on those nine Bedcabins that is in readiness for

Shipwrecked seamen. We have found every comfort that we desire at the Life Boat Hotel except as stated above Feeling much obliged to Mr. Brown for the comforts he has continued towards during our stay here We remain Gentlemen Yours Most Respectfully,

Edward Jones Master of Schooner Betsey of Yarmouth
Richard Burgess Master and Part Owner of the Ark, Schooner of Yarmouth
John F. Wilkinson Master of the Frances of Ipswich
George Hill master of the Nautilus of Boston
Robert Kirby master of Schooner Betsey of Yarmouth
Robert Wilson Master and Owner of the Providence of Boston."

The letter reveals a strange situation where the men were very well cared for, but there were no bed coverings. Trinity House immediately ordered twelve pairs of blankets to be provided. Equally there is no report of any kind from Brown about any calls for assistance or wrecks or even any sighting of these vessels. Perhaps if the records were complete there would be such a report.

The lifeboat was launched at 1.0am on Sunday 22nd March 1846, a light having been seen on or near the Binks. The crew rowed all night and found nothing, but on returning to Spurn found the crew of the Duchess of Beaufort, of Brixham, landing from their own boats. They told Brown the Master had been drowned by the fall of the foretopmast on the Saturday night and the ship then ran aground. The crew took to their own boat and showed a light when clear of the Binks. This probably explains why the lifeboat crew searched in vain. On April 5th the schooner George and Thomas was lost on the Inner Binks. The lifeboat was towed out by the Pilot Cutter No. 6 and saved the entire crew of six men. During this service the sea broke four oars and caused the lifeboat to drag her anchor. Brown asked for a heavier one of three hundredweights. In June he informed Trinity House of the damaged state of the tender and that he had still not received a sail, oars or another anchor for the lifeboat, nor blankets and mattresses for the inn. Some of these items were delivered two weeks later.

The condition of the tender deteriorated and in October 1847 Brown informed Trinity House that the planks in her bottom were only a quarter of an inch thick and that she was "very unsafe for use." In August 1848 the lifeboat was damaged by the Newsand Light Ship which was being towed by the Trinity Steam Yacht. The lifeboat had to be taken to Hull for repairs.

The final blow for Brown came in September 1848 when he applied at Patrington for the renewal of his licences. The Chief Magistrate, Reverend Christopher Sykes, refused to renew the licence to sell on the beaches. This meant Brown could no longer supply the vessels loading gravel and cobbles and he knew his livelihood was finished. He wrote his letter of resignation on September 13th 1848 and a further note a week later confirmed that the resignation would be effective from the end of October.

Robert Brown left Spurn at a time of great financial difficulty for the crew and his successor and when morale was very low. The post was advertised and in spite of the problems there were nine applicants. On the 14th October Michael Hansley Welburn was appointed to be Master of the Life Boat at Spurn, to take up his duties on the 1st November 1848.

MICHAEL HANSLEY WELBURN
1st NOVEMBER 1848 - MARCH 1853

When Michael Hansley Welburn applied for the position of Master of the Life Boat at Spurn he was thirty two years of age, a married man with no children. He had been at sea nineteen years "in every capacity" and had sailed out of the Humber for twelve years. Like Joseph Davey he was a young man, but certainly had many years of experience at sea.

Welburn joined the station at a time of great depression because of the declining gravel trade, almost complete absence of earnings for the crew and problems of the peninsula being broken by the sea and the lifeboat station being on an isolated island. Most of the letters from Welburn to Trinity House are concerning the desperate plight of the crew and himself and appealing for relief. There were many weeks with no earnings of any kind, families were going hungry and some crew members left in search of better conditions .

The crew did earn small amounts of money from time to time for unloading chalk stone to protect the cottages or to try to fill the breaches in Spurn, but this work was spasmodic and certainly poorly paid. On two occasions, in March and April 1852, ten men worked for five days unloading and positioning two hundred and forty tons of chalk. In each case the men were paid eight shillings each for their efforts. Some work was available making a concrete base for a new Low Light on Spurn, but again it was not regular work and the families suffered. It was not until May 1852 that the gravel trade began to improve, but this was short-lived. The attempt to close the breaches in Spurn sometimes stopped for six or eight weeks at a time and then was renewed using "outside" labour based on the landward side of the gaps. Meanwhile the sea had widened the breaches once more. The houses were becoming very dilapidated and Welburn feared for the safety of the inn. It was against this background that Welburn had to battle to motivate and lead the crew. The fact that he faced and shared all the same problems and hardships probably made it easier for him to succeed.

The first record of any kind of service was on December 5th 1848 when the lifeboat went off to the brig Genoa Packet, Captain Dolmahoy, laden with coal from Shields to Le Havre. The brig struck the Binks and later ran ashore to become a complete wreck. The crew of the brig got ashore at 5am and the lifeboat crew tried to salvage as much as possible of the brig and its cargo.

The next recorded service took place on 17th April 1849 to the schooner Enterprise, of Pakefield, Captain Jenkinson.

"On Tuesday night about 9pm, in the height of the Snow Storm wind at NW she parted from her anchor only having 25 fathoms of chain and one anchor they set the fore Lugg. Hearing cries of distress I went down and saw a light so large as I took it to be a ship on fire, but we soon lost sight of it, but seeing the vessel through the snow they had run her on shore on Old Den. While some of our men was getting the tender to go off to her, the boat came on shore with the crew, two men and a boy. I asked them what they had left her for, they said she was half full of water and on her beam ends and wanted assistance which I went to the boat to try and get on board but could not. The men went to our House and called for something to eat, when I was taken so ill I could scarce walk Home. When I made more enquiries about the vessel the little boy said he did not think there was any water in her, so we found was the fact. I left orders as soon as possible the Crew was to get on board and I would send a kedge and warps and let them know how things was going on. It appears as the tide flowed she drove over the Den and came to the beach when our Crew got on board and held her off until 2am when the wind setting to the Eastwards she blew off when I told them to go and look out or she would be blown to sea, they would not go near her all they kept saying they wish they had their clothes out of her she might go where she liked. When I found they were so careless I thought it became our duty to do the best we could to save the property which was entrusted in the Masters hands. I wrote to inform you expecting they would fetch Hull but appears only Grimsby where they gave her up to Mr. N. Chapman, Receiver of Droits, which he says will come under the salvage act ...My brother has to write this for me for I am not able to sit over end."

Captain Jenkinson refused to sign the certificate acknowledging assistance and Welburn asked Trinity House to arrange payment for the service.

The sloop Eagle, Captain Durrants, from Brancaster bound for Goole with a cargo of barley, showed signals of distress on the night of 11th January 1850 after getting into difficulties on Trinity Sand. The lifeboat crew launched the tender to go to the lifeboat but battled for four hours against the wind and sea and could not reach the lifeboat. In the struggle three oars were broken and Welburn "had the misfortune to slip the knee joint out of my right leg." The light on the Eagle was no longer being shown and the captain and crew reached the shore safely in their own boat. The Eagle drove hard onto Trinity Sand and filled with water. The next day the lifeboat crew discharged the cargo and sent it to Goole. This report again shows the power of the elements even on the river side of Spurn. Welburn appeared to be none the worse for the injury to his leg.

The difficulties faced by pulling and sailing boats are again illustrated by a service on Friday 5th April 1850.

"At 3pm on Friday 5th April a Foreign schooner run in upon the clays S by E from us, without anchors and appeared much distressed . It blowing very heavy at the time from SW by W manned the Life Boat to see if they wanted assistance, which particulars I shall state how we performed our duty. Launched the tender the sea very high and broken took the Main Lug Sail and nine of the crew with great and good Exertion got her out of the Land swell when the two port oars was broke by the sea striking the Boat which sent her about seven fathoms astern and half filled the Boat, let her come on shore again baled her out and took four oars more in her determined to try what we could do. When ready tried again when we got on the edge of the Ground swell away went two oars more then with the hardest struggle succeeded in reaching the boat. Got her underweigh just slipt her when she was gathering her way when the Heel of the mast broke off and hurt John Brantons leg very bad. Let go the Anchor dragged the fragments in, having a good one in the boat cut the Heel off, takes in a reef, sets the sail, weighs the Anchor, just taking the weight of her canvas away goes the mast again by the thwart. Let go the Anchor again, could not be more than sixteen fathoms from the shore. I was so pleased to see her perform so well tried again, cut away the shattered part and made another Heel, set the sail, when ready, all depending on the smartness of dragging the Anchor up and getting her to cast the right way, two weather oars being shipped. The order given and instantly obeyed she took her canvas and was off like a bird in fifteen minutes was alongside of the schooner when we found there was a pilot on board and had sent word to Grimsby for Anchors and a steam boat, so we returned the flood coming in could not reach our Moorings, brought up until the next tide, and moored, cleaned the boat &c."

The mast, and oars were broken, one man was injured and a great deal of effort was made only to find that the schooner had already taken a pilot on board and did not need assistance. This was followed by a long wait in the boat until the tides allowed the crew to reach the moorings and then the shore. The whole episode must have been one of great frustration, coupled with the knowledge that the lifeboat had been on the spot had it been required.

Robert Brown had reported to Trinity House in 1847 that the tender was in a bad state of repair and "very unsafe for use." On 30th September 1850 Welburn wrote to Trinity House listing the dimensions of the tender as being sixteen feet three inches in length from inside of stem to inside of stern post, overall breadth six feet and depth from top of gunwale to keel two feet five inches, and rowed four oars. As a replacement he suggested

"a boat would be much better to get off this beach under the following dimensions twenty two feet long, six feet beam and two feet nine inches deep, to row six oars, she will require to have a flat floor in Midships and two bold ends, a Bollard forwards to hang the Life Boats moorings when the Life Boat is away, a good strong Iron plate on her keel to save it when launching up and down the beach."

He also considered it would be "very handy if there was sprit sails."

A new tender must have been ordered by Trinity House, but what the dimensions were or where it was built are not known.

The fishing smack Alert, of Hull, ran onto the Inner Binks at 9.30pm on Monday 21st October 1850 and the lifeboat was launched. The report continues

"...not being water over the Banks for our boat came to anchor off the Banks until low water, then went on the Banks alongside by wading. I begged of the crew to leave her as it was blowing hard and a heavy sea making. They would not although I told them we would ride by them and put them on board if she held together while she drifted off but of no avail. At 3am tried to get to her, could not until she drifted over and them in the rigging. When we got to her she was full of water just going down. We took five of the crew off when she went down ten minutes after, had no time to get their clothes being thankful they saved their lives being very much exhausted. Returned and moored the Life Boat at 5am."

Welburn concludes his report by asking for the new tender as soon as possible as the present one was leaking badly and appeared " to fail all over alike at once with old age."

Tragedy struck whilst the tender was being used to rescue the crew of the brig Cumberland, of Newcastle, which had run ashore near Kilnsea in a sinking state. Welburn wrote

"proceeded to the place with rockets &c and carried over to the vessel our tender to go on board at Low Water when we got a Rocket over her to haul the boat off, went off four times but the boat half-filled - tried the fifth, succeeded in saving five hands, sixth time filled, the seventh time the boat turned over end burying myself, J. Welburn and J. Branton swam on shore but Branton drowned, the boat went away to sea so we are without. Captain Lister of fishing smack lent us his boat, saved the remainder of the crew nine in number. (Master drowned)."

This brief account greatly understates the repeated efforts of the crew to man-haul the tender along the line through the breakers to the wreck to take off the crew. John Branton was the first crew member to lose his life whilst on service. A public subscription raised forty two pounds, eleven shillings and sixpence for his widow, who had to leave her house at Spurn and make a claim on her parish. Welburn hoped she would receive some support from the Board of Trinity House

Following this tragedy Mr. A. G. Carte wrote the following to the secretary to the Board of Trinity House on 29th October

“I trust the Brethren will pardon me if on this Melancholy occasion I call their attention to the omission by which this poor man probably lost his life - I allude to the want of the Life Belts which at my suggestion were some years since furnished to the station at Spurn Point - In 1847 the Master represented to me that he thought the belts were not sufficiently Buoyant, and I immediately furnished him with Five layer ones, with directions that the men who wore the others should each put on two this precaution appears on the Thursday to have been totally neglected; and it was the more necessary, because the Master and Men were obliged to use the Tender to the Life Boat by which they incurred a much greater risk, and which was unfortunately upset and lost.

The conduct of the Master of the Boat in his attempts to save the Crew has been highly praised by all who witnessed it; but I think an enquiry will be made to ascertain why means of safety which the Brethren had been at the expense of providing should be totally neglected at the only time in which they could possibly be of service, and that strict orders will be given that in future no man shall embark on the Life Boat or Tender for the purpose of going to a wreck without wearing his life belt.”

At some time during November an old boat was sent to Spurn as a temporary replacement for the tender which had been swept away during the rescue from the Cumberland. Welburn complained that it was useless as it leaked so badly it would not float for three hours . He asked for another boat as soon as possible “fitting for our service.”

A new reporting system began in January 1857 whereby the Master was required each month to send to Trinity House a statement of the wind, weather, activities of the pilot cutters and services by the lifeboat, all in the form of a table. The report for that month begins

Wed	1	SSW	Very stormy & rain at intervals. Brig Dorothea of Sunderland ran onshore at Kilnsea.
Thur	2	WSW	Moderate weather. The brig got off at night all well.
			At 6am saw a sloop on the Banks, the W.W.Gooding from Woodbridge to Newcastle loaded saphtolite. Succeeded in getting her off the Banks & took her up to Hull - with head sails split.
Fri	3	Variable	Fore part moderate wind southly, at night Easterly, sleet & rain, pilot cutter on duty.

It is recorded that the new tender was received on Tuesday 7th January, but on February 15th Welburn wrote to Trinity House

"We have been off twice to go a buoying with the new tender, with having no keel cannot keep her head to wind, when in a swell we shall have no chance ...If the boat remains she must have a keel put on and stem and stern made up with dead wood."

There are no further service reports for the remainder of Welburn's stay at Spurn. There are brief statements in the monthly summary reports and either Welburn thought this sufficient or the reports no longer exist.

On Friday 21st March 1851, the wind south east and very strong, with heavy seas, the crew "dragged two hands off the Celerity, being two hours in the rigging." Later in the same month the brig Ann drove ashore and filled with water at the Point. The lifeboat crew pumped her out and got her off the beach. Friday 13th June 1851 saw the lifeboat go to assist two lighters blown ashore to the north, with very heavy seas. The boat capsized and all the men were "very narrowly saved." On October 17th very high seas drove the sloop GG ashore and the lifeboatmen saved the crew by means of ropes. Three men were taken from the Banks on November 16th, but in what circumstances is not known.

Welburn, on March 1st 1852, received a copy of the "Challenge" from Mr. H. T. Richardson, concerning the Tubular Life Boat. The Spurn boat did not compete.

A letter from Welburn to Trinity House on 17th March 1852 was to inform the Brethren of the death of the Mate, John Welburn who had "never recovered from injury he received in rescuing the crew of the Cumberland. He was with me in seven attempts and was in the boat when she overended ...He left Spurn on 12th inst for advice and died on 13th with effusion on the brain - leaving a widow and two children."

George Scott, a crew member, was appointed Mate.

Evidence of the tourist industry comes in a somewhat surprising statement in the report for Thursday 20th May 1852. We read "Dense fog and fresh breezes. A great tea party about 1600 landed." Perhaps the lifeboat families were able to earn something by providing some refreshments for the visitors.

During the first week of September 1852 Mr. Bee went to North and South Shields on behalf of Trinity House for an exhibition of lifeboats. There were three locally built Shields boats and five built in H.M.Dock Yards exhibited by Captain Washington. The Shields boats were similar to the current Spurn boat and Mr. Bee considered them "fine boats for the build and found them highly spoken of by those entrusted with their management." The boats built in H.M.Dock Yards were slightly smaller than the Shields boats and their pulling qualities were tested along with two Shields boats by being pulled out of the harbour against the wind and tide. However, Mr. Bee "was much disappointed that the qualities of Captain Washington's Boats were not further tested for one of them was built after the Model which had the prize awarded to her, given last year by the Duke of Northumberland for possessing the best properties for righting herself in the event of being upset and for emptying herself quickly of water and for possessing every other property superior to the great number of models competing for his Grace's Prize but none of these properties were tested and the exhibition was to me altogether void of interest."

The schooner Liberty, of Leith, drove onto the Banks in heavy rain and with strong winds from NNE on Sunday 19th September 1852. The lifeboat was launched to her assistance and the schooner was eventually towed off by the steam tug Peep a Day Boy. This is the earliest reference to a steam tug being involved with and assisting the lifeboat whilst it was on service.

There were six other occasions in the remainder of 1852 when the lifeboat assisted vessels in difficulty, mostly on the Binks, including one steamer, the Neptune from Newcastle. On January 10th 1853 the brig Ann Moore, of Shields, was abandoned on the Binks with three feet of water inside her. The lifeboat crew pumped her out and prepared to get her off. On the following day the brig came off the Binks and was taken to anchor in Grimsby Roads. An increasing gale carried away the fore yard. On January 12th a tug was sent to tow the Ann Moore into Grimsby.

The lifeboat launched on service once more with Welburn in command. On 25th January 1853, with strong winds from the north and north east, and snow showers, the boat went to assist the Amazon, of Hull, on the Binks. This was the final service for Welburn who died sometime during March, but the date and cause of death are not recorded.

Michael Hansley Welburn served as master for almost four and a half years at a time of great poverty and deteriorating living conditions for the crew. For most of the time the lifeboat station was cut off from the mainland because Spurn had been breached and this only made life more difficult. He did fight hard on behalf of his crew but his untimely death brought an abrupt end to a very promising career.

The position of Master of the Life Boat at Spurn was advertised by Trinity House on 19th April 1853 and on 30th April John Calvert was appointed. It is probable that George Scott, Mate of the lifeboat, acted as Master from the time of Welburn's death until Calvert was able to take up his appointment.

Visitors landing onto the beaches at Spurn, about 1900. *Courtesy Mrs. D. Lawrence*

Visitors landing at Spurn, about 1910. *Courtesy of Mr.&Mrs R. Robinson*

John Calvert appointed
30th April 1853.

TRINITY HOUSE,

KINGSTON-UPON-HULL,

19*th April*, 1853.

WANTED

A Master of the Life Boat,

STATIONED AT SPURN POINT.

Persons who intend to offer themselves as Candidates for the situation, must deliver in their names and ages, with Testimonials of their Character and Qualifications, at the Office of the Warden's Clerk in this House, on or before the 29th day April instant, and must also personally attend at this House on the following day, Saturday, the 30th day of April instant, at Four o'Clock in the Afternoon, being the day of Election.

By Order,

EDWARD S. WILSON,

Secretary.

NEW LIFE BOAT.

TO BOAT BUILDERS AND OTHERS.

Trinity-House, Hull,
11*th July*, 1853.

NOTICE is hereby given, that Persons desirous of Contracting for Building a New Life Boat, to be stationed at Spurn Point, at the Entrance of the Humber, are requested to deliver Tenders for the same, sealed up and addressed "Tender for building Life Boat," at the Wardens' Clerk's Office, in the Trinity-House, on or before the 22nd day of July instant.

A Model of the intended Boat, and a Specification of the Boat Stores and Materials, are laid at the Wardens' Clerk's Office, and may be seen by Persons desirous of Contracting for the Work, every day, from 10 A.M. to 4 P.M.

By Order,

EDWARD S. WILSON,
SECRETARY.

JOHN CALVERT 1st MAY 1853 - DECEMBER 1853

John Calvert applied for the position of Master of the Life Boat at Spurn on 23rd April 1853. He supported his application by saying that he had already served Trinity House for twelve years. For most of that time he had been Mate of the Trinity House Yacht and had gained a thorough knowledge of that part of the Humber where the lifeboat was mostly required. His character and abilities must have been already known to the Board and he was appointed on 30th April and was able to take up his duties immediately.

The first service recorded was on Sunday 22nd May when the Dutch sloop Arenida came inside the Binks taking in water. She broke her back and "four planks in each side." The tender was launched and escorted the sloop into Grimsby.

An advertisement for a new lifeboat for Spurn was published on 11th July 1853 with a closing date for receiving tenders on 22nd July. Earlier, on May 13th, Mr. Robert Anderson of South Shields had sent an estimate, with a model to follow, for a thirty two feet long boat "built of the best materials, and all Copper fastened and nailed." Unfortunately the estimate is no longer to be found. Mr . T. C. Clarkson offered one of his newly patented boats for the sum of ninety pounds and was prepared to put it to any test to prove its efficiency. The tender from Hallett & Co. of Hull was for one hundred and twelve pounds, eighteen shillings and sixpence. This last tender was accepted in August. It is not recorded when the new lifeboat was delivered to Spurn, but it must have been in late 1853 or early 1854 as a letter from the Gutta Percha Company of London, on June 12th 1854, concerned the repair of air cells in the "new boat."

Through the autumn of 1853 the lifeboat was launched on several occasions to stand by vessels until they came off sand banks, or to go to vessels which then did not require assistance. Once or twice the crew helped to discharge cargo to lighten a ship, but earnings were very low. On Saturday 5th November the brig Acorn, of Guernsey, timber loaded from Danzig, grounded on the Inner Binks. The lifeboat was launched and got her off the sand and into the Humber.

In December 1853 John Calvert submitted his resignation from his position as Master of the Life Boat. This was because of the lack of earnings for the crew and himself and the great poverty suffered by the families. There was almost no gravel trade, there had been very little salvage work, the houses were in a very poor condition, Spurn was still breached and the families cut off from the mainland. Calvert and the crew appealed repeatedly to Trinity House for some relief and finally Calvert resigned to become a Humber Pilot, where he hoped for a better life.

GEORGE GRANT 1st JANUARY 1854 - 31st JULY 1856

When George Grant applied from Cleethorpes for the position of Master of the Life Boat at Spurn he was thirty four years old. He had been a fisherman on the Humber all his life and said he knew the banks well. He was appointed and took up the post as Master on January 1st 1854.

This was still a time of great poverty at Spurn and living conditions continued to worsen. Grant had to fight hard to keep a crew and maintain the morale in face of great difficulties.

A heavy gale from east south east on 4th January caused an un-named schooner to founder on the Outer Binks and all hands were lost. The brig Isabella foundered on the Inner Binks on the evening of 25th January, but the entire crew, nine in number, reached shore safely in their own boat.

On the last day of January work to close the breaches in Spurn began again in earnest. Three and four ships a day brought chalk stone, but much of it was washed away by gales in February. During the gale on 18th February the steamer Scandinavian went aground on the Inner Binks. The lifeboat launched, two oars were broken in trying to reach the ship, but she got off without assistance. A French lugger drove onto the Inner Binks and became a total wreck. Fortunately the crewmen were all picked up by a steamer. At 11pm on the same day the sloop Dahlia went ashore on the Humber side of Spurn having lost its anchors and all the crew were saved.

A letter written on March 24th 1854 accompanied plans and elevations

"for the Master's House and Ten Cottages for the Life Boat Master and Men at Spurn Point. To carry the above named Plans into execution I estimate will cost about the Sum of Two Thousand Pounds, exclusive of the expense of the Superintending or Surveying the erection of the same."

The matter was considered by the Board of Trinity House on 1st April and referred back to the committee on account of the expense. Nothing more appeared to happen until January 1857.

At 4am on 21st April the schooner Greyhound ran aground on the Inner Binks. The tender was launched, but assistance was not required. There was on this occasion a problem with the crew of the lifeboat at first refusing to man the tender -

"when the Crew of the Life Boat were called they refused to attend to my summons - but ultimately they made their appearance and when I desired them to man the Life Boat's Tender some of them refused to do so and as I have experienced a difficulty on previous occasions in getting the Tender manned I am induced to ask if you expect the Crew to go in the Tender in a case of emergency, when it is not practicable to get off with the Life Boat. I may add that when the Crew were desired to proceed in the Tender on the 21st inst the weather was fine."

There is no record of the reply from Trinity House.

A report from Grant to Trinity House written on 27th January 1855 briefly described a service to the brig Tiberius. The watchman saw the brig's lights on Bull Sand at three o' clock in the morning and the tender was launched. The crew boarded the Tiberius, got her afloat and into Grimsby even though she "was making twelve inches water every hour." The important sentence in the report reads

"agreed with the Captain for one hundred pounds for our assistance in getting the ship afloat."

This represents a change in the rules governing the station, as previously all financial arrangements had to be made through the Board of Trinity House. Indeed, Joseph Davey had previously been dismissed for making his own financial arrangements with a ship's captain.

The Board of Trade sent a brief circular to Trinity House in September 1854 concerning the powers given to the Board by the Merchant Shipping Act of 1854 relating to the saving of life from shipwreck. A much longer and more detailed document was received in Hull in February 1855 which set out the requirements and conditions for the assistance of and rewards from the Board of Trade. It is obvious that Trinity House must have written to the Board of Trade in March questioning the position of the Spurn station in the light of the circular. The reply written on 11th April clearly states "there is no desire, on the part of the Board, to interfere with the Local arrangements..." but the letter went on to say that requests for financial assistance could only be considered if all the conditions of the circular were satisfied. When later Trinity House did apply for a grant the request was refused because the organisation did not meet all the conditions set out in the circular. This was, of course, true of the committee which operated the station.

Another letter received in Hull at almost the same time was a reply from the Coast Guard Office to a request for the establishment of a Coast Guard Station at Spurn. The request was refused because of the difficulty of accommodating any men sent to Spurn and also because there was a shortage of coastguards

"owing to the withdrawal of the more active and efficient portion of the Coast Guard Force for service in the Royal Navy, and the want of seamen to supply existing vacancies in this service generally."

An un-named schooner went ashore on the Inner Binks at about 2.30am on the morning of Thursday 22nd March 1855 and burned a tar barrel. The lifeboat crew answered with two red lights and launched the lifeboat to assist, but "on account of the flood tide he got off before we got to him. We broke two of the Life Boat oars and one of our men (Megginson) got his hand severely hurt."

Throughout the whole of the time since Grant had been appointed the families suffered great hardships. Earnings were very low and the men depended on the relief paid by Trinity House. There was no prospect of work on Spurn, but some members of the Board of Trinity House must have visited the station in early June 1855 and made an offer to loan money to buy a fishing boat and equipment. Grant wrote to Trinity House on June 23rd pointing out that he was three crew members short - one had left, one was about to leave and Megginson was still in Hull as a result of his injury. Grant had held a meeting with the rest of the crew, who had agreed to stay at Spurn provided the loan was made and the men could go fishing. The money was provided, the fishing boat and gear were bought, but the limits imposed on where the men could fish meant that almost nothing was caught and more men left Spurn. On September 18th 1855 an advertisement was published for five fishermen to fill the vacancies in the crew and this was when Trinity House decided to pay the men ten pounds per annum. Some men were found, but conditions were such that several would not stay for long at Spurn.

An un-named barque went aground on the Inner Binks on Tuesday 30th October 1855, flying a flag for assistance. The report reads -

"We went off to him with the Life Boat, let go the Anchor and carried away our Bollard and fore thwart. The sea being so heavy the Life Boat filled five times, broke two oars, lost a boat hook and lost four or five fenders along side the ship and a great deal of damage done to the Life Boat along side the ship getting the crew out. The ship coming off the Binks at six o' clock with fore and main mast cut away. We brought her to anchor above the Bull buoy with a heavy gale of wind. Went on pumping till the pumps were choked and then went on bailing with buckets."

The lifeboat crew stayed on board and continued bailing on the following day until they were forced to let the barque drift on shore. They continued working on the vessel for a further week. The damaged lifeboat was examined by the Buoy Master, Mr. James Todd, who listed the following -

"The top strake on the Port side damaged about 12 feet along from forward.

The cases or coverings over the Gutta Percha Boxes are all started and damaged on the Port side and want refitting.

The Head Bollard broken and fore thwart damaged.

One of the trap doors in the bottom is broken off, the other is damaged.

One of the planks on the Port side is shaken and will want repairing."

Some two weeks after this report there was further damage to the lifeboat, but more tragically, two crew members were drowned.

There was a fresh wind from the east south east when the schooner Zabina, of Ipswich, went ashore on the Inner Binks at half past three on the morning of the 19th November 1855. The Zabina showed flares and lights for assistance, which were answered by a blue light from the lifeboat crew. The lifeboat was launched "with all possible speed", showed another blue light and made all speed to the vessel with the assistance of a smack. The crew "bent two warps to the Boat, one on each Bow of the vessel and as the water flowed hauled the Boat under the Lee of the vessel." It is probable that most of the lifeboat crew boarded the Zabina , leaving only two men in the lifeboat, because the report goes on to say "the Boat capsized and drowned Henry Holmes and John Combes." There is no mention of anyone else being involved in the capsize. The crew got the schooner off the Binks and took her into Grimsby. A fishing boat, number 184, towed the damaged lifeboat to Grimsby.

On the following day Mr. James Todd, Buoy Master, went to Grimsby to inspect the damaged lifeboat and "found her laying bottom up on the White Chalk Stones, just below Grimsby Piers.

Half the stem is gone, and the plank ends started off to below the Copper, the Stern Post is off, as far down as the Pintail; her Port side is completely gone, down to below the Platform deck on the Inside; the Starboard side is all of it shaken and damaged, the Boat looking a complete wreck."

The lifeboat was turned over on November 21st and towed up to Hull for repairs before being returned to Spurn.

A public subscription for Martha Holmes, widow of John Holmes, raised thirty three pounds, two shillings and sixpence, but in January 1856 the Lords of the Committee of the Privy Council for Trade authorized the payment of a gratuity of ten pounds to add to that total. A further ten pounds were received on 1st March 1856 from the RNLI. John Combes was a single man and there was no subscription list opened for his family.

No other lifeboatmen at Spurn lost their lives on service prior to the RNLI taking over the station in May 1911.

A letter was written to Trinity House on the 14th January 1856 on behalf of Thomas Jenkinson, captain of the Filey coble York, and his crew of nine, asking for some remuneration for their efforts in towing the damaged lifeboat to Grimsby.

"After a deal of trouble we succeeded in taking the Life Boat in Tow by our Coble, and by her not turning herself, we were obliged to tow her sideways on.

We had her in Tow Five Hours and broke our Warps Three Times and at last on account of the number of vessels near Grimsby, were obliged to let her go on shore with 40 fathoms of four and a half inch warp to her, which we had to cut adrift."

The Board of Trinity House awarded the sum of eight pounds to be given to Thomas Jenkinson and his crew.

The brig William and Jane, of Sunderland, coal loaded, went ashore on the Inner Binks on the evening of December 28th 1855. The lifeboat launched immediately and went to the brig, but did not succeed in getting her off on the next tide. The lifeboat crew stayed on board throwing cargo overboard to lighten the brig until she was towed off by a steam tug at half past ten at night on December 31st and taken to Grimsby.

Commander W. Ward, Inspector of Life Boats and inventor of a new cork life belt, wrote to Trinity House on January 12th 1856 following the tragedy with the Zabina, pointing out that belts were issued to all crewmen of the RNLI and that the men were under strict orders to wear the belts every time the lifeboat went afloat, either for practice or on service. He urged Trinity House to try one of these belts, but emphasised that he personally made no profit from their sale. They were said to have double the buoyancy of the belts made by Carte, but were the same price, namely fourteen shillings each.

Commander Ward wrote again in March 1856 when one belt was ordered, but the Carte belts which the crew already had continued to be used for some time.

George Grant wrote to Trinity House on April 8th in reply to a letter sent to him on the previous day, concerning the terms and conditions for the crew at Spurn. He referred to a statement in the Trinity House letter of a crew of eight men plus the Mate and Master and this must have been the time when the total number in the crew was reduced from twelve to ten. This was probably in response to the difficulty of finding men to serve because of the poverty and difficult conditions and at the time of the letter there were at Spurn only the Master, Mate and four men.

On April 7th 1856 Trinity House recommended the wages to be one pound ten shillings per month, but devised a share system for the earnings from fishing and

CAPT. WARD'S CORK WAIST LIFE BELT.

Life Boat (Inspector to the Royal National Life Boat Institution.)

THE ADVANTAGES OF THIS BELT ARE—

1. It secures a large amount of buoyancy, without inconveniencing the wearer, when properly put on.

2. It is perfectly flexible.

3. It affords great protection to the body of the wearer against injury when in the water, and preserves it from cold in severe weather.

4. It is very durable, and unliable to injury, but readily repaired, if injured.

5. From being secured tightly round the waist, it cannot slip upwards or downwards, when in the water.

RULES TO BE OBSERVED.

Cross the upper corner strings over the opposite shoulders, as braces are worn, and tie them to the short strings in front, pulling the Belt close up under the arms. Pass the waist strings round the waist, and tie them tightly together in front.

Buoyancy, 24 lbs.

To test however its full advantages, and its amount of buoyant power, it must be worn in the water.

Manufactured by J. BIRT, Jun.,

CORK LIFE BELT AND BUOY MAKER,

No. 4, WELLCLOSE SQUARE, LONDON.

the lifeboat. The earnings from the fishing smack were to be divided into fifty shares, with each of the eight crew members to receive four shares, the Mate to receive five and the Master to have the remaining thirteen. The earnings from the lifeboat were to be divided into fifty five shares, with each crewman receiving four and a half shares, the Mate six shares, the Master eight and the remaining five to be for the lifeboat. This provided some income to help to cover the cost of operating the lifeboat station.

The final letter from Grant to Trinity House was on the last day of July 1856. He reported on the appearance of the beach and the protective banks and sent the July summary of weather and shipping activities. He must then have resigned his position as there is no further correspondence from him. On August 15th Richard Parrott, a former member of the lifeboat crew, applied for the situation of Master of the Life Boat at Spurn and was subsequently appointed. It would appear, however, that Parrott did not take up his duties until October 1st as William Long, Mate of the lifeboat, reported the destruction of the Master's house by the sea on 18th and 19th August and also provided the monthly reports for August and September. There is no record of the lifeboat being launched during this time.

RICHARD PARROTT 1st OCTOBER 1856 - JULY 1857

Richard Parrott took up his position as Master of the Life Boat at Spurn on 1st October 1856 and was at Spurn for only ten months. The difficult conditions of low earnings and the poor state of the cottages continued and there were frequent changes in crew members.

The first letter from Parrott to Trinity House records the resignation of one crewman, by the end of October a second had left and a third was discharged early in November. The first service took place on the night of November 26th. There was a strong gale from east north east, with snow showers, and a brig, the Earl of Wemyss, bound for Aberdeen, ran aground on the Inner Binks and showed distress signals. The lifeboat was launched and took off the crew of eight men and landed them at Spurn "some of them being near starving to Death." Meanwhile the Earl of Wemyss went off the Binks, collided with another brig, causing great damage. The following day the crew was put back on board and the Earl of Wemyss taken to Grimsby for repairs.

In January 1857 Mr.W. Foale submitted plans and drawings for ten new cottages at Spurn for the lifeboat families. The Master's house was to be at one end of the row, the Mate's at the other and the eight crewmen in between. The estimated cost was twelve hundred pounds. The firm of Ellis and Johnson of Grimsby was awarded the contract in May and the final cost was to be thirteen hundred and fifty pounds.

On the evening of January 6th the lifeboat stood by an un-named vessel on the Inner Binks until it floated off, but there is no record of any other service before Parrott left Spurn.

Through the first half of 1857 the men earned some money driving piles for protecting Spurn and the lighthouse, and unloading chalkstone. They also spent a lot of time practising in the lifeboat. There were several changes of crew members during this time and one man was dismissed "for being drunk and going off the island and stopping away all night besides insulting one of Mr. John Homelay men cutting his face in a dreadful manner."

The lifeboat received some damage whilst at its moorings on May 21st when the lighter Young William collided with it.

The monthly report for June was compiled by Richard Parrott, but there is no further correspondence from him. Early in July he was made a Humber Pilot and Trinity House asked the Mate, William Long, to act as Master once again until a new appointment was made.

WILLIAM WILLIS 12th AUGUST 1857 - 30th SEPTEMBER 1865

William Willis applied for the position of Master of the Life Boat at Spurn on July 30th 1857, when he was fifty seven years old. He had served as Shipmaster sailing out of Hull and he supported his application with testimonials from various shipowners who had employed him, one of them for fifteen years. All described him as being honest, sober and industrious and one said he was a very suitable man "for any situation requiring honesty, sobriety or humanity in cases of distress." Willis was appointed and took up his duties on 12th August 1857.

The time of Willis's appointment coincided with the work of building new cottages for the crew and money was earned unloading materials from ships. Throughout his stay at Spurn there was work driving piles for groynes and working to protect the lighthouse and the cottages. The crewmen were more settled both in the new houses and financially for most of the time, but other problems did arise. Within a month of going to Spurn Willis dismissed one man for being drunk and for giving the Master abuse.

After going off to three or four vessels only to find assistance was refused or not required the first real service was to the Norwegian vessel Aegir, loaded with deals, which went aground on the Stony Binks late on the night of Saturday 24th October 1857. At 1.30am on the Sunday morning a light was shown as a signal of distress and the lifeboat was launched immediately. There was a strong wind from the east, "the breakers were running very high," but when the lifeboat was close to the Aegir it could not go alongside because it was low tide and the water was too shallow.

"After daylight got alongside and asked for a rope which was refused. After riding within ten yards of her for two hours our crew being half perished with cold, hailed the ship and asked if any assistance was required, but the Captain declined receiving any."

The lifeboat went ashore for the crew to recover. Conditions moderated and at noon the lifeboat returned to the Aegir only to find the Captain had gone ashore in a fishing boat, along with two crewmen who had "shipped by the run in America" and now considered the voyage at an end. The rest of the crew wanted to leave the ship, but Willis persuaded them to stay, at least until the Captain returned, by promising them the lifeboat would stand by all night and by taking their clothes and belongings ashore.

The Captain returned on Monday 26th and two steamers from Hull tried to tow off the Aegir, but failed, and it was decided to lighten the ship. On Tuesday morning the lifeboat crew began off-loading cargo and other men began dismantling the rigging and masts. During the afternoon conditions worsened and waves were breaking right over the vessel. Later that night the crew of the Aegir asked to be taken off and this was done, but it was not possible for the lifeboat to go alongside. A spar was lashed across the ship to "project fourteen feet clear of the ship's side" and the men were lowered from it into the lifeboat and taken safely ashore.

On Wednesday 28th October conditions had eased, the morning was spent removing more cargo, and at 1.30pm a steamer managed to tow off the Aegir, so ending a prolonged service.

Early in January 1858 the crew and their families began moving into the new houses, as the building and painting were finished. They were delighted with their "very convenient, comfortable houses."

On April 1st 1858 the Tulloch Castle, a barque from Sunderland, coal-loaded for Aden, was taking in water and put into the Humber. In doing so she struck on the Bull Sand and the lifeboat was launched at 3.0pm. The Captain asked the lifeboat to stand by his vessel, which it did until 9.0am the following morning. At 11.0pm that night a brig called the Stockton Packet went aground on the Inner Binks and the lifeboat again launched and took off the crew. The lifeboat's anchor was damaged during this service. For the next two weeks the lifeboat crew was employed discharging the brig's cargo of iron, but it was a further three weeks before she was towed off the Inner Binks.

In July the Captain of the Stockton Packet disputed the account by Willis and the claim for salvage. Willis, in a letter to Trinity House, again detailed the service and the lifeboat crew members all signed the letter in support and the dispute ended.

The schooner Saucy Lass, of London, ran aground on the Inner Binks on the evening of 26th May, but no signal of distress was shown. On the following day the crew got safely ashore in the ship's boat and the schooner became a complete wreck.

One member of the lifeboat crew, Samuel Smith, died at Spurn in April and in June William Todd died of apoplexy and was buried at Kilnsea. Todd's widow was left to pay a bill for four pounds, two shillings and sixpence for medical treatment for her husband during his illness and this amount was far beyond her means. An appeal to the doctor brought a reduction of ten shillings but this still left Mrs. Todd with a demand she could not meet. Mrs. Todd also lost her house at Spurn and a replacement in the crew was appointed almost immediately.

Willis wrote to Trinity House on June 14th 1858 stating his intention to dismiss one of the crew because of insubordination, refusing to keep watch and generally causing dissatisfaction amongst the men. Willis was convinced there was a plot against him from the beginning and did not feel safe -

"If I can place confidence in respected parties there has been a deep laid plot for me even before I set my foot on shore at Spurn. I do not consider either character or life safe with some of them, never was a greater combination, however let the result be what it may I shall commence and clear out some of them by degrees to give them all their notice. At once I must confess it is more than I dare do - imagine what a time I should have amongst such a lot until the expiration of their notice - I being alone and without protection of any sort."

Two days later Willis wrote again because the crewman refused to accept his notice, claiming he was employed by Trinity House and not the Master of the lifeboat. Willis clearly had a low opinion of many of the crew as his letter continues-

"..it plainly appears that they have never been under any control previous. It does not suit them for me to be strict about them keeping the Watch properly kept. However, Grumble they may but go they shall. I feel confident some of them would think nothing about swearing falsely even to taking my life away to suit their own purposes.

I cannot find a better specimen of a bad man than the man Bell who has come to the House only a short time ago. He was bound over to keep the peace towards his own Brother - his usage to his former wife anything but manly and thinks no shame to boast about other feats of rascality. His language generally indecent so much unfit for anyone to hear who has the least spark of decency about them. But upon the whole a more dissatisfied lot of men it never was my fate to be among previous to this."

At least part of the unrest was caused, Willis suggested, by the assistant keeper of the Low Light, who had been sent to Spurn as a punishment - "none of the respectable people either in the Light House or elsewhere will associate with him. Our crew has been his sole companions." Fortunately the man was about to leave Spurn. The man Bell and one other were dismissed and life settled down for a few months.

A new tender was delivered to Spurn on June 22nd 1858 to replace the one badly damaged in March when it sank at its moorings during heavy gales from the north west.

At the beginning of November 1858 Willis asked Trinity House for six new life belts, an old ship's bell to be used to muster the crew and a "look out House." Detailed specifications were drawn up "The Box to be six feet long, four feet wide and seven feet high in clear." Estimates of cost were received and the wooden hut was eventually erected. This must have been a considerable improvement for the men who had previously been on the beach.

The morning of November 5th was dull with light breezes. Later in the day there was heavy rain and in the evening the wind "flew round to the north and blew very hard." At 8.0pm four brigs ran aground on the Binks at the same time and the lifeboat was launched immediately. Willis took the boat to one brig but thought it was in no danger and moved to one in greater difficulty. It was an ebb tide and there was not sufficient water to get close to the brig. The anchor was let go and the crew waited for the tide to flood. At about 3.0am on November 6th three of the brigs managed to get off, but some thirty minutes later the masts of the fourth brig crashed down and she became a total wreck. It was thought the crew must have gone aboard one of the other brigs at low water as no trace of the men was found. The wrecked brig was the Ythan, of Whitby.

Two days later there was again trouble with the man Bell, who had been dismissed in June, the Mate Long and two crewmen, Mearns and Hopper. Willis was sitting at dinner with three visitors when the group, with Mrs. Long, Mrs. Mearns and Mrs. Hopper, went to his house and picked a quarrel "when Bell abused me most shamefully. Had the Police been near I would have given him in charge, but finally I was compelled to stand in my own defence or run the risk of being maimed." Willis was convinced there was "a premeditated conspiracy" and described the wives, who urged on Bell, as "three viragos of the first class, a disgrace to their sex." Willis thought the episode had taken place because he had "put a stop to their thievish practices and it does not suit." He also pointed out that Long had expected to be appointed Master rather than Willis himself and it had been planned that Mearns should become Mate. He also blamed Mearns for stirring up trouble amongst the crew and accusing the Master falsely of theft, and said that Long, as Mate, lacked energy and drive. Willis did put in a plea for Hopper on account of his large family and the possible suffering if the family lost the house at Spurn. Long and Mearns were dismissed and John King, not previously a member of the crew, was appointed Mate. Having left Spurn Long wrote to Trinity House asking for repayment of five shillings for his wife washing blankets, five shillings for papering the inside of his house and eight shillings for fencing round the house. He received eight shillings only.

The crew of the brig Miaza, of Sunderland, landed on the beach at Spurn early on the morning of February 9th 1859, having abandoned the Miaza on the Inner Binks. The brig had gone aground at about midnight but no signals had been given or lights shown as the crew expected she would come off without damage. The crew left when she filled with water. At 10.0am the captain of the Miaza, having agreed with Willis and the lifeboat crew to strip her, went back on board only to find George Grant, once Master of the lifeboat and now a fisherman, had taken charge of her and insisted on stripping her and would not accept the captain's authority. Some of the lifeboat crew, unknown to Willis at the time, made an agreement to help Grant for a fixed sum of money. Whilst the men were working on the Miaza

Willis kept permanent watch at Spurn so that they could be called and the lifeboat be launched if necessary. When Grant paid the men there was nothing for Willis and he felt he should have been given something for his watch keeping which allowed the men to work. This led to more bad feeling between Willis and his crew.

The problem arose again in October. The men had been paid salvage money for the brig, but nothing for the cargo. On October 21st Grant appeared at Spurn and told the men that salvage money for the cargo of coals was now awaiting collection at Grimsby. Willis gave permission for the Mate, King, and two men to go to Grimsby, provided they returned by two o'clock in the afternoon. One man returned at 5.0am the following morning, perfectly sober, but said King and Brown had gone on a spree. Brown returned on October 25th and King on October 27th and although they sent letters of apology to Trinity House both were dismissed from the service. Fewson Hopper was appointed to be Mate.

In November the lifeboat took off the crew of the schooner Rebecca and Elizabeth, of Hartlepool, as she filled with water on the Binks. Later it was possible to pump out the schooner and a steam tug towed her to Grimsby. The brig St. Hilda, also of Hartlepool, ran aground on the Inner Binks three weeks later and became a total wreck. The crew was saved by the lifeboat.

Immediately after Christmas 1859 Willis received a letter expressing disappointment that no report had been received at Trinity House concerning the wreck of the Amalthea, a barque, on 20th December. Willis replied on December 27th apologizing and explaining that for several days his hands had been too swollen for him to be able to hold a pen, as a result of that service. The Amalthea, laden with linseed, ran aground on the Inner Binks at about 8.0pm when there was a very strong wind from south south west and heavy falls of snow. The letter continues -

"myself and Crew got into the Life Boat Tender to go off to the Life Boat and when within reach of her the man in the Bow of the Boat attempted to hook her but his Boat Hook being turned wrong-side up he missed her and strange to say we could not again reach her, a Gale of wind right ahead and a strong tide. We pulled the whole night but could not keep the Boat head to the wind, sometimes the wind being off one Bow and then the other, sometimes falling in with ice of which there was a great quantity, and finally was obliged to abandon the Boat near Kilnsea, full four miles from Spurn at 6.0am on the 21st - and from the Land nearly a mile beset in the ice. There was no alternative, we must either leave the Boat or starve. In going ashore sometimes we were waist deep in mud and water, other times for a great distance we had to crawl upon our hands and knees on the ice, it not being sufficiently strong to walk upon and being dark could not see where to place our footsteps - I believe a little more melancholy tale would have to be told - however, at last we all got safe on shore and got to a House and got some refreshment and walked to Spurn and when arrived the Barque was hard and dry. We walked off to her and when night came on no one would stay on board of her - the Captain being completely exhausted - however at his request and my own will I called all our people together at two o'clock the following morning and went off to her with the Life Boat as a safeguard. At daylight I sent the Ship Boat for the Captain - he brought with him George Grant and a lot of Fishermen and made an agreement with our assistance to get her off and the matter to be settled by arbitration and had it still kept smooth no doubt she would have been got off but upon the following tide a fearful gale set in, the ship actually twisting like a snake. The Life Boat was at Anchor ahead of the ship in readiness. At last we were obliged to abandon her, some from a rope off the Jib Boom and others jumped in from the Cut Water. Finally all got in safe and went on shore. At low water went off to her again - her decks was all blown up and not a particle of Cargo left, the ship entirely on her broad side. We cut the masts away in hopes she would float away the next tide but all to no avail. On Saturday night she came on the beach a total wreck."

Soon after daylight on January 22nd 1860, with a strong wind from the north west, a vessel was seen driving from the westward, apparently from Grimsby Roads, towards Spurn Point and as it approached it was realised there was no one on board. The lifeboat was launched and Willis and some of the crew boarded her and found she had been in collision forward and that her rudder had been carried away. She turned out to be the brig Tranby, of North Shields. Willis ordered his men to set sails to reach her inshore and whilst that was being done he went into the cabin. He found every appearance of a hasty departure, with bed clothes turned back, clothes on the floor and a bundle of clothes and a bag. He also found water was pouring in. He snatched up the belongings, went on deck and ordered everyone back into the lifeboat. The Tranby sank within five minutes. Two days later there was still no information concerning the crew of the Tranby. Three days were spent salvaging everything possible from the wreck.

At noon on October 3rd 1860 a smack ran aground on the lower end of Trinity Sand and the lifeboat crew launched the Tender to go off to the lifeboat

"A sea breached right over the Boat and upset her and left us to our own resources. I found the benefit of the New Life Belt you kindly sent me down for trial. Had we had far to have swam I am confident the Old Belts would not have kept a person up for any length of time ...I am glad to say we are all alright excepting a few slight bruises."

The smack floated off and proceeded up the Humber unharmed.

LIFE BELTS FOR LIFE BOATS.

CAPTAIN WARD'S R. N.

(Life Boat Inspector to the Royal National Life Boat Institution.)

CORK WAIST LIFE BELT.

THE ADVANTAGES OF THIS BELT ARE—

1. It secures a large amount of buoyancy, without inconvenience to the wearer, when properly put on.
2. It is perfectly flexible.
3. It affords great protection to the body of the wearer against injury when in the water, and preserves it from cold in severe weather.
4. It is very durable, and not liable to injury, but readily repaired if injured.
5. From being secured tightly round the waist, it cannot slip upwards or downwards when in the water.

☞ These Belts possess buoyant power equal to 24lbs. being double that of ordinary Cork Belts.

RULES TO BE OBSERVED.

Cross the upper corner strings over the opposite shoulders, as braces are worn, and tie them to the short strings in front, pulling the Belt up under the arms. Pass the waist strings round the waist, and tie them tightly together in front.

⁂ This Belt needs to be put on to be appreciated, since though somewhat cumbersome in appearance, it is not felt when on, to be more so than a waistcoat.

To test, however, its full advantages, and its amount of buoyant power, it must be worn in the water.

MANUFACTURED BY

J. BIRT, Jun., Cork Life Belt & Buoy Maker,

5, WELLCLOSE SQUARE, LONDON, E.

N.B.—Tie the Strings as they are when sent, but tighten them to suit the wearer. Those with the striped strings are the larger size, and the green the smaller.

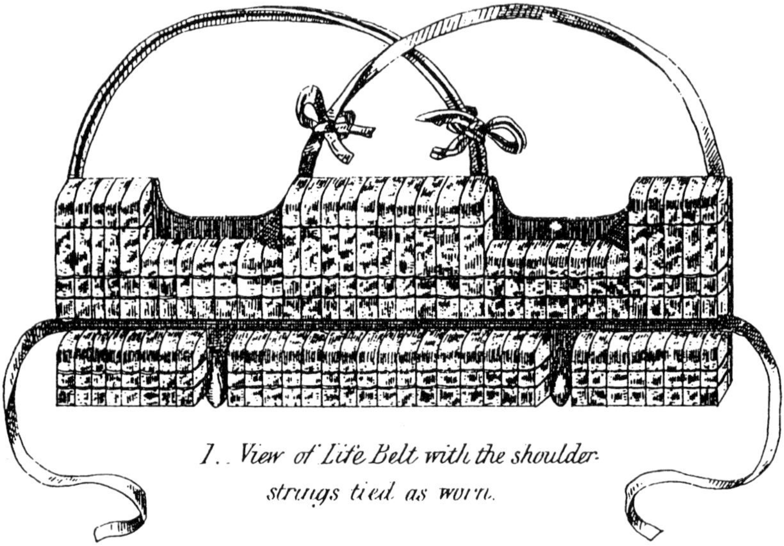

1. View of Life Belt with the shoulder-strings tied as worn.

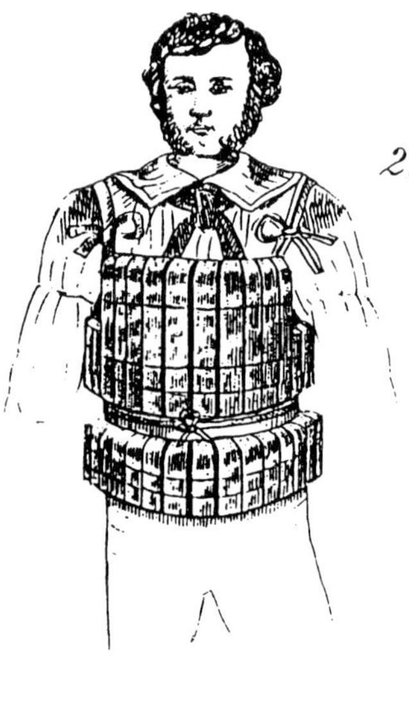

2 & 3. Life Belt as worn: Front and Back view.

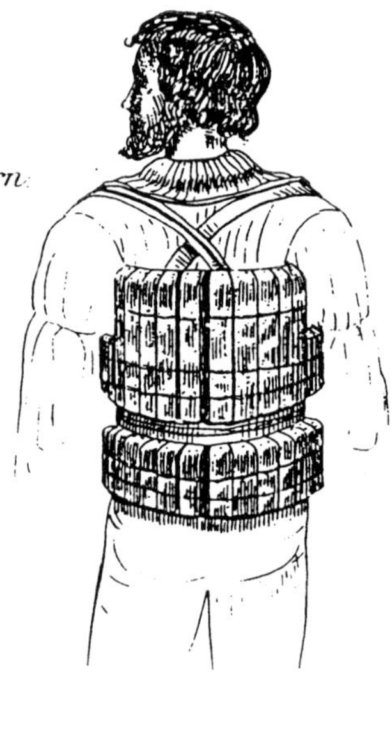

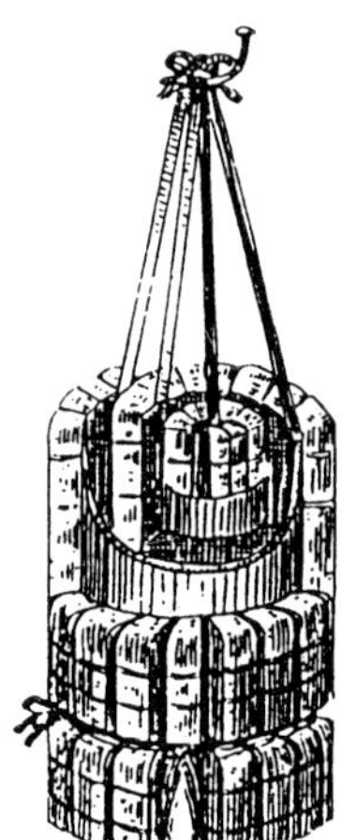

4. Life Belt rolled-up.

Sole Maker of these Belts J. BIRT Jun.r 5, Wellclose Square, London.

The year 1861 began with very cold weather, a lot of frost, heavy snow and on January 12th "A great quantity of floating ice in the Hawk Roads." At about 1.0am on January 15th the trawling smack Renown, of Grimsby, ran aground on the Stony Binks, but no signal was seen from the shore. At 4.0am the captain and crew landed at Spurn having abandoned the Renown, which had sunk without trace by day light.

On January 16th the trawling smack Industry, of Hull, showed signals of distress at 1.0am from the Stony Binks and the lifeboat launched and took off the crew of five. The lifeboat then rode by the Industry until she floated off on the next tide and put the crew back on board along with eight of the lifeboat's crew. The men pumped her out, set sails, and got her in a safe condition to go up to Hull. The lifeboat crew then left her, about half way between Bull Island and Grimsby and returned to Spurn, arriving at about 9.0am on the 17th. "We were thoroughly drenched the whole time. The first sea at the edge of the Breakers filled the Boat and lost some of the oars - it freezing very keen at the time...It is evident life would have been lost had we not been there."

A month later a brig, the Countess of Zetland, drove aground at night on the lower end of Trinity Sand and took in water. A light was shown as a signal of distress, but the watchman at Spurn thought it was a bonfire on the shore and ignored it. The London Trinity Corporation Steam Tender was anchored close by and fired a gun to attract attention, but the watchman thought it was a signal for a pilot and did nothing. Willis knew nothing of these events until after daylight when the vessel was seen. Willis launched a boat and went to the brig and the Steam Tender to find that the crew had been taken off by a smack. The watchman had completely disregarded all orders, but fortunately no further damage was caused and no lives were lost.

Mr. Joseph Birt, of London, on March 21st 1861, dispatched twelve Cork Waist Life Belts, with the latest improvements, to Trinity House in Hull for the crew of the Spurn lifeboat, at a cost of eight pounds eight shillings. These were the belts praised by Willis when the tender was overturned when trying to reach the lifeboat.

The lifeboat crew carried out a rescue from the beach with rocket line on July 23rd. The ballast lighter Good Intent drove on the beach after loading gravel on the Binks, There was heavy rain at the time and it began to blow hard from the south south west and " the crew were in imminent danger of their lives." A rocket line was fired over the lighter from the beach and the men were hauled ashore through the breakers. At low water the lifeboat men discharged the cargo, "patched her up and got her off on the following tide, very much shaken" and took her to shelter on the river side of Spurn.

At half past eleven on the night of September 27th the schooner Clementina, of Lyme Regis, went aground on the Binks when there was a strong southerly wind and heavy rain. The lifeboat launched immediately, stood by the schooner and took off the crew at 6.0am on September 28th and landed the men safely ashore. The vessel was blown onto the beach full of water and when the weather moderated the men discharged the cargo of coal. Almost a week later the Clementina came off the beach and was taken to Grimsby.

During the weekend of November 2nd and 3rd, with a heavy gale from the north west, the steam tug Hotspur, of Hull, was blown ashore at Spurn and became a complete wreck. A schooner, a yacht and a lighter were also blown ashore along with "a great quantity of wreck" which was washed onto the beach. The bodies of two men were found on the beach and on the next day the body of a boy.

The first three months of 1862 proved difficult for the lifeboat crew as they earned nothing during that time and only three pounds at the end of April. This was the worst time financially whilst Willis was at Spurn. The only service was on January 20th to the brig Heroine, of Shoreham, which grounded on the Stony Binks. The lifeboat was launched and tried to get the vessel off, but she filled with water and Willis "took the crew from the vessel at considerable hazard." For a week the wreck was constantly shifted by the sea and whenever possible materials were saved. On January 29th the wreck drove to sea, it was taken in tow off Kilnsea by a steamer and towed to Grimsby.

A similar service was carried out for the schooner Dart, of Sunderland, on May 4th on the Stony Binks. The crew was taken safely ashore, but the schooner was completely broken up by the sea.

The new Withernsea lifeboat station was to be opened in August 1862 and the crew from Spurn wrote to Trinity House asking for permission to attend. They proposed travelling to Withernsea in the tender, wind and weather permitting. Permission was not granted as the Board of Trinity House decided the Spurn station could not be left unmanned for the length of time proposed.

The schooner Thomas and Martha got into difficulties on the Binks early in the evening of November 19th. The lifeboat went to assist, took off the crew and landed them at Spurn at 9.30pm. At 2.30am the following morning the schooner sank and later in the day the crewmen were taken to Grimsby.

Late in December 1862 there were heavy gales coupled with high tides and Willis wrote to Trinity House that the tides were the highest he had ever seen at Spurn. The new houses were in danger of having the foundations undermined and it was decided to protect them by placing some three hundred tons of stone as a barrier. The work was done in June the following year, with the lifeboat crew providing the labour. The stone cost one shilling and four pence per ton, one shilling a ton for transport and the men were paid about one pound ten shillings - to share between them - for unloading each lighter of about sixty tons.

December 3rd 1863 proved to be a day of severe losses of shipping and life because of heavy gales. The day began with the wind blowing hard from a westerly direction. By mid-morning it was a heavy gale from the north west and at noon "a perfect hurricane." There was also very heavy rain and very poor visibility. Willis said it was impossible to launch the lifeboat or even the tender because the wind was "dead upon the beach." Even a large steamer could not go to windward and had to go out to sea to ride out the storm. The report by Willis, written on December 4th, continues -

"About 10.0am a sloop came on shore near the Old Cottages and not a living thing on board. She is a French vessel called Neptune, Captain Gournay, of Gravelines. She is coal laden. About 10.0pm a large Norwegian vessel, 550 tons, barque run on shore in the Old Den with his Fore and Main mast cut away. She is called the Levant, Captain Gluckstadt, from Hull in ballast. Last night I picked up two Boats, one marked the Betsy, of Blyth, the other the Robert, of Ipswich. During the height of the Gale a Boat drove near the Point and as soon as she touched the beach the wind took hold of her and blew her up to the Bents like a shaving. Another Boat was picked up near to the two with a man dead in the bottom, no doubt starved to death. One schooner crew landed in their Boat at Kilnsea with the loss of the Mate, being knocked overboard. There are several wrecks, I understand, on the upper part of the Trinity I have not seen. A Quantity of wreck from large vessels has washed on shore here but the vessels we never saw. I fear the loss of life has been great."

On the morning of December 4th it was found that there were five vessels on the Trinity Sands, two on their broadsides and the others full of water. The lifeboat crew spent a lot of time during the month working on the wrecks, and although strong winds were frequent there were no more tragedies.

At the beginning of March 1864 a box of twelve pound and a box of nine pound rockets, with all their equipment, were ordered from a new supplier, Mr. Horatio Dennett of the Isle of Wight. The problem was that many of the railway companies refused to carry "combustible stores" and others only carried them on one day a week. Water transport was therefore necessary, but even this could not be guaranteed.

The trawling smack Albion, of Hull, went aground on the Binks at eight o'clock on the morning of October 2nd 1864. The lifeboat took off the crew and the Albion filled with water. The lifeboat cable broke and when a week later Trinity House asked about it Willis replied that it had been spliced and replaced, that the Albion

DENNETT'S

Double or Coupled Rockets.

This contrivance is designed to obtain a greater range than a Single Rocket is capable of making, it does not interfere with the ordinary arrangement of the apparatus, and can be applied to any of the Rockets supplied during the last three years.

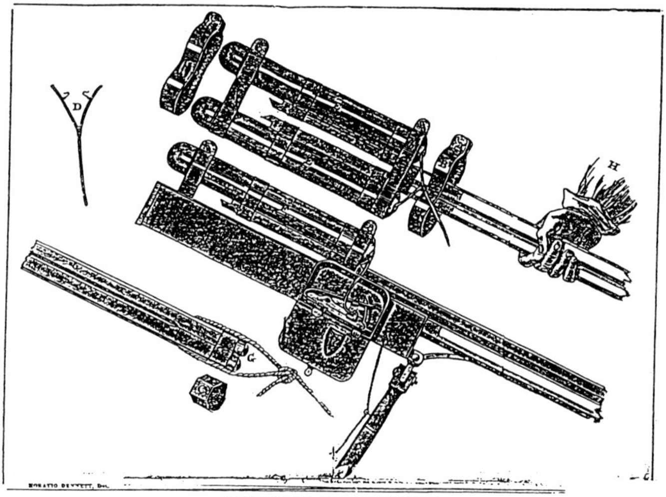

HORATIO DENNETT, Del.

DESCRIPTION OF THE FIGURES.

A Perspective view of Head Coupler: it is provided with two set screws.

B Ditto of Mouth Couplers, having but one screw.

C Ditto of Pole Coupler, is slit on its lower edge, so that it may accommodate itself to any slight irregularity in the size of the poles.

D Improved Forked Waterproof Leader, furnished with two small copper hooks, which hooking into the small holes made in the bottom of each Rocket, secures it to their mouths; the lower end is furnished with a percussion tube, which is fired by the lock.

E E Two Rockets united by the Couplers a and b and the leader attached ready for laying into the frame.

G The ends of the Poles coupled by c, and the line rove and secured by the bowline-knot.

F The Rockets in the frame ready for firing, shewing the manner of bringing the leader to the lock: the frame and poles are shewn as broken, to save room.

INSTRUCTIONS FOR COUPLING AND FIRING.

CUT the seizing and strip off the canvas caps of two Rockets, ship and pin both poles as usual, one person then takes hold of the poles with the right hand, about a foot below the mouths, see H, and with the left at a convenient distance below it, keeping the backs of the poles close together, and the Rockets exactly even and flush with each other, and as nearly as possible in the same plane, or " Out of Winding," a second person takes the Head Coupler A, and slips it over the heads of the Rockets to see it square and gently turn up the *upper screw* to close but not to tighten it, then pass the Mouth Coupler B up the poles to the lower loops of the Rockets, and gently turn up the screw, now see that the Rockets are out of winding with each other, and set the top screws fast, and tighten up the middle screw of the Head Coupler, slip on the Pole Coupler, keeping the slit edge of it towards the ends of the poles, reeve the line, after wetting two or three fathoms of its end, through the holes in the heels of the poles, and secure it by a bowline-knot, carefully middling the bight.

Take a Leader and INSERT one of its legs into the MOUTH of the lower Rocket, hook the hook into the hole in the mouth of the case, and pinch the hook close between the finger and thumb, take the other leg and INSERT it into the MOUTH of the upper Rocket, hook it into its place and close the hook as before, lay the Rockets into the frame, taking care not to jamb the leader between the bottom of the Rocket and the end of the shaft of the frame inside, pass the loose end of the leader down through the hole in the Lock-case, and insert the *small end* of the percussion tube into the vent-hole (for steadiness only,) and close the jaw upon the seizing where the paper joins the quill, or if the lock-case has no hole, bring it down over the edge of the casing to the jaws, but in this case the cover of the case must be left open.

The hole in the rim of the Lock-case for the admission of the leader can be made by any handy man at the Station, with a marlin-spike or pricker, and should be placed before, and just clear of the hasp fastening the cover (when shut,) when through the copper, the marlin-spike should be worked from the inside of the case so as to raise a burr or little rim round the hole, which will prevent the water from running into it.

The Coupled Rocket will require a greater elevation than a single one, (about 35 degrees will probably give the longest range) because the flight being quicker, it will go to a greater height without expending its power at such a distance from the earth, as to be over-come and drawn back by the force of the wind in falling.

If the Frame will not come up to the elevation required, remove a few inches of earth for the trail to drop into, but be careful to set the spur fast as usual.

In Coupling keep the Screws UPWARDS, and the Leader on the left side of the poles, its legs into the mouths of the Rockets; if from shrinkage of the poles the lower coupler should be too slack, place an inch of rope-yarn, or a bit of folded paper between them at a few inches from their ends, so that it may jamb hand tight.

As it is not advisable that a Rocket should be uncapped until it is to be fired, and as the poles cannot ship pleasantly, or the leader be applied whilst the cap remains in its place, it is recommended that two old cases should be kept for the purpose of practice or instruction in Coupling, and a dumb leader (made of line only, that it may not be mistaken for a proper one) will accompany the couplers, should the small holes be burnt through at the edge, they may easily be drawn or closed together by a few blows with the pane of a hammer, sufficiently to hold the hooks of the dumb leader.

The operation of Coupling is exceedingly simple, and can be performed in a few minutes.

Carisbrooke, Isle of Wight.

HORATIO DENNETT.

YELF & Co., PRINTERS, HOLYROOD STREET, NEWPORT.

had broken up and "Part of her Broadside washed ashore near the Point. It was under my charge. I am sorry to say the best and principal part of it was stolen by a quantity of Dutch Fishermen. There was about 80 sail of them on shore. Nothing would they leave alone they could move.

Our Peoples gardens suffered considerably, potatoes, carrots &c. They took the advantage to steal the wreck when we were all away with the Life Boat...perhaps the Gentlemen might represent it to the Dutch Consul."

The outcome is not known.

When a large party of visitors was expected at Spurn the wives of the lifeboat crew earned some money by providing refreshments. Before the visit a small group sailed to Grimsby to buy in provisions and preparations were made. During the first few days of July 1865 Willis received a letter from Mr. Hollingworth, Master of the New Holland Steamers, asking if the people on Spurn could cope with a visit of three hundred men, all employees of Messrs Foster and Andrews, on a works outing on Monday 10th July. The reply was positive and on Friday 7th July John Marshall, Richard Bland and his wife set sail for Grimsby for supplies. When they were half way a cross the Humber there was a sudden and "serious storm of Thunder and Lightning." They immediately returned to Spurn. On the following morning "the weather being fine the same party started again and was overtaken by another storm of Thunder and Lightning - when Marshall gently slid or partly laid upon the Boats Thwarts and breathed his last - he never spoke another word.

The other man Bland immediately bore up, his wife employed in attending to Marshall, rubbing him and loosening his Neck-Tie, but all to no purpose, life was extinct. I am exceedingly sorry. He had been the longest of any person here and was a good and faithful servant. I cannot sufficiently express my sorrow for him. He has left Four children, the Eldest about eight years of age and the youngest about two or three. I do not think he was struck with Lightning, there is not a bruise about him nor yet discoloured. I think it was fear, his nerves could not bear the shock. Only a few minutes previous he had been remarking how very frightened he was the day previous."

John Marshall was buried at Kilnsea but his widow and children were left destitute and in want of clothing. Willis wrote to Trinity House

"I have got a subscription up amongst ourselves and a casual friend or two which will get a few clothes for her but I am afraid I shall not have funds sufficient to pay for the Funeral. I will strain every nerve to get sufficient. I am given to understand if the Parish pay the Funeral expenses they will reimburse themselves out of her furniture. If they do that God knows what will become of her and her poor children - she will not have the means to get them a living. However I will put myself to great inconvenience rather than that shall be done. I was not aware we had any person so badly off at Spurn. Their outward appearance was always clean. I believe their liberality has been above their means.

The Grocer's Bill amounts to about ten pounds - he is going to take his Boat and sundry articles in part payment and will not press her any further, which is very kind. Friends she has none, her Father lives in Leeds - a poor man. Where she will live in Hull I do not know. A party here has offered to sell her a mangle but money to pay for it is out of the question. I hope God will take them under his care."

The situation described in the letter was probably not uncommon at that time and the other lifeboat families were not in any position to give very much practical help. Even before Marshall's funeral someone had applied to fill the vacancy in the crew, and therefore occupy the house, and an appointment was made almost immediately.

The RNLI wrote to the Board of Trinity House in Hull on 4th August 1865 to say that "The Commercial Travellers have raised the cost of a lifeboat which they have presented to this Institution and they wish that their boat should be stationed in the North part of England if possible." The letter continued that no new stations were then required in northern England but the boat could be stationed at Spurn if Trinity House would cease to operate at Spurn and allow it to be taken over as a normal RNLI station with all the usual organisation. Trinity House was offered fifty per cent representation on the local Committee of Management which would be established. Trinity House declined the offer and continued to fund and operate the lifeboat.

In July William Willis heard that the position of light keeper at Killingholme was becoming available and he asked Mr. Gill, Secretary to the Board of Trinity House in Hull, to speak for him. In September Willis was appointed to that position and resigned from the lifeboat service. He had served for eight years at Spurn, mostly at a time of greater financial security, but he did have other problems to face. Relationships with the crew were not always sound and he appeared to see plots against him - imagined or real - whenever any criticism was made against him, but he did try to maintain a high standard of service to mariners in distress.

FEWSON HOPPER 1st OCTOBER 1865 - 31st DECEMBER 1877

When it was known that Willaim Willis had been appointed Keeper of the Light at Killingholme Fewson Hopper wrote to the Board of Trinity House in Hull on September 27th 1865 offering himself for the situation of Master of the Life Boat at Spurn. He had served on the lifeboat three years as seaman and six years as Mate. He was forty two years of age and said he had been constantly on the Humber since the age of thirteen and had a good knowledge of the waters. His application was supported by William Willis and the two lighthouse keepers on Spurn. On 30th September Hopper was appointed Master and took up his duties on the following day. John Best was appointed to the lifeboat as Mate on 6th October 1865.

The first service after Hopper's appointment took place on Saturday 28th October 1865 during hail storms with a squally northerly wind. The schooner Superior, "with a cargo of slates from Port Maddoc to Middlesbrough" ran aground on the Stony Binks at 2.0am. The lifeboat was launched and with great difficulty succeeded in saving the crew of five men and a boy from the rigging, where they had gone for safety, as waves were breaking right over the schooner and had swept everything from the deck and filled the vessel with water. At 10.0am the Superior broke up completely.

The smack Frolic, of Grimsby, went aground on the Outer Binks very early on November 9th, but as the tide was ebbing and there was no danger no light was shown. At 4.0am a light was shown for assistance as the flooding tide with heavy sea carried away the boom, mainsail and ship's boat and disabled the smack. The lifeboat was launched but the Frolic finally floated off and was towed to Grimsby by two Pilot Cutters.

Around midnight on 2nd January 1866 two lights were seen by the watchman. The lifeboat was launched and went to the first schooner, the Wave, on passage from Lowestoft to Goole. Despite "a terrific Gale of wind and rain" from the west south west and a heavy sea all the crew of the Wave were taken into the lifeboat which then went to the second schooner, the Pearl, from Honfleur to Goole. Both vessels were grain loaded. The crew, three men, with one woman and three children, were all in a small boat and were quickly taken into the lifeboat. Some of the lifeboat crew boarded the Pearl, manned the pumps and took her safely into Grimsby.

The steamship Gibraltar, from Valencia to Hull with fruit, grounded on the Inner Binks on the evening of December 3rd 1866. The lifeboat went to assist and the Captain asked Hopper to stay by the ship till she floated off, to prevent his crew from leaving, as they were afraid. The Captain promised some payment for the service. The lifeboat stood by until 2.0am when the Gibraltar floated off and continued on its voyage, without the lifeboat crew receiving anything, the Captain saying "we have done with you." Fortunately not all captains behaved in this way, but this was not an isolated incident.

Five days later three vessels drove onto the Trinity Sand at midnight during a strong south westerly gale. Signals were shown at 3.0am and the lifeboat went to assist. Hopper boarded the brig Nelson and the brigantine Rising Sun and advised them how to proceed. He then went to the schooner Mary Ann and some of his crew went on board with him. They pumped all night, but the vessel filled with the rising tide and he took off the crew and landed them at Spurn. From there they were sent home by the Fishermen and Mariners Benevolent Society.

Severe weather at the end of November and in early December 1867 caused several ships to run ashore. The lifeboat assisted the sloop Baltic and the schooner Fidelity, but did not have to take off the crews. A smack was dismasted near the Bull Light and a screw steamer saved the crew.

Early on the morning of 19th January 1868, with a strong south west wind, a vessel was seen to be grounded on the Inner Binks. Because of the water conditions the men could not get the lifeboat round the Point to go to assist and therefore man-handled the tender across Spurn and launched from the beach direct into the sea and went to the ship, the Newcastle, bound for Hull, only for the Captain to refuse all assistance.

The men at Spurn were given a very busy time over the weekend at the end of January into February 1868 when the weather was extremely severe. Hopper wrote "I have never experienced such a gale since I have been at Spurn." On Friday January 31st

"we were called out to a Barque which was on shore on the Inner Bank on Friday morning at one o'clock and we had to remain by her on the Friday night and Saturday morning in the most terrific gale that I have experienced for some time."

The barque was the Echo, on passage from Buenos Aires to Hull with a cargo of bones and bone dust. The report continues

"we stayed by her all the day and the wind increasing towards nightfall to a heavy gale with squalls of rain. The Crew leaving the ship went to Grimsby by a tug boat, the Captain and Mate landing at Spurn. Unbent what sails we could at the time and brought them on shore with other stores that we could save according to circumstances and the situation the ship was in we stayed by the vessel, the wind increasing to a complete Hurricane. About midnight or a little after prepared to leave the ship.

Sat. 1st February.

Blowing the most awful hurricane with squalls of rain. About 2.0am succeeded in getting in the Life Boat, at the same time saw the illumination of a signal of distress across the Spurn Point on the Trinity Sand but it being ebb tide we could make no assistance till the break of day, the wind continuing with the utmost fury. Made sail and off the Point our sail gave way at the throat cringle ; lowered and secured it and getting up abreast of the lower middle buoy it split from the bottom near to the top. Got alongside the vessel, the schooner Henry, of Goole. She was striking very heavy, expecting the Masts to go by the board every minute. Made an agreement with the Captain to get his Anchor and take his vessel into safety, for the sum of fifty pounds."

The schooner was deliberately run ashore on "the beaching grounds at Kilnsea" and made safe.

"I left the Mate on board with four men and proceeded to Spurn by land for another sail for the Life Boat. As the wind was lewardly and as fierce as ever was obliged to leave the boat. We had scarce got to Spurn before another Barque named Kyanite drove on shore on the Point without a soul on board. Got another boat launched with the few hands and all the women - succeeded in boarding her. She appeared to have been in collision, her spars some of them being gone and her Bulwark and Cathead stove in. Got her kedge and Spare Anchor out and moored her, the weather moderating at night."

On the Sunday the men began stripping the Kyanite and in the afternoon a steam tug arrived with the crew of the Kyanite, these men having taken refuge on the New Sand Float.

Monday 3rd February was taken up stripping sails and cutting away the masts of the Echo to save the ship if possible, but heavy seas on 9th February broke her up completely. The men did succeed in saving the Kyanite, getting her off the beach on 8th February and taking her up to Hull, having first discharged the cargo to lighten the vessel.

This brought to an end a very busy period and also this was the first time any reference was made to the women helping to launch a boat.

The last day of July 1868 saw two men visiting Spurn in connection with the possibility of establishing a post office there and this was sanctioned by the Post Master General on 5th August. John Quinton, the keeper of the Lifeboat Inn, wrote to Trinity House in Hull asking to be considered for the position of postmaster, but a letter from Lord Hotham to Trinity House on 14th August made it clear that married women and innkeepers were not eligible for the position. In fact Eliza Hopper, daughter of the Master of the Life Boat, was appointed and retained the position until the post office was closed in 1920.

George Foster, Master of the smack Jason, of Hull, lost his life needlessly on the night of November 10th 1868 by refusing to listen to Hopper's advice. The smack ran aground on the Binks at 7.0pm and the lifeboat launched immediately. On reaching the casualty Hopper asked if the master and crew would go into the lifeboat or stay on the Jason. The Master said they would stay. Hopper pointed out the very dangerous situation and tried to persuade the men to join the lifeboat, even promising to stand by all night and return the crew if the vessel floated off. The five crewmen heeded his advice and climbed into the lifeboat, but Foster refused. At that point a heavy sea broke the line between the lifeboat and the Jason and the lifeboat was driven away by the sea and was unable to return because of the conditions. The crew dropped an anchor and rode until the sea broke up the Jason, and Foster was drowned. The survivors were taken to Spurn for the night and then to Grimsby the following morning to be put on the packet for Hull. Hopper asked for the Captain's behaviour to be made public as a warning to others not to ignore his advice.

A man dressed as a Coastguard went around the village of Paull in mid-August collecting money. He claimed the money was to buy a new pair of wheels for a carriage for the lifeboat at Spurn. Major Pricket gave him one pound ten shillings, Mr. Wray and others gave him a pound, but he was an imposter. The matter was reported to the police, but whether or not he was caught is not known.

The watchman reported a vessel aground on the Stony Binks at 2.30am on January 2nd 1869. The state of the tide and the sea made it impossible to launch the lifeboat at the time, but Hopper burned two blue lights as a signal. As he received no reply it was assumed the vessel had floated off. At 4.30am the Captain and crew landed on the beach in their own boat and said the vessel, the Cautious, of Whitstable, was filling with water. The lifeboat crew mustered and went off to the ship, boarded her and found only three or four feet of water in her. They pumped her dry, set sail and took the Cautious to Grimsby. At 1.0am on 29th January the lifeboat crew was called to the keel Betsy. Her cargo of coal was on fire. "By means of plenty of buckets and water soon got the fire out."

Three men were saved from the rigging of the wreck of the Traveller, from London, which had gone aground on the Middle Binks on January 16th 1871. There was a heavy gale from the south and it was a difficult service for the lifeboat against the flood tide. The Traveller became a total wreck and the survivors were left with only the clothes they were wearing.

An electric telegraph system was opened at the post office at Spurn on Wednesday 25th January 1871 and Eliza Hopper was responsible for its operation.

Permission for this link had been granted in September 1870 and the work had been going on since that date.

A very heavy gale from the south south east with blinding sleet and snow blew all day on February 10th. At about 2.0pm the crew of the schooner Sarah landed on the beach near Kilnsea and made their way to the Life Boat Inn. Two hours later the vessel was broken up by the sea.

"About midnight a flaring light was seen from the Middle Banks. We manned the Life Boat and after a hard struggle with wind and sea we succeeded in saving the crew of the Fortune Teller, six in number, belonging to Fowey, coal laden for Plymouth. The men were very much exhausted, being swollen in their hands and feet by the frost. When they got onshore I administered Brandy which soon brought them round and I passed them on through the Benevolent Societies Officer."

Two days later the lifeboat men were busy salvaging as much as possible from the wreck of the Fortune Teller.

The last week of September 1872 was a time of strong westerly gales and many ships parted from their anchors in the Humber and had to go out to sea to ride out the storms. The schooner Ariel parted from her anchor, collided with another vessel and totally dismasted her and then ran ashore near the lighthouse. The lifeboat tender was launched and the crew boarded the Ariel and gave her assistance. The schooner Henry ran onto the chalk bank and a crewman was lost, washed overboard from another ship whilst recovering the anchor in the Hawk Roads. When the weather moderated a steam tug assisted in getting the Ariel and the Henry afloat. The Ariel was taken to Grimsby and the Henry continued on passage to Whitby.

Two more crews were saved in November, the schooner Maria going aground during a heavy northerly gale and the crew being rescued. Ten days later the schooner Teignmouth grounded whilst "it was blowing a terrific gale" from the south. The lifeboat saved the crew of six men.

Once again lives were lost unnecessarily when men refused to leave ships and go into the lifeboat. There were strong easterly gales all day on Sunday 16th March 1873 with a very heavy sea on the Binks.

"About 11.0pm the Watch on the Look Out reported a vessel on shore on the Binks showing blue lights and sky rockets. I answered with the same and proceeded off with the Life Boat and was soon on the spot and found it to be the steamer Aberdeenshire, of Hull. The crew contained of thirteen hands ten of which were taken into the Life Boat. Three men refused to leave the ship. With great risk we got clear and anchored about a quarter of a mile from her. Shortly after we saw a Rocket go up and then a blue light - two boats drove past us and a quantity of deck cargo.

A little while after the ship came off, we boarded her, made sail and got her on the Trinity Sands. We found her low in the water, her fires out, water two feet above the stoke hole. The three men have been washed overboard as they were not to be found on board the vessel."

Over the next two years the lifeboat was launched on many occasions to offer assistance and stand by vessels which had gone aground in heavy weather. On several occasions captains refused any kind of assistance and on others no assistance was necessary and the vessel floated off unharmed. On Saturday 13th November 1875 with a strong south west wind blowing the watchman reported a vessel on the Binks burning a tar barrel. Hopper burned blue lights and fired rockets and launched the lifeboat. They soon reached the ship, the Elizabeth and Susan, of Yarmouth, Captain Carter. There was now very heavy rain with the wind, but the crew of four men were taken into the lifeboat and almost immediately the ship fell over. At daybreak there was nothing to be seen. On the following day, the gale continuing, three vessels went aground on the Trinity Sand and the tender was launched to give assistance. The crews of two ships left in their own boats and reached the beach safely. The lifeboat men boarded the third vessel and manned the pumps all night and until mid-day, when a steam tug took her to Grimsby. Yet another service was carried out on 19th November during a terrific gale from the north. The fishing smack Jane, of Grimsby, had had her sails blown out and bowsprit carried away and was riding at anchor in a dangerous position. The lifeboat tender was launched and reached the Jane "after a hard pull" and Hopper decided it was advisable to slip the anchor and run the Jane onto the beach near the lifeboat cottages. This was done and the ship and crew were safe.

A number of businessmen, mostly connected with shipping companies, made a small collection and gave the money to Hopper and the lifeboat crew on 26th November 1875 in recognition of their services. Part of the letter which accompanied the money reads as follows

"Annexed we hand you a list of a few donations amounting to fourteen pounds ten shillings from the several contributions named for Captain Hopper and crew of the Spurn Life Boat in slight acknowledgement of the noble manner in which they fulfil their perilous duties."

There was an additional donation of ten shillings and sixpence in January 1876 and the whole gesture was much appreciated by the men at Spurn.

The crew of six men were saved from the smack Undaunted, of Grimsby, on February 4th 1876, when the vessel ran aground on the Binks and quickly became a total wreck.

The strong north east winds on Thursday 13th April increased to gale force during the evening. At 11.0pm the watchman reported a vessel on shore on the Inner Binks. Hopper burned blue lights and fired rockets and put off with the tender -

"After Great difficulty succeeded in reaching the Life Boat. It then blowing a terrific gale. Notwithstanding we succeeded in getting within two or three hundred yards of the vessel but owing to the wind being so heavy the crew was unable to pull the boat against it and we got drifted down to Leeward. I thought it advisable to make for Grimsby and fearing the crew was still in the rigging I engaged the steam tug Victor to tow us down to the Binks, but it was only to see that the ship had gone to pieces. Returned with the Life Boat to her moorings, fears are entertained as regards the safety of the crew, but think they may have got clear in their own boat."

Obviously a disappointing and frustrating result after a great struggle in difficult conditions.

The lifeboat was not launched on service at any other time during April or May 1876 and yet the following short letter was sent to Trinity House -

"I am concerned to hear that the Spurn Life Boat in her noble effort to save the Shipwrecked crew was upset twice - I wish you would kindly inform the Hull Trinity House that the National Life Boat Institution is prepared to place at Spurn Point one of its best Life Boats free of any charge to them, on the understanding that they will contribute to the Institution annually the amount which it now costs them to maintain an inefficient Life Boat.

I am Yours very truly,

R. Lewis.

Submitted to the Hull Trinity House 10th May 1876

J.E. Fisher
Local Secretary
Grimsby.

Later documents show the casualty to have been the "Miss Nightingale" and make it very clear that the tender was washed onto the beach and upset twice whilst the crew tried to reach the lifeboat, but the lifeboat itself never suffered that way during the service.

Mr. Richard Lewis was the secretary to the RNLI at the time and although Mr. Fisher signs himself as "Local Secretary" there was no lifeboat station at Grimsby at the time. Perhaps the letter sent to Trinity House was simply a copy of part of a longer letter from Mr. Lewis. It is possible that the reference to "an inefficient Life Boat" prompted someone at Trinity House to produce the following note in defence of the station, which has neither signature nor address -

"The Life Boat at Spurn was established in 1810 and upwards of 760 lives were saved by this Boat since then down to about 1854, and also in 1853 HMS "Medea" with a Crew of 280 men was rescued from a perilous position and piloted up the Humber by the Master of the Life Boat. Since then many valuable services have been rendered to Life and Shipping."

There is no documentary evidence still in existence to support these claims and the whole episode is somewhat mysterious.

Another strange happening was on June 19th when a man named Riches jumped from the steam tug, Pride of the Day, into the water in front of the lifeboat cottages and immediately drowned. His body was recovered four days later.

Christmas morning 1876 dawned with a heavy easterly gale with showers of snow and sleet and a heavy sea on the Binks. At daybreak the watchman reported a vessel sunk on the Binks and the lifeboat was launched. The report continues -

"..owing to the strong flood tide running over the Binks, the crew was unable to pull the Boat against it. No 3 Pilot Cutter took us in tow and tried to tow us out, but failed to do so. He transferred us over to the Swanland (a steam ship) then entering the Humber. I asked him if he would tow us out to the Middle Bink Buoy, which he kindly did. We then got under canvas and shook out to wind ward of the sunken vessel. When we got there we found it to be the Grace Darling, of Goole, with three men in the rigging, all in a Pitiable Condition, being exposed there for twelve hours. They were not able to show distress signals as the vessel sunk immediately after she struck, the sea making a clear Breach over her. With great difficulty we succeeded in getting the men into the Life Boat. The Captain was so benumbed that he could not help himself out, so one of the Life Boat Men, E. Wheldrake, went into the rigging and got a rope round his waist and by that means we were able to get him into the Boat.

They were forwarded home by the Shipwrecked Mariners Society."

Edward Wheldrake was dismissed from the lifeboat service on March 6th 1877 because he was one of a group of men who accused the Master of cowardice. On April 27th the Secretary to the Board of Trinity House in Hull wrote to Wheldrake asking him to attend at the House on the following day as the RNLI had awarded him the Silver Medal for his gallantry during the rescue from the Grace Darling. Unfortunately the citation was incorrect -

Patrington Mothers' Union outing to Spurn, 1st September, 1904
Courtesy of Mr. J. Kirkwood

Outing from Patrington 1906. Group at Kilnsea Warren, at the northern end of Spurn.
Courtesy of Mr. J. Kirkwood

“Resolved That the Silver Medal of the Royal National Lifeboat Institution be presented to Mr. Ed. Weldrake one of the crew of the Spurn point Life Boat in acknowledgement of his humane and intrepid conduct in jumping into the Sea from the Life Boat and Saving the Master of the Boat “Grace Darling” of Hull which was wrecked on the Middle Banks off Spurn point during a Strong Gale from the E and in a heavy sea on Christmas Day 1876.

Thomas Chapman Chairman. Rich. Lewis Secretary.”

Wheldrake did not jump into the sea from the lifeboat, nor did he ever claim to have done so. When he attended at Trinity House there was an inquiry and he was questioned about his actions, with the following result -

“Ed. Weldrake stated to the Warden that in jumping into the rigging the sea curled upon him - that the Master of the Grace Darling was so benumbed with the cold that after getting the Rope fast round his body he had to force his fingers clear of the rigging - he admitted that he did not jump overboard.”

At the end of the inquiry it was decided that the award should be made and the Warden presented Wheldrake with the Silver Medal.

(The spelling of the name “Wheldrake” depended on who wrote it. The man himself usually included the letter ‘h’, other people missed out the letter, hence the spelling on the citation.)

The month of March was occupied by an unhappy episode when bitter accusations and counter-accusations were made between several members of the crew and the Master, Fewson Hopper. The Mate, John Best, received his discharge notice from Hopper on January 24th 1877. On March 5th he wrote to Trinity House in Hull lodging a complaint against Hopper, repeated in a later letter. Thomas Hodgson handed in his notice of resignation on March 9th “feeling that I cannot put up with his (Hopper’s) ill conduct any longer. I have been in the Life Boat Service now eleven years.” James Barnby handed in his resignation on the following day “as I do not feel that I can settle down, or any longer bear the ill-will of the Captain.” John Parrott resigned on March 12th because “I consider his conduct in a great many things that have passed as not at all right.

The crew have always been able to agree quite well together, and any disturbance that has taken place has been usually caused by the Captain. On the morning when I took him my discharge I said to him previously that I supposed it was no use beginning to set my garden and he said to me that it quite depended on what side I was with regard to the loss of life by the wreck of the schooner Miss Nightingale, and also the recent collision between the Albatross and the Newsand light-ship.

I then told him I was on Truth side, and he said I might go."

In a long letter written to Trinity House on March 11th Best accused Hopper of foul language, verbal and physical abuse to himself and others, of having no qualifications or experience as a seaman, only ever having sailed on the Humber, of being very pleasant whilst money was being earned by the crew, but being ready to pick a quarrel with anyone when earnings dropped, and "cursing, ramping and swearing... foaming like a mad bull." He also accused Hopper of stealing wreckage, keeping the crew under threat of dismissal " and no one seems to dare appeal against such treatment for fear of failing and having to go, as all of us know that he is held in such high estimation that anything we may say will have very little effect we fear."

This was followed by another letter from Best, part of which is quoted below, referring to the loss of the crew of the "Miss Nightingale".

"Gentlemen, our own crew has made no secret of it, for it was and still is said that had he (Mr. Hopper) been from home we could have saved that crew of seven poor fellows and I believe the same. Gentlemen, on the 13th day of April last about 10.40pm the watch called all hands and we mustered at the boat shed as quick as possible waiting for Mr. Hopper bringing the key as he told me he would bring it as he had to go into his house. We were coming down from the watch house at the time and I did not see him for more than half an hour after that. When he came we got the boat out as quick as possible, but broke an oar just outside the shed, replaced it and got the boat down to the water and all hands jumping into her before she was properly afloat. She struck on her heel and came on shore with us. She was launched again and next time an oar was broke and it being a lee one the boat came on shore a second time. All this occurred Gentlemen in a very short space of time and while I ran up to the boat shed for an oar Mr. Hopper went home to light the lamp. I was as quick as I could for I knew the ebb tide was spending and the gale seemed to increase every moment with blinding snow and sleet. When I got back with an oar we launched the boat once more and as Mr. Hopper had not come down we waded the boat up towards the low Light House that is abreast of it, the gale being from the NE and increasing in fury all the time, and every few minutes the sky was in an illumination (from the flares from the ship in distress) and we were waiting expecting every moment he would be coming, but no Gentlemen. If we were waiting five minutes we were waiting an hour after I had taken the oar down and when he came he said that his heart failed him and that his nerve was gone and that he had rather be in a Union House than have to go off a night like that, and that there ought to be a younger man in his situation.

Indeed Gentlemen, after he had said that before all hands, I never supposed he would have stayed another winter at Spurn. It was not half ebb when we were all mustered but one stoppage or another for Mr. Hopper to throw an hour and a half away and no one knew the reason till he came and confessed that he was afraid. The wind by this time was about ENE and fiercer than ever. We got off to the Life Boat and after I had slipped her I noticed a reef in her sail as it was being set and I made the remark that it was the first time for near twelve years that I had seen the sail reefed, especially with the wind dead against you and the ebb tide near spent, that we should not reach the wreck."

Best continued by saying that there were never enough supplies of rope, or equipment in the lifeboat, and that everything he said was the truth and would be supported by most of the crew, but -

"..there may be an exception, the one who is expecting my situation, and there may be others afraid to speak for fear as I have said before."

On the following day Wheldrake wrote saying the same things as Best and adding an accusation that two lives were lost when the Albatross collided with the Newsand Light, which could have been saved had the lifeboat been launched. Another crew member, Joseph Wilkinson, wrote to Trinity House on March 13th repeating what Wheldrake had said and on March 15th a letter signed by John Best, John Parrott, James Barnby, Edward Wheldrake and Joseph Wilkinson, was sent to Mr. Wilson, Secretary to the Board of Trinity House in Hull. This repeated all the accusations, but with reference to the Albatross -

"And again I wish to call attention to the loss of two more lives sacrificed. I allude to the collision of the Albatross of Lowestoft and the Spurn light ship on Friday 19th January last, about 10.0pm when the light was put out for one hour and twenty minutes. Part of the crew got on board the light ship firing guns and sending rockets. The watch on duty duly reported to the Master and he answered their signals with a blue light, but neglected to put off. Consequently two poor fellows sank with the ship. Now sir all this has been reported and on being asked by the Master if we intended to abide by our decision and on being told we did we are summarily dismissed and cannot prevail on the house to give us a hearing it matters little how they decide we should like our characters vindicating if you Sir will kindly try to obtain for us a hearing we shall feel grateful."

The only statement in the summary report for 19th January 1877 reads -

"Blowing a gale throughout. 10.0pm the Spurn Light Vessel light went out and continued so until 11.30. It appeared to be owing to a vessel running into her."

Thomas Winson, who had been appointed Mate after the dismissal of Best was the only crew member to write in support of Hopper. He stated that the watchman called the crew at about eleven o'clock on the night of Thursday 13th April 1876.

There was a fearful gale from the north east with blinding squalls of snow and hail. Some of the crew went to the boat house, some to the watch house. The Master burned a blue light and fired a rocket and the crew all went to the boat house to get out the tender, when it was customary for the Mate to unlock the shed, but on the night in question he did not do this and the crew waited about twenty minutes. Hopper had gone home to put on his Life Boat suit and when he returned -

"..he remonstrated with the Mate for not fetching the key he then either fetched it himself or sent one of the Crew I cannot say which. Subsequently we succeeded in getting the boat out and down the Beach. We then attempted to put off to the Life Boat but we could not get the Tender through the surf clear of the Beach. In the mean time the wind and Tide kept driving us towards the Point. We were obliged to Beach the Boat and Track her up to windward again. On the second attempt we could not get the Boat clear of the wash of the Beach. Eventually one of the Crew broke an oar, consequently the Boat went ashore a second time, not before she had drifted some distance to leeward again. All this occupied a great deal of time. The Mate had to go to the Boat Shed to get another oar in the place of the broken one, the Captain going up home at the same time to light the Boat Lantern which had gone out. In the mean time he ordered us to Track the Tender to windward again. We then waited about a quarter of an hour or twenty (minutes) when the Captain returned with the lamp lighted. We then made a third attempt to get off and succeeded in reaching the Life Boat and getting her under canvas with all the haste we could. We tried to sail the Boat to the ship but failed to do so. We then lowered the sail and tried to pull the Life Boat to the ship but owing to the force of the Gale we blew further to leeward still. All our efforts were unfortunately in vain, we were obliged to let go the Anchor again, we then knew it was impossible for us to get out to the ship. The flood Tide making we set sail and tried to fetch the Life Boat moorings but could not beat in. At last we had to run away to Grimsby, the force of the wind was so great that we could not pull the Boat round head to wind but was obliged to wear her round before it.

Gentlemen

Allow me to state that I have been in the Life Boat Service nearly seven years I have never had an angry word with Mr. Hopper during the whole time but always found him Indulgent, a very Sober and persevering man, it is very evident that three or four of the Crew have conspired together to agitate and do him all the harm they can through spite and base Fabrications they have spread about the country to annoy him."

Fewson Hopper wrote his own account of events on that night and it is the same as Winson's up to the firing of the rocket. It continues -

"I sent up the Rocket and held the Blue light until it burnt out, then proceeded home, on the way I met one of the crew which asked what was the matter. I answered something ashore on the Binks, then dressed myself in my Life Boat Suit, lit my lamp and proceeded to the Boat Shed. On arriving there I found the Crew loitering about the Shed. I said what is the matter then. Its no use making any bones about it we shall have to go. Some answered they could not get into the Boat Shed. I said what was the reason the Mate had not brought the key, where was he. Some of them said Best is here. I said to him what is the reason you have not got the key and got the Boat out. He answered in an abrupt manner that key ought to be at my House. I said that key is not going to be at your House and made my way home to fetch the key, then we succeeded in getting out the Boat. There was one oar broke, it was soon replaced with another. We got down to the waters edge. I gave orders for them to wade the Boat up to windward, which was done. We all got into the Boat and struck out for the Life Boat. It was Hailing at this time and the wind had increased to an Hurricane. The Boat soon drifted down below the Life Boat and we could not reach her. I ordered them to back ashore and wade her up to windward again. We did so and then struck out again. I said the Boat is drifting down like a ball again, then one of the men broke an oar. We then had to back ashore again and go up to the Boat Shed to get the broken oar replaced. In the meantime I had lost my light and had to go up home to get it replaced and left orders to wade the Boat up again to windward. We struck out again and succeeded in reaching the Life Boat. I ordered them to take the reef in the Sail and slip the Boat from her moorings. We stood out abreast of the stranded vessel. I ordered the Sail to be lowered and the Anchor let go. There was a strong ebb tide running - I said to the Crew do you think you can pull her, some of them said no I am sure we cannot. I said shift the Sail over, we got under way and stood into about two fathoms of water close under the Bink edges, the vessel then being about two hundred yards from us. I said drop the Anchor and lower the Sail down. I said now can you pull her think you, they answered we will try. They got on their oars and pulled for a considerable time till I found she was drifting to leeward. I said give a cast of lead, she had dropped off into nine fathoms water. I said let go the Anchor and we rode there a short time and then got under way and stood into the Humber. The wind was so heavy that we could not get the tack of the Sail down and when I wanted to heave about the Crew could not pull her round for the weight of wind and sea and I had to wear her round and in doing so we lost a mile dead to Leeward. I then made for Grimsby and engaged a Steam Tug to tow us down and when I knew the ship had gone to pieces it was then when I said I would rather live in A Union House than have such work to do."

All these statements were considered by the Board of Trinity House in Hull and the decision was made in favour of Fewson Hopper, the Master. Thomas Winson remained as Mate and the crew members who had complained were all dismissed.

Early in April 1877 it was decided to have a new tender at Spurn. The boat was ordered from Mr. Lewis Emery, of Sheringham in Norfolk. The boat was to have an overall length of twenty feet and a beam of seven feet three inches amidships. The cost was to be twenty pounds plus a further eighteen shillings for all the iron work, but Mr. Emery could not make the boat before August because of other commitments. In the third week of August Mr. Emery wrote to apologise for a delay -

"We have had a setback as a Gentleman's Reaping Machine broke down and I had to repair it or the boat would have been forwarder."

The tender was completed on September 11th and because of the difficulty and cost of transporting it to Hull by rail the Trinity House Yacht was sent to collect it and it was delivered to Spurn on 25th September 1877.

At the beginning of June 1877 John Quinton, tenant and keeper of the Life Boat Inn on Spurn, gave notice to Trinity House that he would leave in July. Fewson Hopper applied for and was granted the position and took over as inn keeper when Quinton left on 19th July.

During the second half of the year 1877 the lifeboat was launched on several occasions to stand by vessels until they floated off, or to find that a steam tug had reached the casualty first and that the lifeboat was not needed. Early in December, after only a short time as inn keeper, Hopper was appointed to be Keeper of the Saltend Light House. He sent his resignation to Trinity House and left the lifeboat service at the end of the month. He was succeeded as Master by Thomas Winson, Mate of the lifeboat, who took up his position on 1st January 1878.

Hopper had served twenty one years at Spurn, twelve of them as Master of the lifeboat. In his early days in the crew he had suffered financial and physical hardships along with the others, but during his time as Master conditions had improved for everyone. He did have other problems to contend with, notably the charge of cowardice and neglect of duty, but he emerged from that with a largely new crew and the dissension came to an end. He saw big improvements in the communication links between Spurn and Hull and overall left the station in good heart for Thomas Winson.

THOMAS WINSON 1st JANUARY 1878 - 18th MARCH 1894

Thomas Winson first became a member of the lifeboat crew in December 1865, but left the service in February 1869. He was re-appointed to the crew in September 1873 and became Mate in March 1877 following the dismissal of John Best. When Fewson Hopper left the lifeboat service to become a lighthouse keeper Thomas Winson was appointed to be Master of the Life Boat at Spurn.

Winson took up his appointment at a time when life was relatively settled and the families were not suffering the financial hardships of the past. For the first ten years of office there were very few changes in the crew and the problems he faced were those connected with the sea and ships.

The first launch was only four days after he took up his appointment, to check the Bull Light Ship Fog Bell, which was not working. He discovered it had been hit by the Gleaner, a Hull smack, on the previous night. This was followed by two launches in February which were ineffective, the first when the watchman reported "a vessel showing a flaring light on the Binks." When the lifeboat arrived there was no trace of any ship. A week later the lifeboat launched to assist the steam tug Unity, which had gone aground on the Binks, but no assistance was required.

The watchman reported a vessel showing distress signals on the Binks at 11.0pm on Monday 8th April 1878, whilst there was a very strong breeze from the south-east. The lifeboat was launched to assist and found the Earnest, a new smack built at Rye and on her passage to Hull. The lifeboat stood by the smack until it floated off, and whilst there, a schooner was observed trying to enter the Humber, but it grounded on the Binks. When the smack floated it was made secure and the crew taken into the lifeboat, which then went to assist the schooner. This was the Freedom, from Fowey to Hull with a cargo of china clay. The schooner had filled with water and the crew were in the rigging. The lifeboat men succeeded, after a difficult struggle, in getting the crew into the lifeboat and all the men were landed safely at Spurn. The lifeboat then went back to the smack and with the help of the Goole tug boat No. 3 succeeded in getting the Earnest off the Binks and it was towed up to Hull. The Freedom was forty five years old and appears to have become a total wreck.

During September 1878 the lifeboat was launched to assist the Myrtle, a small steam pleasure yacht aground on the Binks, with four young men on board. The lifeboat succeeded in getting her clear and into the Humber to Grimsby. Later in the month the lifeboat was launched again to assist two herring luggers loaded with a catch. The Three Sisters and the Florence Nightingale floated off without assistance and made their way to Grimsby.

A gale was blowing on the night of November 8th when a vessel showing signals of distress was sighted on the Lincolnshire coast. The lifeboat was launched at about 10.30pm and found a brig with her mainmast gone. On going close to the brig it was found that the crew had left her earlier in their own boat. As the lifeboat was about to leave the brig a second vessel close into the shore was seen to fire a rocket and show a flaring light. The lifeboat went to assist and found the schooner Triumph, of Liverpool, riding in fifteen feet of water. The Captain denied showing any signals and refused all assistance, but as the Spurn lifeboat left the scene it met the Cleethorpes lifeboat going out to the same vessel. There was a very heavy sea running on the Lincolnshire coast and the lifeboat returned to Spurn at 3.3 0am on 9th November "after a very rough night."

The lifeboat was launched at 5.30am on the morning of Saturday, 16th November, flaring lights having been seen on the Lincolnshire coast. On arrival the crew found a brigantine on fire, which had been abandoned, and the lifeboat returned to its moorings. At 8.30pm on the same evening a vessel was seen in the Hawk Roads "showing flaring lights and firing rockets" and the lifeboat was launched immediately. The crew found the German brig Marie, of Barth, coal laden, had collided with a light brig, the Agricola, of Aberdeen. Both vessels had sustained some damage and the lifeboat men helped to clear the debris, but on finding that neither ship was taking in water the lifeboat returned to Spurn.

The cod fishing smack Reliance, of Grimsby, ran aground on the Outer Binks at 9.0pm on Saturday 22nd March 1879 and the lifeboat was launched immediately. The vessel was reached at about 10.0pm and the entire crew of eleven hands taken into the lifeboat, which then stood by until 3.30am. By that time the Reliance had filled with water and the lifeboat returned to Spurn. The smack quickly be came a complete wreck and during the morning the eleven hands returned to Grimsby by tug boat.

There was a dense fog on the morning of 27th April when the Norwegian brig Diamanten grounded on the beach a mile and a half from Spurn. The brig was timber laden from Arendal for Kings Lynn. The lifeboat was launched and tried to get the Diamanten off the beach, but failed. On the following day cargo was thrown overboard to lighten the ship, but three steam tugs were needed to pull the vessel clear of the sand.

The men at Spurn depended on salvage to supplement their income, but from time to time services were carried out and no charge was made. On 5th May 1879 a sloop, the New Hope, of Hull, drove onto the Stone Bank inside Spurn and the Tender was launched to assist. "We succeeded on getting her off, did not charge the owner anything, being a poor man."

Robert Tennison, one of the crew members, was discharged from the lifeboat service in May, "being too old, over sixty years of age."

The year 1880 proved to be quite busy with a number of launches to assist vessels in distress. Some ships were pulled off sand banks and helped to Grimsby, others, which had been abandoned by their crews, were pumped dry and taken by the lifeboat crew or by tug to Grimsby and docked safely.

The end of January 1881 proved to be very cold and Winson recorded "large quantity of floating ice in the Humber." The cold weather continued into February and on Monday 7th February at 8.0am there was a moderate breeze from the south, but this later developed into a full gale with snow and sleet. The fishing smack Loyal, of Hull, went aground on the Trinity Sands and the lifeboat crew launched the Tender and went to assist. They found the Captain in the cabin, with a broken leg, and agreed to run out an anchor and try to get the vessel off. This they failed to do and returned to Spurn at about 3.30pm, "when it was blowing a very keen Gale." At about 5.0pm the men returned to the Loyal, this time with the lifeboat, to take off the crew, but they did not want to leave. The weather moderated and the lifeboat stood by until high tide and again tried to get the vessel off, but there was not sufficient water. At about midnight the tug Samson arrived with the agent for the Loyal, who told the lifeboat men their services were no longer required. The lifeboat returned to Spurn, arriving about 1.0am on February 8th. Hardly had the boat been moored when distress signals were seen on the smack. The lifeboat was launched again and the Loyal was found to be filling rapidly with water. The four hands making up the crew were taken into the lifeboat and landed safely at Spurn at 4.0am. The service had lasted about twenty hours. Two days later the Loyal was emptied, pulled off the sand and taken to Grimsby.

At 5.30am on the morning of 10th February news was brought to Spurn that a vessel was ashore on the beach near Kilnsea Beacon. The ship, the Premier, of Hull, had gone aground late the previous night during a heavy snow squall with a strong south south east breeze. The lifeboat was launched immediately, but on reaching the Premier could not help immediately because it was low water. The tug Charm came on the scene and with great difficulty in heavy seas the lifeboat crew took a warp from the Premier to the tug. In less than half an hour the tug had to cast off the warp to keep itself out of danger in the bad conditions. Later the lifeboat again carried a warp to the tug and at this time a second tug from Grimsby, the Garibalda, arrived and at high water the two tugs managed to pull off the vessel.

The brigantine Lord Exmouth, of Lowestoft, coal loaded, went aground on the Binks at about 8.30pm on Monday 14th February and showed distress signals. There was a strong breeze from the south east with squalls of rain and a heavy sea at the time. The lifeboat was launched immediately, found the ship's boat had been washed away and succeeded in saving the crew of four men. The lifeboat returned safely to Spurn at about 11.0pm and the Lord Exmouth filled with water.

Winson wrote to Trinity House in Hull on March 18th 1881, obviously in answer to a letter from the Board, saying that everyone at Spurn was "very pleased to hear that the old Boat is about to be replaced by a new one." He asked to be allowed to delay sending dimensions and details until he had had time to examine the lifeboat at Cleethorpes. A week later Winson wrote again saying that there was nothing in the Cleethorpes boat he wanted to build into the new boat for Spurn. He said the new boat should be thirty two feet six inches overall length, nine feet eight inches beam amidships and three feet six inches overall depth amidships. He also asked for a trysail and foresail instead of the lug sail of the old boat, as well as other specifications.

In April Trinity House was offered a lifeboat already built by Wouldhave and Johnson at South Shields. The cost of the boat was one hundred pounds, but extra work and fittings were needed to make it fit and acceptable for use at Spurn. Three weeks later the offer was declined and the reason given was that the boat was too heavy for use at Spurn.

Tenders were invited from shipbuilders in June and finally on 27th July the tender of J.E.Cooper, Boatbuilder of Garrison Side, Hull, was accepted. The final dimensions were to be thirty two feet six inches overall length, nine feet eight inches beam amidships and four feet deep amidships. To be copper fastened throughout, copper sheathed two feet high from underside of the keel and to have thirty copper air-tight tanks. The gunwales and timbers to be Quebec elm and the planking to be English oak. The whole to receive three coats of best white lead and oil paint. The total cost on delivery to be one hundred and ninety five pounds.

The sloop Sarah, of Hull, signalled for assistance at about 9.30pm on May 21st 1881, having gone aground on the Binks. There was a moderate south easterly, but the sea had broken the hatches and filled the sloop with water. The sea was washing right over the vessel when the lifeboat arrived. The captain of the Sarah and the mate, together with the captain's wife and two children, were taken into the lifeboat, which then stood by until the sloop floated off with the tide. The lifeboat men succeeded in pumping her out and taking her to a safe anchorage in the Humber, when the crew and the captain's family returned on board. Winson concluded his report by writing -

"I beg to say we do not intend to charge anything for our services on the present occasion as the Captain is a very poor man and has been ill in bed during the whole of last winter."

Three weeks later on 11th June the fishing smack Ben Ledi, from Hull, returning to port loaded with fish from the fleet, ran aground on the Inner Binks. The lifeboat was launched at 8.0am into a north east wind and very rough seas. On reaching the vessel Winson advised the captain to batten down everything as conditions would worsen. When a steam tug sailed by it was engaged to tow off the Ben Ledi. The lifeboat men took the tow rope to the tug and stood by as conditions became rougher. The captain and four crewmen were taken into the lifeboat as a precaution and the tow rope broke. It was only with very great difficulty that the lifeboat crew managed to connect a second rope, but eventually the Ben Ledi was pulled off the Inner Binks. She was found to be taking in water and the lifeboat men pumped her all the way to Grimsby, only managing to balance the leak, and moored her safely. When they returned to Spurn the service had lasted about twelve hours.

Monday 15th August 1881 was when the Duke of Edinburgh visited Spurn and was taken fishing by Winson. This must have been one of the high points in the lives of the people living at Spurn at the time.

All five members of the crew of the fishing smack Agile, of Grimsby, were rescued by the lifeboat when the smack went aground on the Inner Binks on October 2nd. There was a very strong east south east wind and very heavy seas at the time. Three days later when the lifeboat was launched in more difficult conditions Winson wrote in his report -

"I was obliged to lay the Boat to several times for her to free herself of water as it was very often half way up the air boxes."

The crew must have been sitting in water whilst they rowed.

December 1881 proved to be a busy month for the lifeboat with several calls for assistance. On the last day of the month the new lifeboat was handed over by Mr.J.E.Cooper to Trinity House and it was taken to Spurn by the steam yacht Duke of Edinburgh on January 6th 1882. The boat was tested and telegrams were sent to Hull saying that all was well. On January 17th Mr.Cooper, the boat builder, wrote to Trinity House pointing out that the agreement had been for the account to be settled within fourteen days of the boat being handed over, but it was now eighteen days since the boat had been delivered, he had been twice to Trinity House, but the account still had not been settled. He added that he was going to lose ten pounds on the contract and could not afford to be kept waiting for payment as he had bills to pay.

Another letter on January 19th from Mr. Cooper showed that Trinity House had made payment, but had deducted three pounds thirteen shillings and sixpence from the bill. Mr. Cooper listed various items which were not in the original contract, but which had been agreed to at a later date and for which he required payment. The letter continues -

"The next item is nine shillings for the four iron cleets. I beg to remind you that the cleets which were first put on were passed by your surveyor before they were put on and therefor the four for which I only charge you the blacksmith's price and which were put on at the wish of Captain Winson and under your supervision I cannot allow, as your surveyor passed the first four and all else must be considered extra. I am sorry that your committee should have attempted to deal so grudgingly with me, especially after the loss I am sustaining through the contract, and I must remind you that if I had attempted to make a bill of extras I could have soon done so. As you must remember first that we raised the deck four inches at each end after the bearers were in, then we had to double the main thwart as you altered your minds in the placing of the Mast, then we supplied a New Mast Step. All these things and several others I have not been paid for, but shall certainly expect paying for if your committee insist upon taking off my account that which I have a perfect and honest right to."

In the records there is no further correspondence on the matter - can it be assumed that the bill was paid in full ?

The new lifeboat was kept busy over the following months and Winson was pleased with its performance. Many ships were assisted, crews were taken off and then returned and vessels were pulled off the Binks and taken into the Humber. The first life-saving service took place on December 18th 1882. Winson's report tells the story -

"...at 8.30am I received information that a vessel was ashore near Kilnsea Beacon and that the crew was in the rigging, the vessel being full of water. The Rocket apparatus could not render any assistance. The wind at the time being SSE, flood tide, our greatest difficulty being getting round the Point against the wind and tide. After several attempts to turn the Boat out past the Point so that we could sail over the Binks and along the coast the Steam Boat Lorne of Hull was coming into the river and the Captain kindly towed us half way out to the Inner Bink Buoy so that we could sail over the Binks and along the coast. We had about seven miles to go against the tide but we did our best with rowing and sailing to get there as quick as possible. On arriving at the vessel found all the crew, twelve in number, still in the rigging. There was a very heavy sea on the beach making a clean breach over the vessel. After letting go Life Boat's Anchor in position the Life Boat was filled nearly every sea, we was in the worst place just where the heaviest sea curled over into us. Slacked the Life Boat within four yards of the vessels rigging, we effected the rescue with two heaving lines, we had to pull them all through the water after letting go our anchor. We had all the crew in the Life Boat in about twenty minutes, it would be about 10.40am high water when we got them all in. We had the ebb tide to turn against to Spurn. We arrived safe at Spurn about 4.30pm all safe. I am sorry to say we got an oar broke during the time we were getting the crew off. The vessel is the cod smack Mary Anne of Grimsby."

A year later at the beginning of December 1883 Winson received the following letter from Mr. Mundahl, the owner of the smack -

" I have bought a book each for yourself and your crew as a small acknowledgement of your services in the saving of the crew of my smack "Mary Anne" in December last, and shall be glad if you will accept them. The reading of them may interest you in your some what secluded homes and also in a humble way that your good work is not altogether forgotten. As I do not know the best way to send them I shall be glad if when the boat comes up some one would please to call at my office for them."

During the night of March 11th/12th there was a northerly gale and a very high tide. Water washed completely over the cottages, fortunately without damaging them, but land was washed away and groynes were damaged. The major casualty was the watch house, which "was washed down the cliff, turned over and partly broke to pieces." Winson suggested that a replacement should be ten or twelve feet square, made of wood or zinc, and made in sections in Hull so that it could be erected by the crew at Spurn. He also suggested that it should be set up on piles about four feet above ground level, so that the sea could wash underneath it, the hut could be easily moved if necessary and the men on watch would be raised up above most of the wind-blown sand and "would not be blinded so much."

In the same letter Winson gave the correct facts of an incident which had been wrongly reported in the press. The newspaper account said that two Scarborough brigs had gone ashore three miles from Spurn, the crews had been rescued by rocket apparatus, but one man had been washed overboard and drowned. The facts from Winson were that the brigs came into the Humber during a gale, were deliberately run into the river muds near Kilnsea and the crews never at any time left the vessels as there was no danger. One man was washed overboard but that happened at sea before the brigs entered the Humber.

During July 1883 there was the incident of the two young boys who had been adrift in the Humber all night in a very small boat. Fortunately the incident ended with the boys safe.

Nine men, the crew of the barque Foringen, were rescued by the Spurn lifeboat on October 4th 1883. The barque was loaded with deals for Grimsby and Winson saw it part from its anchor across the Humber near the Lincolnshire coast. A second anchor was let go, but "all the masts went by the board." The lifeboat was launched immediately and sailed across the Humber, receiving some damage herself on the

Spurn lifeboat about 1883. Mr. thomas Winson at the helm.
Courtesy of Mrs. D. Lawrence

way. On reaching the Foringen the lifeboat dropped anchor and slacked towards the vessel and succeeded in saving the crew. The lifeboat could not go too close because of all the "masts, yards, sails and rigging all alongside the vessel." As the barque drove, Winson had to cut the lifeboat's anchor cable and leave the anchor, because of the danger to the lifeboat. The men were all landed safely at Spurn and were taken to the Lifeboat Inn. The following day the lifeboat and the tug Champion went back to the barque, cleared all the wreckage and towed the vessel to Grimsby. The Captain and crew of the Foringen were put on another tug and taken to Grimsby.

Very early on the morning of Saturday, October 6th, the watchman reported a vessel in the Humber showing flares. Winson checked and saw what he thought was a burning tar barrel and called all his crew. The lifeboat was launched and reached the vessel at about 4.50am. the casualty was the steam ship Empress, of Hull, and the ship was ablaze.

"All the fore part of the vessel was then on fire as far aft as the bridge. The tug Flying Sand was already on the scene and shortly after daybreak the London Boat came and lay by."

One crewman from the Empress had had his legs broken and was very badly burned and the lifeboat took him to the London Boat. The lifeboat also carried passengers to the tug for transport to Hull and tried to put out the fire, but was unable to do so. When all the passengers and crew, except the captain and mate, had been transferred to the tug the lifeboat lay by the vessel, still trying to extinguish the blaze. After it had burnt out a cable and anchor were attached to the hulk to prevent it from floating off into the Humber. On 14th October the lifeboat assisted three tugs to get the hulk afloat and tow it to Hull. Because of the ebb tide they were compelled to run the vessel onto the mud at Saltend and wait for the next tide to complete the journey.

Winson wrote the following to the Board of Trinity House on 12th December 1883

"I beg respectfully to inform you that during the heavy gale of this morning some time between 12.30 and 6.30am this morning I am afraid the Life Boat has broke her Mooring Chain and driven out to sea as I cannot see her anywhere. I think the Boat must have broken her chain about an hour and a half after high water as the Tide would be going out very strong and the sea very heavy. We did not know she was gone until dawn of day when we got the Tender down to the water for the purpose of putting off with the Life Boat to a large Barque riding close in shore between the Trinity Sand and the beach."

The Grimsby lifeboat took the crew from the barque as it was not possible for the Spurn men to assist with the Tender. Nothing more was heard of the lifeboat for some time and the old one was patched up and put into service, in spite of it leaking rather badly. New and stronger moorings were put in place.

A telegram was received by Winson on December 31st telling him that the lifeboat had been found and the following paragraph appeared in the Eastern Morning News on 7th January 1884 -

"SPURN LIFEBOAT - A telegram has been received from Mr. Matthew Brown, Chairman of the Buoyage and Beaconage Committee of the Hull Trinity House, stating that the Spurn lifeboat, which was broken from her moorings during the heavy gale on the night of the 11th of December, and driven out to sea, and picked up by Dutch fishermen near the Island of Texel, and finally taken into Nieuwe Dieppe, may be expected in Hull to-day, on board the steam ship European, which steamer left Amsterdam yesterday about noon. Mr Brown left Hull on Wednesday night for Nieuwe Dieppe to arrange for the salvage and bringing home of the boat."

On arriving in Hull the lifeboat was taken to be repaired and was returned to station at Spurn on January 24th 1884.

Most of the year was quiet, with few calls for the lifeboat, but she was launched five times on service in December. On the night of Tuesday 23rd December at about 11.15pm the lifeboat was launched to assist the barque Athenian, of Grimsby, loaded with ice from Norway.

Spurn Lifeboat crew about 1885. Man on extreme right is Thomas Hodgson Jarrett, grandfather of Mrs. D. Lawrence, who Kindly loaned the photograph.

There was a fresh breeze from the east and a considerable sea running. The barque had a crew of eleven men. The captain asked the lifeboat to lay by and assist if necessary. At high tide there was not sufficient water for the barque to float off and three tugs were engaged to tow her off, but they failed. Winson advised the captain to lighten the ship. As the captain went in one of the tugs to Grimsby to receive instructions and bring back gangs of men to throw out the cargo, Winson and the lifeboat crew returned to Spurn for refreshment after eleven hours in the boat. After low water the lifeboat returned, as requested, to the Athenian to see men throwing ice overboard. As conditions moderated the lifeboat was no longer required and returned to Spurn. After one hundred and fifty tons of ice had been thrown out the tugs succeeded in pulling off the vessel on the next high tide and taking her into Grimsby.

During 1885 the lifeboat was launched on service ten times. On seven of these occasions the boat reached the vessel in distress, several times after a hard battle with the sea and weather, only to be told that assistance was not required. One such launch was to the cod smack Alma, of Grimsby. On reaching the vessel the captain claimed he was signalling for a tug, but Winson commented in his report "that is always the case when out of danger."

On January 19th 1885 at about 11.0am the smack Gladstone, of Grimsby, was seen to be sinking in mid-channel. The lifeboat crew launched the Tender and went to the Gladstone, which was by then full of water, to find it had been taken in tow by the tug United. The tug took the Gladstone onto the Inner Binks and left her and returned to Grimsby for assistance. The lifeboat offer was refused and the Tender returned to Spurn. At about 1.0pm the Tender was launched again and as the tide was rising and the crew of the Gladstone could not cope with the leak the offer of assistance was accepted. With the extra help the water level in the vessel was reduced and the Tender pulled her free before the tug returned. The lifeboat men continued to assist and by keeping two pumps and eight buckets working all the time the Gladstone was towed to Grimsby, where she filled with water as soon as the pumping stopped.

The man on watch reported a vessel aground on the Inner Binks and showing signals of distress at 12.45am on the morning of Friday 16th October. The lifeboat was launched immediately into a strong breeze and big seas. The vessel proved to be the Norwegian brig Nordstjernen from Christiania bound for Newcastle with timber. When the lifeboat reached her she had lost her masts overboard and had eight feet of water in her hold. The lifeboat men succeeded in taking off the captain and his crew of seven hands and then laid by the vessel until 6.30am, when they returned to Spurn and landed the survivors at 7.30am. The lifeboat put off again to the Nordstjernen, expecting her to come off the banks, but she was full of water and starting to break up. The lifeboat again returned to Spurn. On October 17th the lifeboat men went back to the vessel and threw out deck cargo to lighten her, but tugs failed to pull her off. Another attempt was made at 2.0am on the 19th October by the tug Anglia, with the lifeboat men assisting, but things went wrong in the heavy seas -

"After we had boarded the brig for the purpose of making Tugs Rope fast when the heaving line was thrown on board the Tug should have gone ahead to have kept clear of the brig and the broken water, but owing to some defect in the machinery the Tug went full speed astern instead of ahead. The consequence was she collided with the brigs quarter and went stern first into the Binks when they let go their Anchor and hailed our Boat to fetch them off. The Tug shipped two heavy seas then the machinery came right itself and went full speed ahead, when she came off dragging her Anchor with her. Eventually we got the Tow Rope on board but failed to pull the vessel."

Another three attempts failed and it was not until the afternoon of Wednesday 21st October that the two tugs Victor and Champion succeeded in pulling off the disintegrating wreck and managed to take her into the Humber and up to Hull.

The smack Pansy, of Grimsby, got into difficulties near the Lincolnshire coast early on January 14th 1886. There was a strong northerly wind, squalls of sleet and a heavy sea at the time and her signals of distress were seen at Spurn. The lifeboat was launched immediately and the entire crew of five men were rescued and landed safely at Spurn.

The German barque Marie, of Rostock, went aground on the Inner Binks at 9.0pm on January 22nd when there was a strong north east wind with squalls of sleet and rain and heavy seas. Although no signals were seen the lifeboat was launched as Winson knew the sea conditions would worsen with the tide. On reaching the vessel Winson took off the entire crew of eleven men -

"...with the intention or rowing clear of the Binks and dropping Anchor again when clear of them, but in doing so we had a very heavy sea to encounter and all broken water to row through. We got a very severe washing, the Life Boat was filled with water repeatedly, the heavy sea breaking three oars and washed one away, but I am pleased to say the Life Boat behaved admirably, emptying herself instantly."

At about 6.0am the following morning, in spite of the battering by the sea, the Marie began to float off, and was found to have twelve feet of water in her holds. The tugs Liverpool and May, with the lifeboat in attendance, succeeded in towing the vessel to Grimsby.

The watchman reported a vessel showing signals of distress on the Inner Binks at about 9.30pm on Saturday 6th March 1866. There was a strong north west breeze and a very heavy sea at the time. The vessel was the smack Humber with a crew of five hands. The lifeboat was launched and found the smack, but there was no one on board - the crew had left in their own boat. The lifeboat men rowed about for an hour, hoping to find the crew, and eventually heard them shouting and found them on a dry sand bank. They were in an exhausted state, having tried to wade ashore through the very cold, rough water, as there was a sharp frost throughout the night. They had had some very narrow escapes in their attempts to reach the shore, but finally the lifeboat men were able to help them and they reached Spurn at about midnight. After giving the men refreshments and attending to their needs the lifeboat men returned to the smack, but she was broken up by the sea at about 7.0am on March 7th.

During the remainder of the year the lifeboat was launched on several occasions, but was able to assist only once. At all other times the crewmen were told that assistance was not required.

The lifeboat was launched at 1.30am on the morning of Friday 13th May 1887 to go to the assistance of a three-masted Norwegian schooner, the Hanna, from

Arendal for Hull with a cargo of pit props. The schooner was seen to go aground on the Inner Binks at about midnight when there was a strong breeze from north north east and heavy squalls of rain, but no signals were shown. As conditions worsened Winson decided to launch the lifeboat in case it was needed. On reaching the Hanna Winson found the captain, plus eight crewmen and a Humber Pilot, ten men in all. He managed to put them into the lifeboat and then backed away from the broken water near the schooner and lay by until 7.30am, when the Hanna began to break up.

A week later Winson wrote to Trinity House in Hull pointing out errors in a press report of the incident. This claimed that signals had been shown for assistance immediately the Hanna grounded, but Winson insisted he had watched the vessel for over an hour before launching the lifeboat and there had not been a single light. The ten men having got into the lifeboat, the captain of the Hanna remembered he had left his gold watch in his cabin. Winson transferred the other nine men to the tug Conqueror, which was nearby expecting to be called into service, and then took Captain Wiig back to the wreck to find the watch. This he did and was then landed at Spurn.

In July Trinity House gave each member of the lifeboat crew five shillings as a special gift to mark the Royal Jubilee.

Robert Tennyson died on July 6th after being ill for six months and having served for twenty one years in the lifeboat. His widow's only possessions were the pieces of house furniture and Trinity House allowed her a pension of three shillings and sixpence a week.

The Hull smack Good and Blanchard, made of iron, eighty seven tons register and nearly new, ran aground on the beach about a quarter of a mile north east of Spurn light at about 4.0pm on Thursday 12th January 1888. There was a light breeze from the south west and a dense fog. The lifeboat crew launched the Tender and on reaching the smack found that the crew had abandoned her and left in their own boat. They had taken with them all their clothes and the cabin fittings, including the "clock, weatherglass and log." The lifeboat men could not see or hear anything of the crew of the smack and waited for some time for them to return. The crew did not land on the beach or return to the smack so Winson telegraphed for a tug and threw out about fifteen tons of ballast to lighten the ship. At about 4.30am on Friday 13th January the tug Humber pulled the vessel off the beach and she was taken safely to Grimsby. The smack "had a cargo of fish on board."

There was a moderate westerly gale on Thursday 26th January and at about 4.0am the Bull Lightship broke from her station and was driven out to the edge of the Inner Binks, when she fired a rocket for assistance. The lifeboat was launched and reached the lightship despite the difficult conditions. Unfortunately the lifeboat was swept away from the lightship before a line could be made fast and the men found it impossible to return to her without assistance. The tug Champion towed the lifeboat back at dawn and it made fast to the lightship. The crew gave all the assistance they could to make the lightship safe and then returned to Spurn with a telegram to be sent to Trinity House. When the reply came the men returned to the lightship in the Tender, not the lifeboat, and made fast to her stern. They helped to get on board a warp from a tug and then to get the lightship's anchor. The tug then began towing the vessel and Tender to the Humber, with the lifeboat men on board the lightship -

"All went well until the Lightship was towed before the heavy swell against the flood tide when all at once the Tender in running in on a sea took a broad sheer off and was capsized. We tried to pull the boat close up but could not owing to the heavy chain. The painter which was nearly new soon broke and the Boat drifted up the Humber. The tug tried to get the Tender afterwards but eventually pulled her stern out."

The wreck of the Tender was swept away.

A new Tender was ordered from Mr. Lewis Emery of Sheringham. She was to be twenty one feet long, seven feet six inches beam amidships and three feet three inches deep amidships. The keel, stem and stern posts were to be oak, the planking to be good larch and all other timber either oak or American elm, and she was to have a mast. The boat was painted with "two good coats of paint in oil" and "the whole of the work to be done in a workmanship like manner." The cost was twenty one pounds and the boat was to be completed in three months. The cost was increased by six shillings because of alterations which were asked for to the thwarts. The order was made in February and the new Tender was delivered to Spurn on Wednesday 23rd May 1888.

In the meantime the wreck of the Tender was washed ashore on the beach near Dunwich, south of Great Yarmouth, in mid-March. The Receiver of Wrecks described it as "much damaged" and valued it at five shillings. Trinity House decided nothing could be done with the boat except to abandon it.

At about 10.30pm on February 14th, when there was a strong north east breeze, with squalls of snow and rain, a vessel was seen aground on the Inner Binks, showing signals of distress. The vessel proved to be the schooner Winifred, bound from London to Aberdeen with a cargo of superphosphate. The lifeboat was launched and succeeded in taking off Captain Williams and his crew of four hands, five men in all. The lifeboat lay by the vessel until about 3.30am, when some of the

NOTICE

TO

MASTERS OF SMACKS.

IN consequence of the Dangers to Life and Property, and serious losses that have happened from time to time amongst Fishing Vessels owing to the foolish practice of exhibiting Lights contrary to Board of Trade regulations, the NAVIGATION COMMITTEE OF AMALGAMATED INSURANCES OF GRIMSBY hereby call upon all Masters of Vessels connected with them to do all that lies in their power to put a stop to such practices, and to give information of any cases coming under their notice.

The attention of Masters holding certificates is specially called to the fact that under the Merchant Shipping Act severe penalties may be inflicted on Persons offending, as set forth in the following letter received from the Hull Trinity Board:---

TRINITY HOUSE, HULL,
28th July, 1888.

SIR,—I am directed by the Board of this Corporation to inform you that the Master of the Life Boat at Spurn has reported that the Life Boat Men are frequently called out at night by the exhibition of red lights, flares, and rockets, which appear to be signals of distress, but which are found on arriving out to have been exhibited merely for sport by the crews of Fishing Smacks. This thoughtless and reckless conduct on the part of the crews of Fishing Smacks has caused much unnecessary labour and trouble to the crew of the Spurn Life Boat, and might result in serious consequences.

I am desired to request you to be good enough to bring the matter before the Directors or Committee of your Society with a view to the Masters and Crews of the Fishing Smacks insured in your Society being warned to desist from the reprehensible and illegal practice in question.

I am to direct your attention to the provisions of sect. 27 of the Merchant Shipping Act Amendment Act 1862 (25 and 26 Vic., cap. 63), and of sect. 18 of the Merchant Shipping Act 1873 (36 and 37 Vic., cap. 85). I remain, Sir, your most obedient Servant,

EDW. J. WILSON.

Published by order of the Amalgamated Insurances Navigation Committee,

WM. ASHFORD,
CHAIRMAN.

AUGUST 15*th*, 1888.

GEO. N. NUTT, "OBSERVER" PRINTING WORKS, 77, CLEETHORPE-ROAD, GRIMSBY.

rescued men, being wet and cold, wanted to be landed at Spurn. At the same time it was thought that the schooner could not be saved and would break up. The men were landed at Spurn at about 4.0am and the lifeboat returned to the Binks only to find no sign of the vessel. Winson was later informed that the schooner had floated off and been found by the tug May and taken to Grimsby.

During July 1888 Mr. Edward Wilson, Secretary to the Board of Trinity House in Hull, wrote to all ship owners and Ship Owners' Associations in Hull and Grimsby, asking them to instruct their captains to stop the crew members from firing red flares or signals at night just for the sport of seeing the Spurn lifeboat launched on a fruitless journey. This foolish behaviour had continued for some time before these letters from Mr. Wilson and the activities were at least checked by the official poster warning of severe penalties if the practice continued.

The lifeboat was launched several times during the year to give assistance to vessels in distress and on some occasions assistance was refused. On October 5th the lifeboat launched to a fishing smack and assistance was not required, but the captain thanked Winson and his crew for putting off. This Winson described as "an incident very unusual for fishermen."

The first service by the lifeboat in 1889 was to the keel Arthur, of Hull, on February 9th. The vessel was loaded with barley and got into difficulties near the Inner Binks and signalled for assistance. The lifeboat was launched and took off the crew of three men and landed them at Spurn. Some time later the tug Humber towed away the keel and deliberately ran it aground inside the Humber on the Trinity Sands. On the following day the lifeboat crew helped to get out part of the cargo and assisted the vessel to Grimsby.

The remainder of the year was very quiet, with the lifeboat being launched on only three other occasions. Two men were saved by heaving line from a small vessel which ran aground at the southern end of Spurn in August.

Six men were saved from the cod smack Smelt, of Grimsby, on the evening of Saturday 16th February 1890. The vessel showed distress signals from the Middle Binks at about 6.30pm and the lifeboat was launched to assist. Winson saw the Smelt leave the Middle Binks and sail northwards in heavy seas with a strong east north east wind. The vessel eventually stranded on the beach about half a mile north of Spurn lighthouse. As the wind and tide were against the lifeboat it was some time before the vessel was reached. By then the tide had made up and there was a very heavy sea running and it was with great difficulty that the men were rescued, and then only by using the heaving line, as it was impossible to hold the lifeboat alongside the smack. The lifeboat returned to Spurn at about 9 .40pm and the Smelt became a total wreck.

Another four men were rescued from the Grimsby whelk smack Mermaid on 18th April. The smack fired distress signals from the Inner Binks at about 9.0pm and the lifeboat was launched. The four men were saved and landed at Spurn at about 1.30am the following morning and the smack disappeared. The Mermaid was later picked up by the steam trawler Staghound in the Humber near Killingholme and was put ashore at Withernsea, having sustained only slight damage.

In August all the crewmen at Spurn signed a letter sent to Trinity House in Hull asking for a rise in wages. The men pointed out that provisions at Spurn cost fifteen per cent more than elsewhere, that fishing was not so good, there was little salvage and they could "not make ends meet in winter." They asked for the sum of four pounds per month, but the Board of Trinity House refused the request.

The watchman saw a vessel in difficulties on the Inner Binks at 4.30am on the morning of Friday 7th November, but no signals were shown. Winson mustered the crew and launched the lifeboat and found the vessel to be the ketch Vacuna, from London to Scotland with a cargo of whitening. The ketch had grounded and quickly filled with water as heavy seas broke right over her. The lifeboat men succeeded in saving Captain Hopkinson and his two crewmen and landed them at Spurn. The vessel was expected to become a total wreck.

Twice, in November and December, the lifeboat was launched after the watchman reported seeing flares or signals of distress. On each occasion many hours were spent searching in difficult conditions, but no trace of a vessel was found.

The year 1891 began optimistically with the opening of the new school but in mid February five of the lifeboat crew resigned at the same time. This was because storms around the Norfolk coast had damaged the fishing grounds and crab fishermen from Sheringham moved north and cleaned out the fishing grounds near Spurn. The crewmen left to become fishermen elsewhere or to find work with better prospects. After four of the men had been paid off and were being transported to Withernsea by fishing boat they came across the Grimsby smack Henry Freeman, ashore on the beach, and were able to give assistance and get her off before the lifeboat arrived. By mid March the crew was again complete.

Winson wrote to the Board of Trinity House on July 25th asking to be considered for a position as lighthouse keeper when such a vacancy occurred. He said he was suffering from rheumatism which sometimes made it impossible for him to raise his right arm, and the condition was made worse by being soaked in the lifeboat. It was to be another three years before he finally left the service.

Distress signals were seen coming from the Inner Binks at about 6.0pm on Tuesday 13th October. There was a very heavy southerly gale with rain at the time.

The lifeboat was launched and found the Grimsby trawling smack Petrel full of water, with the sails blown away and suffering other damage. The entire crew of six men was saved and landed safely at Spurn at about 10.30pm. The Petrel became a total wreck.

Another four men were saved on November 11th from the schooner Caroline, bound for Wells with a cargo of coal. The vessel was riding at anchor in the Humber during a strong westerly gale when she parted from her anchor. She was driven down river, grounded on Trinity Sand, beat over the sands and went ashore on the beach north east of the lifeboat mooring. The lifeboat men found it very difficult to launch the Tender because of the conditions, but finally reached the schooner and rescued the crew. Late that night the tug Humber arrived and after midnight succeeded in towing the Caroline off the beach and taking her to Grimsby.

A further seven men were saved from the Grimsby cod smack John Fildes on 30th November. The vessel went aground on the Inner Binks in a strong southerly breeze and began to take in water. The crew fired distress signals and the Spurn lifeboat was launched. The John Fildes was half full of water when the lifeboat arrived and the crew was successfully taken off and landed at Spurn. The smack became a complete wreck.

During the last two weeks of January 1892 the lifeboat was launched on four occasions to go to the assistance of vessels in difficulty. The lifeboat was successful on each occasion in helping the vessels, but no lives were saved.

When one of the lifeboat crewmen left in February to train as a naval reserve man Winson signed his son Thomas Charles Winson, aged twenty four, as a crew member. This was to have repercussions when Winson retired.

On the evening of January 14th 1893 the lifeboat was launched to a vessel seen to be aground on the outer edge of the Inner Binks. On reaching the vessel she proved to be the Grimsby trawl smack Specimen, abandoned by her crew, with the helm lashed hard a starboard. There was a strong wind and considerable sea which made conditions very difficult, but as the Specimen floated off some lifeboat men succeeded in boarding her and putting the helm to port just in time to prevent her from going back onto the Inner Binks. They managed to sail the smack into Grimsby.

The lifeboat gave assistance to vessels on two other occasions in the first half of the year, but a surprise came on June 23rd in the form of a letter from Winson to Trinity House informing the Board he was about to dismiss the Mate of the lifeboat. The letter is quoted in full -

"Gentlemen,

I beg respectfully to inform you that it is my intention to discharge the Mate of the Life Boat as he is very little use to me as a Mate, in fact I ought to have got rid of him years since. I have kept the Mate on through Charity more than anything else. He, the Mate, John Liversedge, is very quiet but no Energy, no Push, in fact I have never had a Mate at all and I am sorry to say the Man is Ruptured very bad and has been nearly all his life. A short time back I shipped two of the Mate's, Mr. Liversedge, sons in the Life Boat as they had nothing to do. One was a Docker. Now I find that I did wrong as I have too many of them, in fact I do not get common civility from them. I find it is generally the way as soon as they earn a few pounds they are too Independent. As regards my Mate being of no use to me as a Mate, I have named it to Captain Boxhall once or twice more than twelve months since and as the Mate is no acquisition to me I think it is only right that I get rid of him and ship a Mate that is some use to me."

John Liversedge wrote to Trinity House asking for an explanation of his dismissal, pointing out that he was only fifty four years of age and therefore not too old, that he had served at Spurn for twenty six years and had no dispute with Winson.

There is no record of any reply from Trinity House and Liversedge left the lifeboat service on July 10th 1893 and James Bishop joined the crew as Mate.

It is interesting to note that in September 1892 Mrs. Curtis, the wife of one of the crew members, wrote to Trinity House complaining of trouble caused by the Liversedge family and saying that there were too many of them at Spurn. Winson dismissed her as a mischief-maker.

On Tuesday 13th June the Archbishop of York visited Spurn and conducted a service there. On Friday 30th June there was a visit by Prince Louis of Battenberg and his party.

A telephone line was connected to Winson's house from the coastguard stations at Kilnsea and Easington on Tuesday 24th October, obviously giving rapid communications between the rescue services. The building of a new lighthouse began.

A vessel went aground on the Inner Binks at about 7.0pm on the evening of Wednesday 20th December and fired signals of distress. These were answered and the lifeboat was launched to assist. On arriving out they found the vessel to be the schooner Mary Louisa, of Brixham, bound from Ghent to South Shields with a cargo of potatoes. There was a strong breeze from the north and the vessel already had three feet of water in the holds. The lifeboat men succeeded in taking off the entire crew of six men and landing them safely at Spurn at about 10.0pm. The Mary Louisa became a complete wreck. The six men were sent on to their destination on the following day by the Ship Wreck Society.

At the end of February 1894 Thomas Winson resigned from his position as master of the Life Boat at Spurn. He had served just over sixteen years as Master, had successfully carried out many rescues and was generally respected. However, immediately prior to his retirement he recommended to Trinity House that his son, Thomas Charles Winson, a crew member, should be appointed to succeed him as Master and the Board made this appointment. Immediately all the other members of the crew signed a letter which was sent to Trinity House and part of which is quoted below -

"Gentlemen,

We the undersigned Crew of the Life Boat at Spurn beg most Respectfully to Petition against the recent appointment of Mr. Thomas Winson Junior to the position of Coxswain of the Life Boat stationed here. We consider if called upon at any time to a Wreck that we are simply placing our Lives in danger and also the lives of the ship-wrecked crew, should we be so fortunate as to save them. We consider that he is not qualified for the position, having had no experience in sea faring life or boating and no man of the crew has any confidence in him whatsoever in such a position of trust. We beg most respectfully to call your attention to the fact that he has only been a member of the crew for two years and in our humble opinion that time does not qualify a man having as we have previously pointed out no experience whatsoever for such a position of trust. We humbly venture to call your attention to the fact that there are members of the crew who have been years at Spurn and have had a life's experience in boating and are fully and thoroughly acquainted with the coast and sets of tides round Spurn and in whom we have every confidence, and would readily and willingly risk our lives to save others under a qualified and experienced man. We beg most respectfully to inform the Elder Brethren that if the position is to be held by Mr. Winson Junior every member of the Crew will resign as we will not go round the Point under his charge. We humbly Pray that the Board will be pleased to take our memorial into serious consideration and your humble servants ever Pray

William Chapman
George William Liversedge
John Henry Branton
Chas. Peacock Raspin
James Robert Liversedge
Charles Crask
Fred Hopper."

The only ones not to sign were the Mate, Bishop, and the two Winsons.

This letter was followed by a similar one two days later and on March 7th 1894 Thomas Charles Winson resigned from his position "as Appointed Master of the Spurn Life Boat, with the advice of my Father the late Master, owing to the envious disposition of the Mate and crew." He went on to say he would be very pleased to accept the position as Mate, his father recommended this, and he was so appointed.

Trinity House advertised in the press on March 8th 1894 for a new Master of the Life Boat to succeed Thomas Winson, who continued as Master until a new appointment was made. All the crew members were officially discharged, but as they were given fourteen days notice to leave, the lifeboat could still be manned. Winson wrote to Trinity House asking to be allowed to be present at the appointment of the new Master and his letter contained some bitter comments about the crew and their action in refusing to accept his son as Master. Trinity House made it quite clear that Winson's presence was not required.

There were ten applicants for the position of Master of the Life Boat at Spurn and David Pye, a fisherman of Easington, who had served for nine months in the Withernsea lifeboat, was appointed. He took up his duties on March 19th 1894.

TREATMENT OF THE APPARENTLY DROWNED.

ROYAL NATIONAL LIFE-BOAT INSTITUTION.

INCORPORATED BY ROYAL CHARTER.—SUPPORTED SOLELY BY VOLUNTARY CONTRIBUTIONS.

Patron—Her Most Gracious Majesty the Queen.

Vice-Patrons { Her Royal Highness The Princess of Wales.
His Royal Highness The Prince of Wales, K.G.
Admiral His Royal Highness The Duke of Edinburgh, K.G.
Commander His Royal Highness The Duke of York, K.G., R.N.

DIRECTIONS FOR RESTORING THE APPARENTLY DROWNED.

The leading principles of the following Directions for the Restoration of the apparently Dead from Drowning are founded on those of the late Dr. MARSHALL HALL, combined with those of Dr. H. R. SILVESTER, and are the result of extensive inquiries which were made by the Institution in 1863-4 amongst Medical Men, Medical Bodies, and Coroners throughout the United Kingdom. These Directions have been extensively circulated by the INSTITUTION throughout the United Kingdom and in the Colonies. They are also in use in Her Majesty's Fleet, in the Coast-guard Service, and at all the Stations of the British Army at home and abroad; in the Light Houses and Vessels of the Corporation of the Trinity House; the Metropolitan and Provincial Police Forces; the Metropolitan School Board Schools; and the St. John Ambulance Association.

I.

Send immediately for medical assistance, blankets, and dry clothing, but proceed to treat the Patient *instantly* on the spot, in the open air, with the face downwards, whether on shore or afloat; exposing the face, neck, and chest to the wind, except in severe weather, and removing all tight clothing from the neck and chest, especially the braces.

The points to be aimed at are—first and *immediately*, the Restoration of Breathing; and secondly, after breathing is restored, the Promotion of Warmth and Circulation.

The efforts to *restore Breathing* must be commenced immediately and energetically, and persevered in for one or two hours, or until a medical man has pronounced that life is extinct. Efforts to promote *Warmth* and *Circulation* beyond removing the wet clothes and drying the skin must not be made until the first appearance of natural breathing. For if circulation of the blood be induced before breathing has recommenced, the restoration to life will be endangered.

II.—TO RESTORE BREATHING.

To Clear the Throat—Place the Patient on the floor or ground with the face downwards, and one of the arms under the forehead, in which position all fluids will more readily escape by the mouth, and the tongue itself will fall forward, leaving the entrance into the windpipe free. Assist this operation by wiping and cleansing the mouth.

If satisfactory breathing commences, use the treatment described below to promote Warmth. If there be only slight breathing—or no breathing—or if the breathing fail, then—

To Excite Breathing—Turn the Patient well and instantly on the side, supporting the head, and—

Excite the nostrils with snuff, hartshorn, and smelling salts, or tickle the throat with a feather, &c., if they are at hand. Rub the chest and face warm, and dash cold water, or cold and hot water alternately, on them.

If there be no success, lose not a moment but instantly

To Imitate Breathing—Replace the Patient on the face, raising and supporting the chest well on a folded coat or other article of dress.

Turn the body very gently on the side and, a little beyond, and then briskly on the face, back again; repeating these measures cautiously, efficiently, and perseveringly about fifteen times in the minute, or once every four or five seconds, occasionally varying the side.

[*By placing the Patient on the chest, the weight of the body forces the air out; when turned on the side, this pressure is removed, and air enters the chest.*]

On each occasion that the body is replaced on the face, make uniform but efficient pressure with brisk movement, on the back between and below the shoulder-blades or bones on each side, removing the pressure immediately before turning the body on the side. During the whole of the operations let one person attend solely to the movements of the head, and of the arm placed under it.

[*The first measure increases the Expiration, the second commences Inspiration.*]

⁂ The result is *Respiration* or *Natural Breathing*;—and if not too late, *Life*.

Whilst the above operations are being proceeded with, dry the hands and feet, and as soon as dry clothing or blankets can be procured, strip the body and cover, or gradually reclothe it, but taking care not to interfere with the efforts to restore breathing.

1.—INSPIRATION.

2.—EXPIRATION.

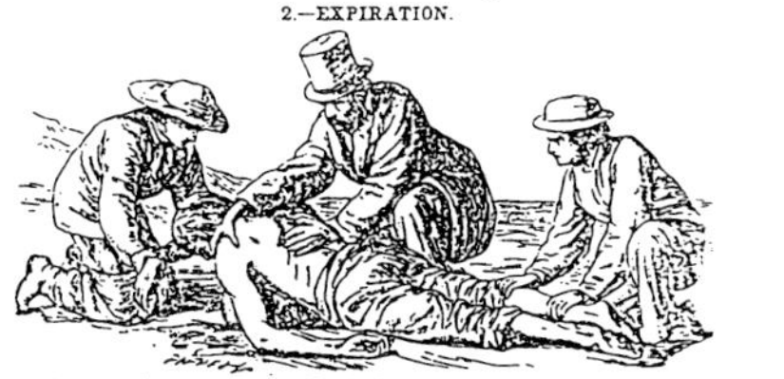

To illustrate the position of the Body during the employment of Dr. Marshall Hall's Method of Inducing Respiration.

III.

Should these efforts not prove successful in the course of from two to five minutes, proceed to imitate breathing by Dr. Silvester's method, as follows:—

Place the Patient on the back on a flat surface, inclined a little upwards from the feet; raise and support the head and shoulders on a small firm cushion or folded article of dress placed under the shoulder-blades.

Draw forward the Patient's tongue, and keep it projecting beyond the lips;—an elastic band over the tongue and under the chin will answer this purpose, or a piece of string or tape may be tied round them, or by raising the lower jaw, the teeth may be made to retain the tongue in that position. Remove all tight clothing from about the neck and chest, especially the braces.

To Imitate the Movements of Breathing—Standing at the Patient's head, grasp the arms just above the elbows, and draw the arms gently and steadily upwards above the head, and *keep them stretched* upwards for two seconds. [*By this means air is drawn into the lungs.*] Then turn down the Patient's arms, and press them gently and firmly for two seconds against the sides of the chest. [*By this means air is pressed out of the lungs.*]

Repeat these measures alternately, deliberately, and perseveringly, about fifteen times in a minute, until a spontaneous effort to respire is perceived, immediately upon which cease to imitate the movements of breathing, and proceed to Induce Circulation and Warmth.

1.—INSPIRATION.

2.—EXPIRATION.

To illustrate the position of the Body during the employment of Dr. Silvester's Method of Inducing Respiration.

IV.—TREATMENT AFTER NATURAL BREATHING HAS BEEN RESTORED.

To promote Warmth and Circulation.—

Commence rubbing the limbs upwards, with firm grasping pressure and energy, using handkerchiefs, flannels, &c. [*By this measure the blood is propelled along the veins towards the heart.*]

The friction must be continued under the blanket or over the dry clothing.

Promote the warmth of the body by the application of hot flannels, bottles, or bladders of hot water, heated bricks, &c., to the pit of the stomach, the arm-pits, between the thighs, and to the soles of the feet.

If the Patient has been carried to a house after respiration has been restored, be careful to let the air play freely about the room.

On the restoration of life, a teaspoonful of warm water should be given; and then, if the power of swallowing have returned, small quantities of wine, warm brandy and water, or coffee, should be administered. The Patient should be kept in bed, and a disposition to sleep encouraged.

GENERAL OBSERVATIONS.—The above treatment should be persevered in for some hours, as it is an erroneous opinion that persons are irrecoverable because life does not soon make its appearance, persons having been restored after persevering for many hours.

APPEARANCES WHICH GENERALLY ACCOMPANY DEATH.

Breathing and the heart's action cease entirely; the eyelids are generally half-closed; the pupils dilated; the tongue approaches to the under edges of the lips, and these, as well as the nostrils, are covered with a frothy mucus. Coldness and pallor of surface increase.

CAUTIONS.

Prevent unnecessary crowding of persons round the body, especially if in an apartment.

Avoid rough usage, and do not allow the body to remain on the back unless the tongue is secured.

Under no circumstances hold the body up by the feet.

On no account place the body in a warm bath, unless under medical direction, and even then it should only be employed as a momentary excitant.

⁂ *These large Placards can be supplied by William Clowes and Sons, Limited, Printers, Charing Cross, London, at a cost little beyond the actual price of the paper on which they are printed, namely, Twelve Shillings per 100 Copies.*

Annual Subscriptions and Donations in aid of the great and national objects of the Life-boat Institution are earnestly solicited, and will be thankfully received by the Bankers of the Institution, *Messrs. Coutts & Co., 59 Strand*; Messrs. Herries, Farquhar, & Co., 16 St. James's Street; Messrs. Hoare, 37 Fleet Street, London; by all the other London and Country Bankers; and by the Secretary, at the Office of the Institution, 14 John Street, Adelphi, London.

Royal National Life-Boat Institution,
London, *July*, 1892.

By order of the Committee,
CHARLES DIBDIN, *Secretary*.

LONDON: PRINTED BY WILLIAM CLOWES AND SONS, LIMITED, STAMFORD STREET AND CHARING CROSS.

DAVID PYE 19th MARCH 1894 - JULY 1912

David Pye applied for the position of Master of the Life Boat at Spurn on 9th March 1894. He said he had spent the last twelve years fishing in the vicinity of Spurn and loading gravel vessels on the Binks and that he knew the tides and currents and various banks. He had served in the Rocket Brigade for a long time and for nine months in the Withernsea lifeboat and considered himself competent to assume the position as Master at Spurn. His application was supported by glowing references from the Station Officer of Kilnsea Coast Guard, tug owners and ship owners, company owners, a surgeon, a Justice of the Peace, a curate and by Thomas Winson. He was appointed on 14th March and took up his duties on 19th March 1894 at Spurn.

The first thing Pye did at Spurn was to appoint a crew. Four of the previous crew members were re-appointed along with several new men. He then sent to Trinity House a list of supplies and materials needed for the lifeboat and a list of repairs needed for the houses.

The lifeboat was launched twice on March 30th, the first time at about 2.0pm to a steamer aground on the Inner Binks. The vessel was the Chester, bound for Grimsby from Antwerp with passengers and general cargo, but assistance was not required. At 5.30pm the boat was again launched, to the Hull fishing smack Invicta, aground on the Inner Binks. The Invicta was got off successfully at about 7.30pm and the lifeboat returned to Spurn.

At the end of April Pye asked Trinity House for a quite extensive supply of medicines and materials for the medical chest. This had previously been very basic and simple, but Pye obviously had new ideas compared with his predecessors.

The first lives were saved by Pye on 16th August 1894. At about 10.0am two herring luggers stranded on the Inner Binks and the lifeboat was launched. The first one, the Result, of Lowestoft, had a crew of nine hands all told. Some of the crew were taken into the lifeboat which stood by until the vessel refloated and the men returned to the lugger. The second one, the Valkyrie, also of Lowestoft, was damaged when the two vessels clashed together as the flood tide returned. All nine crew men were taken into the lifeboat and the Valkyrie became a total wreck.

The Board of Trinity House was asked by the Mayor of Grimsby to allow the Spurn lifeboat to take part in a Life Boat Display and Demonstration off Cleethorpes on 15th September. As well as the displays and demonstrations there were to be lifeboat races. The Board eventually agreed to give permission, provided the weather was fine, and the lifeboat went to the display. The Board received a letter of thanks and a cheque for three pounds, seven shillings and sixpence to be distributed amongst the crew.

Pye applied to Trinity House in June 1895 for new life belts as the old ones were "getting very bad." Trinity House contacted Henry Morrill and Sons, Ships Chandlers, and they sent one to Pye for his approval. Morrill's letter continues -

"he wanted one, same as is used by all the Life Boats generally. We have now got the price of the sort supplied to the Life Boat Institution and find that they run up to about twenty one shillings each, which to say the least, we think very high. We should like you to see the one we have got, or are we to order the above ?"

On 31st August ten new life belts were delivered to Spurn of the type supplied to the Life Boat Institution.

A new set of rules governing the lifeboat station was sent by Trinity House in October 1895 -

Trinity House, Kingston upon Hull, 1895

For the purpose of ensuring good order and proper conduct on the part of the Master and Crew of the Life Boat at Spurn during their continuance in the service of the Corporation of the Trinity House do hereby direct the observance of the following Regulations.

1. The Master of the Life Boat hereinafter called "the Master" is required to be sober and watchful and at all times ready and diligent in the performance of his duty; he must keep with regularity a daily Journal of the Wind and Weather, and the situation of the Pilot Cutters, distinguishing them by their numbers; as also any other occurrences connected with his office; and make his Report thereof to this House not less frequently than once a month. He must make a special and immediate report on all urgent cases and by telegraph when requisite.

2. The Master is invested with the full command of the Boat's Crew.

3. The Master is to see that a regular Watch is kept by night as well as by day.

4. The Master and Crew of the Boat are on all occasions to use their utmost endeavours in the first place to save the Lives of the Crews of such Ships and Vessels as may unfortunately be driven on the Outer or Inner Binks or on shore or be in distress elsewhere at Spurn or in the vicinity thereof; their next care must be the preservation of Ships and their Cargoes, but in no cases whatever is the Life Boat to be made use of for the purpose of carrying out Anchors or Cables, unless the greatest necessity exists for so doing.

5. The Crew of the Life Boat which consists of Ten Men (inclusive of the Master) shall participate in all the benefits, rewards and emoluments arising from the services of the Boat.

6. Whenever the Boat is made use of the Master is to see that she is afterwards properly moored and taken care of.

7. The Master and Mate of the Life Boat shall never be both absent from Spurn at the same time. No member of the Crew of the Boat shall leave Spurn without the consent of the Master.

8. The Master is strictly to enforce these Rules and to cause a copy thereof to be placed in each Cottage, as well as in some conspicuous part of his own home.

By Order

Edward S. Wilson
Secretary.

Very early on the morning of 16th January 1896 the Grimsby smack Achievement parted from her anchor in the Humber and drove ashore at the Point. At 3.0am signals of distress were reported by the watchman and the Tender was launched. The entire crew of the smack was saved and landed safely at Spurn. Pye fully expected the Achievement to become a total wreck, but the lifeboat, with the assistance of the tug Champion, succeeded in getting off the Achievement at about 6.0am on the morning of 31st January.

There was no other effective service until the morning of 17th November 1896. At 6.0am the watchman reported a vessel aground on the Inner Binks, showing signals of distress. The lifeboat was launched immediately but just before reaching the vessel the lifeboat met up with the crew of six leaving the casualty in their own boat. The boat was taken in tow and landed at Spurn and the lifeboat returned to the vessel, the Grimsby oyster dredger, Alfred and Henry, bound to Grimsby from sea. Being unable to do anything the lifeboat went back to Spurn. At 11.30am the Tender was launched to see if the vessel would float off and the tug Humber came alongside and put a man on board the Alfred and Henry to make fast a tow. The vessel was full of water and there was a heavy sea running and the Master of the tug dare not go close enough to take off his crewman. The Spurn men had to take back the Tender and bring out the lifeboat to "rescue" the man and put him back on board the tug. The oyster dredger became a total wreck.

Another set of new rules was drawn up in January 1897 and copies were sent to Spurn to be placed in each cottage.

RULES AND REGULATIONS

FOR THE GOVERNMENT OF THE

MASTER AND CREW OF THE LIFE BOAT

STATIONED AT SPURN.

Trinity House, Kingston-upon-Hull.

16TH JANUARY, 1897.

For the purpose of ensuring good order and proper conduct on the part of the Master and Crew of the Life Boat at Spurn during their continuance in the Service, the Corporation of the Trinity House do hereby direct the strict observance of the following Regulations :—

1. The Master of the Life Boat, hereinafter called " the Master," is required to be sober and watchful and at all times ready and diligent in the performance of his duty ; he must keep with regularity a daily Journal of the Wind and Weather, of the situation of the Pilot Cutters (distinguishing them by their numbers), and of any other circumstances and occurrences connected with his office ; and make his Report thereof to this House not less frequently than once a month. He must make a special and immediate report in all urgent cases and by telegraph when requisite.

2. The Master is invested with the full command of the Boat's Crew.

3. The Master is to see that a regular watch is kept by night as well as by day.

4. The Master or Mate shall meet the Trinity House Yacht whenever she visits Spurn in order that he may answer any enquiry that may be made or render any service that may be requisite. and the man on the watch shall on observing the approach of the Yacht immediately report to the Master or Mate in order that this rule may be carefully observed. If the Yacht shall be flying the Union Jack at her Mainmast Head the Crew shall be mustered and proceed at once to the Yacht in their Tender.

5. The Master and Crew of the Boat are on all occasions to use their utmost endeavours, in the first place, to save the Lives of the Crews of such Ships and Vessels as may unfortunately be driven on the Outer or Inner Binks, or on shore or be in distress elsewhere at Spurn or in the vicinity thereof ; their next care must be the preservation of Ships and their cargoes, but in no case whatever is the Life Boat to be made use of for the purpose of carrying out Anchors or cables, unless the greatest necessity exists for so doing.

6. The Crew of the Life Boat, which consists of Ten Men (inclusive of the Master), shall participate in all the benefits, rewards, and emoluments arising from the services of the Boat. The amount of remuneration received under any Salvage Agreement, or award of Salvage, or for any special work done by the Crew of the Boat or any of them, shall be apportioned between the Crew as follows:—The said amount shall be divided into eleven shares, whereof one shall be paid to each of the ten members of the Crew, and the remaining share shall be paid, as to two-thirds thereof to the Master, and as to one-third thereof to the Mate of the Boat.

7. Whenever the Boat is made use of, the Master is to see that she is afterwards properly moored and taken care of.

8. Once in every year at the least the Life Boat is to be drawn on shore and her bottom carefully examined as she lies on the beach, and any defect that may be found must be at once made good. And whenever she may have touched the ground, or be suspected of having done so, or whenever from any other reason it may be requisite, she must undergo the same examination.

9. Not less frequently than once a month the moorings of the Life Boat are to be lifted, carefully examined and seen to be in proper condition.

10. The Master and Mate of the Life Boat shall never be both absent from Spurn at the same time No member of the Crew of the Boat shall leave Spurn without the consent of the Master.

11. Every member of the Crew of the Boat who shall proceed to Grimsby to sell crabs or fish shall return by the next ebb tide.

12. The Master is strictly to enforce these Rules, and to cause a copy thereof to be placed in each cottage, as well as in some conspicuous part of his own house.

By order,

EDWARD S. WILSON,

Secretary.

The watchman saw distress signals from a vessel in the Humber at 7.30pm on 22nd January. There was a north easterly gale with "blinding snow squalls throughout." Pye and his crew put off in the Tender to go to the vessel but the gale and strong ebb tide drove them ashore near the Point. It was only on the third attempt that they succeeded in reaching the casualty, "which proved to be the steam barge Moonlight, of Hull, which was riding at Anchor off the Point in a helpless condition." The lifeboat succeeded in saving the crew of three and returned to Spurn at 3.0am on 23rd January. The three men were later sent home by the Shipwrecked Mariners Society. Later on the same day the lifeboat and the tug Pendragon took the Moonlight safely to Grimsby.

Three more men were saved from the barge Amy, of Harwich, bound from Newcastle to London with general cargo. The barge got into difficulties in very bad weather on the night of 2nd March and was towed into the Humber by the tug Pole Star and was beached. The lifeboat crew agreed to try to pump the vessel and assist her to Grimsby, but a gale blew up, the barge filled with water and the men had to be rescued. Some time later the barge was pumped out and taken to Grimsby with the assistance of the tug Pole Star.

On 29th April 1897 Thomas Holmes, Commander RN, the District Inspector of Lifeboats for RNLI, wrote to the Secretary to the Board of Trinity House in Hull, stating that the Institution was anxious to place a steam lifeboat at the mouth of the Humber at as early a date as possible. The only two possible sites were Grimsby and Spurn and Commander Holmes was seeking permission to discuss the matter with the Board of Trinity House and also to visit Spurn to look over the lifeboat station and consult the Master, David Pye. A month later plans of the steam lifeboat City of Glasgow were sent to Hull for the Board to study. It is probable that Commander Holmes visited Hull and Spurn at the end of July and on 18th October members of the Board of Trinity House were able to inspect the steam lifeboat Queen when the boat was at Grimsby. Having considered the report by Commander Holmes the Committee of Management of RNLI wrote to Trinity House in Hull agreeing with the members of the Board that Grimsby was not so well placed as Spurn for service, but had much better facilities for accommodation of crew members and for obtaining supplies of coal, oil and water. The committee also accepted the opinion of the Board that the present Spurn lifeboat was more adapted to local conditions than any steam lifeboat could be and as a result of these considerations decided to station a steam lifeboat at Grimsby as an experiment.

There appears to have been a problem in establishing lines of communication at night time between Spurn and Grimsby when the life boat Master, David Pye, required the assistance of a tug. It was eventually decided that the postmistress should telegraph to Hull, the message would go from there to the coastguard station at Cleethorpes and the coastguard would contact Captain Jewitt, Port Master at

Grimsby, who would send a message for a tug. For this service Captain Jewitt was prepared to accept an annual retainer of ten shillings, and a fee of five shillings was to be paid every time a message was delivered. The Chief Officer of Coastguard at Cleethorpes would also contact the Grimsby lifeboat station if that boat should be needed, and he too accepted an annual retainer of ten shillings, with a fee of five shillings for every message delivered.

Following a request from the Board of Trinity House, Hull, the RNLI, on 13th December 1897, sent a copy of the pension scheme operated by the Institution. Despite this information the Board never had a pension scheme for the Masters or crew members of the lifeboat at Spurn.

During the year 1898 the lifeboat was launched on several occasions and gave assistance to vessels which had grounded or were in difficulties, but no lives were saved. The lifeboat also sailed after the Bull Light Ship, which had broken from its moorings, and returned it to its station.

David Pye wrote to Trinity House on 4th October 1899 pointing out the necessity of having a rocket apparatus of some kind stationed at Spurn.

"On Saturday morning last when the Steam Trawler 'Atlantic' was stranded on the beach here, it took the Rocket Brigade nearly three hours to arrive (from Easington) at the seat of the action, which might very easily have proved fatal to the poor fellows on the wreck.

The distance was about six miles and if we had had the apparatus here (about one mile distant) we could have effected a rescue before half that time had elapsed.

I think gentlemen this question is worthy of your most serious consideration."

The members of the Board of Trinity House considered this suggestion seriously and passed on the request to the Board of Trade. A letter from there on 8th November concluded with the following paragraph -

"In reply the Board desire me to inform you that they have carefully enquired into the matter, and, as at present advised, they see no sufficient reason for establishing a Life Saving Apparatus at this place."

Although the lifeboat was launched on several occasions through the year and gave assistance, the only life-saving service took place on Wednesday, 5th December 1899. Two sloops, the Francis Ann and the Horncastle, had loaded gravel on the Binks. As the tide flooded the sea became very rough and both vessels signalled for assistance as the seas were breaking right over them. It was with great difficulty that the lifeboat struggled towards them and as the lifeboat approached, the Francis Ann floated off and was towed into the Humber. The lifeboat went to the Horncastle and succeeded in taking off the two men. The vessel later floated off, with several feet of water inside her, was towed into the Humber inside Spurn where she sank. On the following day at low tide she was pumped out and made ready to proceed on the next high tide.

There was a busy start to the year 1900. On 1st January in dense fog the steam trawler Eddystone, having collided with another steamer in the Humber, had to be beached at the Point of Spurn with the fore compartment full of water. The lifeboat crew assisted to make temporary repairs, pump out the water and help the vessel when she floated off at 4.30am on the following morning.

Late at night on 6th January the SS Ready, with the lighter Experiment, both of and from London to Hull laden with chalk, went aground on the Inner Binks and signalled for assistance. The lifeboat was launched and whilst going out to the vessels saw the schooner Demaris, also chalk loaded from London, near the Inner Bink Buoy showing signals of distress. The lifeboat went first to the Demaris, took off the crew of five and then went on to the lighter Experiment and took off the crew of four. All the men were landed safely at Spurn at 6.0am on 7th January. The lifeboat later returned to assist the vessels, but the Grimsby steam lifeboat took the Demaris in tow. The Spurn men, with the help of a tug, brought the lighter into the Humber inside Spurn, put the crew back on board, along with three lifeboat men to assist the Experiment up to Hull.

During the remainder of the year the lifeboat gave assistance to a number of vessels, but on 20th December a vessel was lost when a trawler captain did not do what the lifeboat Master asked him to do. At 6.30am the watchman reported a vessel showing signals of distress a mile outside the Point. The lifeboat was launched, but on arrival it was found that the Hull steam trawler Lord Kitchener had taken the vessel in tow. The report continues -

"We boarded the vessel and commenced to get the water out - the pumps choked. The water continued to sweep over the vessel and the steering gear broke down and the towage broke. We again connected the trawler and asked the Captain to tow the vessel onto the beach inside Spurn as she was getting very low in the water, but he continued to tow the vessel up the Humber. When about the Lower Middle Buoy he found that the vessel would not bear towing much longer he then asked what to do with her and I told him to tow her on to the Trinity Sand. On turning his vessel the tow rope parted again and the vessel very soon sunk about 11.0am. The masts at that time were not visible, the Lower Middle Buoy bearing south west by west about two cable lengths. We landed the crew at Spurn, three hands all told. The vessel was the steam barge Countess of Erroll, of Newcastle, bound from that port to Boston with a cargo of coal."

Royal National Life-boat Institution.

Retiring Allowances to be Granted on and from 1st January, 1898, to Coxswains, Bowmen and Signalmen of Good Behaviour, and subject to Due and Satisfactory Discharge of Duty.

1. COXSWAIN SUPERINTENDENTS.

PENSIONS.—Retired on account of *old age, ill-health, accident,* or *abolition of post,* after ten years and upwards of service as Coxswain Superintendents: 10*s.* for each year as Coxswain Superintendent, and 5*s.* for each year as Second Coxswain, but the total amount of pension not to exceed £12 per annum.

COMMUTATION OF PENSION.—£2 for every year's service as Coxswain Superintendent, and £1 for each year's service as Second Coxswain.

GRATUITIES.—Retired on account of *old age, ill-health, accident,* or *abolition of post,* after five years' service as Coxswain Superintendent, but with less than ten years of such service, £1 10*s.* for each year, and 15*s.* for each year of service as Second Coxswain.

The salary of a Coxswain Superintendent is usually £8 per annum, irrespective of tank and other allowances.

2. SECOND COXSWAINS.

PENSIONS.—Retired on account of *old age, ill-health, accident,* or *abolition of post,* after ten years and upwards of service as Second Coxswain: 5*s.* for each year, but total amount of pension not to exceed £6 per annum.

COMMUTATION OF PENSION.—£1 for every year's service as Second Coxswain.

GRATUITIES.—Retired on account of *old age, ill-health, accident,* or *abolition of post,* after five years' service as Second Coxswain, but with less than ten years' service, 15*s.* for each year.

The salary of a Second Coxswain is usually £2 per annum, irrespective of tank and other allowances.

3. BOWMEN.

PENSIONS.—Retired on account of *old age, ill-health, accident,* or *abolition of post,* after ten years and upwards of service as Bowman, 2*s.* 6*d.* for each year, but total not to exceed £3 per annum. Bowmen with less than ten years' service as Bowmen to receive nothing on retirement.

COMMUTATION OF PENSION.—10*s.* for every year's service as Bowman.

The salary of a Bowman is £1 10*s.* per annum, irrespective of exercise and service allowances.

4. SIGNALMEN.

PENSIONS.—Retired on account of *old age, ill-health, accident,* or *abolition of post,* after ten years and upwards of service as Signalman, provided he is not already receiving a pension as a retired Coxswain Superintendent or Second Coxswain, 2*s.* for each year, but total not to exceed £2 10*s.* Signalmen with less than ten years' service as Signalmen to receive nothing on retirement.

COMMUTATION OF PENSION. — 8*s.* for every year's service as Signalman.

The salary of a Signalman is £1 per annum, irrespective of other allowances.

Pensions to be paid annually in advance.

All pensions and gratuities to be paid through the Local Honorary Secretary.

Should the pensioner have removed to an address at which there is no Local Branch of the Institution, payment to be made from the Institution direct.

By order of the Committee,

CHARLES DIBDIN,

Secretary.

ROYAL NATIONAL LIFE-BOAT INSTITUTION,
14, JOHN STREET, ADELPHI, LONDON, W.C.
11th November, 1897.

David Pye sent the following letter to Trinity House in Hull on 3rd January 1901.

"Will you please inform the Chairman that the Life Boat is leaking very badly. I have her ashore on some timber but failed to find the leak. It is time that it was found and seen to. She has been leaking for some time but I find it gets much worse and the crew is not satisfied with the present state of the Boat. Until something is done the Boat is not fit to go out in a gale of wind should she be required to do so. The Boat is getting bad to manage when sailing as she does not discharge the water as she should do when sailing she is about half full most of the time if in a strong breeze. I think the Boat has been at Spurn about nineteen years and that is a long time for a Life Boat which has to ride afloat all the time. I think sir that it is time we had a new Life Boat for the Station."

The Board of Trinity House obviously considered the matter and wrote to RNLI in London asking permission to borrow the Grimsby sailing lifeboat whilst the Spurn boat was examined and repaired. A steam lifeboat was based at Grimsby at the time as an experiment. The Chief Inspector of Lifeboats, E.J.Heseltine, granted permission provided that "The Trinity House pay all out of pocket expenses, and all loss or damage to the Boat is to be made good, but no charge will be made for the loan of the Boat." These conditions were accepted and on 22nd January 1901 the Trinity House Yacht brought down the Grimsby sailing lifeboat to Spurn and took away the Spurn boat for repair.

The only time the Grimsby boat was launched whilst at Spurn was on 30th January when it was used for practice. On Friday 8th February the Spurn boat was returned and the Grimsby lifeboat was taken back across the Humber.

At the beginning of March Pye wrote to Trinity House with suggestions for dimensions and fittings for a new lifeboat. Pye thought it should be thirty seven feet six inches in length, ten feet beam and four feet six inches deep amidships. It should have two masts, sets of sails, five thwarts and be fitted with water ballast. It was to be another year before Trinity House asked for tenders for a new lifeboat and placed an order.

Pye wrote to Trinity House at the end of November asking for "a light carriage to run the Tender down to the water. I find that it takes us a long time to carry her down when almost low water and when we have got her down I find the men has not much pull in them for some time. The Boat is so deep that we are not able to carry her clear of the Beach. We break more oars with carrying the Boat down than in any other way. Gentlemen if you consider to supply a carriage it will be a very good improvement on the present system of getting the Boat down as we should save a considerable time when we are required with the Boat."

Grimsby lifeboat, Manchester Unity" at Spurn on loan for two weeks at the end of January 1901. *Courtesy of Mr. M. Welton*

Various tenders were considered and a carriage was ordered from Mr. Gell of Holmpton, Withernsea, and it was delivered to Spurn on 24th June 1902.

The lifeboat was launched four times during November and assisted vessels in difficulties, but no lives were saved.

Pye again wrote to Trinity House on 4th January 1902 about the condition of the lifeboat -

"I beg to ask you again for a new Life Boat for this station. The Crew is very dissatisfied with the present Boat. It is about twelve months ago that I reported to you the state of the Boat and you promised that we should have a new one. When we get into broken water we are just like a raft not like a Life Boat. She cannot clear herself of water that is in a fresh breeze and that gives the Crew a very bad opinion of her. Should we be called for in a gale of wind I shall not be surprised at the Crew refusing to go in her. I think Gentlemen it is time something was done in the matter. If nothing is done we shall not be able to keep a Crew as men will not trust their lives in a boat in the state ours is in. She has been stationed here twenty years come the 6th of this month."

Under Royal Letters Patent.

NORRIS'S TUBULAR LIFE-BOAT.

SELF-RIGHTING AND UNSINKABLE.

This Boat is designed and constructed upon a multitubular principle, which may be aptly termed a series of small cylindrical compartments like the honey-comb in a bee-hive.

All the tubes or cylinders employed are both air and water-tight.

The exterior form of the Boat is somewhat similar to the present Life-Boats in use by the Royal National Life-Boat Institution, but with the additional advantage that every compartment or tank is fitted and filled with a series of water-tight cells or tubes. Thus, in case of collision, or being stove in, no water can enter in bulk, and the Boat's buoyancy is unaffected, and she is practically unsinkable.

These cells or tubes are constructed of a light elastic vegetable material, which is water-proof, and they make no appreciable difference in the weight of the Boat, or in the requirements of air space under the Board of Trade regulations.

By a skilful arrangement and adaptation in construction, the Boat is, even when with mast and sail up, and when turned completely over, self-righting in any circumstances.

For Ordinary Ships' Boats, this patent is adapted for immediate use at small cost, by means of lengths of canvas, to which are fitted the buoyancy tubes, and on an emergency cut to length, and quickly nailed in, when the Boat becomes unsinkable.

An unsinkable Life-Raft may be constructed in the same manner.

The Tubular Life-Belt (under this Patent) has stood every test, and will easily support Three persons in the water.

NORRIS'S PATENT LIFE BELT & BOAT CO.,
(c/o Messrs. FOSKETT & Co.) 9, FENCHURCH STREET,
LONDON, E.C.

This is the Boat I offer you and for which I was awarded the Silver Medal and Diploma of Merit.

Under Royal Letters Patent.

NORRIS'S TUBULAR LIFE-BOAT.

Self-Righting and Unsinkable.

A Boat constructed on this patent is just completed and ready to forward to the Paris Exhibition for competition as to the best "Life-saving device in cases of Disaster at Sea" under the "Anthony Pollok Memorial Prize."

This Boat may be inspected during the next few days at Messrs. Leslie & Hamblin's, Boat Builders, South Dock, New Road, Blackwall, E. London.

Her measurements are as follows:—Length, 20 ft.; breadth, 5 ft. 8 in.; depth, 2 ft. 7½ in.; weight, 18 cwt.; and fitted with all requirements.

She is fitted also with 848 separate watertight, but extremely light, cylinders and in buoyancy capacity almost doubles the Board of Trade requirements.

In an emergency she could carry 20 persons, whilst with 10 in addition hanging on to her life-lines, she is practically unsinkable. This Boat may, with, or without mast and sail, be thrown off the deck of a ship in any position and will at once right herself. Her cost is much less than the usual class of life-boats and even if stove in her safety is but little impaired.

Norris's Boat Belts are adaptable to every kind of boat and are easily fitted and secured.

The boat was highly commended by Capt. [illegible] R.N.
Royal Nat. Lifeboat Institution.

The Board of Trinity House began to collect together the names of boat builders who could be asked to tender for the work of building a new lifeboat, but final specifications were not drawn up until June and it was near the end of July when a tender was accepted. Many companies were approached, but several declined to tender as they already had too much work. Tenders were received, however, from Hartlepool, Cornwall, Birkenhead, East Anglia, Scotland, London and Hull. The Board of Trinity House was invited to consider a steam lifeboat from Newcastle. Mr. E.S.Norris offered his Tubular Life-Boat at a cost of one hundred pounds, but the final decision was to ask Earle's Shipbuilding and Engineering Company of Hull to build the new boat. The price quoted on the tender was seven hundred and fifty pounds.

A steam lifeboat had been stationed at Grimsby experimentally by RNLI in 1898 and in January 1902 Thomas Holmes, District Inspect or of Lifeboats, sent a report on the situation to the Chief Inspector of Lifeboats in London, following a meeting with the local committee in Grimsby. The committee members agreed unanimously that the lifeboat should not be kept in the dock; it was not practicable to provide a berth anywhere else at Grimsby; the boat would be much better placed at Spurn. Mr. Holmes agreed with these findings.

There were certain advantages of Grimsby, namely a good volunteer crew, facilities for coaling, watering, docking and repairs to machinery, good telephone communications all along the coast and accommodation for all crew members.

The disadvantages were that when the lifeboat was in the dock there was no certainty that it could get out when needed. If there was a strong wind from anywhere between east north east and south east the flood gates were closed for one and a half hours on each side of high water to protect other gates and could not be opened. The dock gates were not allowed to be opened with less than twelve feet of water on the sill, which meant that at low spring tides the gates could not be opened for four hours. The berth used in the dock was surrounded by coal hoists and drops and when these were all occupied by steamers the lifeboat could be trapped.

For all these reasons Mr. Holmes recommended that Spurn was a much better place and there were other advantages. At Spurn the boat could be kept afloat, available at all states of the tide, at a safe mooring, she would be five or six miles nearer her work and there was a constant electrical connection between Spurn and Cleethorpes.

It was decided to approach the Board of Trinity House in Hull to arrange a meeting to discuss the possibility of a steam lifeboat at Spurn and the following propositions were made -

1. That RNLI would build and maintain a steam lifeboat at Spurn Point and build cottages for the engine room staff and maintain them.

2. That the Board of Trinity House be asked to allow the Boat to be put under the charge of their Coxswain and Assistant Coxswain and to be worked by their crew; and that the Coxswain have complete discretion as to whether he used the steam Boat or the sailing Boat.

3. That when out in the steam Boat the crew of seven men be paid by the Institution according to that scale of pay.

4. That the Institution pay the Coxswain and Assistant Coxswain a yearly salary.

5. That the Board of Trinity House in Hull should act as Local Committee for the steam lifeboat.

6. The taking of salvage not allowed by RNLI, but the Spurn men to be allowed to do so on condition that any damage to the lifeboat be repaid by Trinity House of Hull.

A coal store would be required and a room as a workshop for the engineer. Fresh water would have to be obtained from Grimsby.

A meeting was arranged in May and it must have been arranged for four engineers from the Institution to stay at Spurn for some time to study the conditions. Unfortunately it was not possible to find accommodation for all of them. In June the Spurn lifeboat crew expressed the opinion that "a good, sound, sailing Boat would answer the purpose best as a steam Life Boat would be too risky to go on or across the hills of the Banks which we have to do in most cases in the night time. The steam Life Boat may be of service to us at times, but in very few instances on the Banks." In July RNLI decided more information was required before any decision could be reached and postponed all further consideration until November. In that month it was decided not to pursue the matter any further and to abandon the idea of a steam lifeboat at Spurn.

Whilst the Board of Trinity House was busy with all these problems the work of the lifeboat continued as usual. The boat was launched to assist vessels in March, April and September and three lives were saved on 29th September. The lifeboat was launched at 7.30 pm on 28th September to a vessel in distress on the Inner Binks. The vessel was the schooner Aquilla, of Goole, with a cargo of scrap iron from Portsmouth to Hull. The three men on the schooner were taken off and the lifeboat lay by until 12.30am on 29th September when the Aquilla sank and became a total wreck.

Lifeboast and crew on the beach in front of the cottages at Spurn. The boat is almost certainly the one built in 1903. *Courtesy of Mr.&Mrs. R. Robinson*

The lifeboat assisted a barquentine at the end of October and on November 21st was launched to a barge, coal loaded, which was on fire. The lifeboat men sailed the barge towards the beach and scuttled her and then began throwing buckets of water onto the fire. This was the only way to save the barge. Late that night they put out the fire. On the following day the men returned, pumped out the water and floated the barge and left her at anchor over night. On 23rd November, with the help of the tug Humber, they took the barge to Grimsby. The vessel was the Olympia, of Faversham.

The Hull trawler Yorkshire stranded on the beach two and a half miles from Spurn towards Easington on the night of 25th November.

Pye received a message that the Easington Rocket Apparatus would be used and the team saved nine men. On the following day Pye arranged with the insurance agents to pull the vessel off the beach with tugs and assist her to Hull, and this he did at 3.30am on 27th November. All this was in his report. Some three weeks later a letter was received at Trinity House in Hull from Easington asking if the Spurn men were allowed to leave their station and assist vessels off the beach when no life-saving was involved. The letter went on to describe the events near Easington, offered details of other similar instances and asked what would have happened had there been a call for the lifeboat. The letter ended by saying that this "never occurred during Mr. Winson's time only for Life Saving. and I think that the Gentlemen of the Hull Trinity House ought to be acquainted." The members of the Board were well aware that what had happened was normal practice.

Through the second half of the year there was a constant stream of correspondence between Trinity House and Earle's Shipbuilding Company, where the new lifeboat was being built. Pye was asked to go to the shipyard and give his opinion on various aspects of the boat and it was finally delivered to Spurn on Thursday 1st January 1903. This was the beginning of a year of frustration concerning the new boat.

When the boat was delivered there were some minor problems. The water ballast tanks would admit water, but the pumps could not pump it out, some copper sheathing was missing, as were two life buoys, and the boat was leaking. Water collected to a depth of eight inches over the first weekend at Spurn and on a later test fourteen inches of water collected over six days. It was thought that the leaking would stop as the timber expanded, but a further check over five days at the beginning of February showed water to a depth of four and a half inches.

From March to the end of August all went well, but very early in September the copper sheathing on the waterline was damaged by "some drifting object." When the lifeboat was beached to be checked for repairs it was found that all the copper sheathing was riddled with holes and apparently eaten away. "The life rods along the keel are all adrift - several of the brackets having already fallen off, others loose." The lifeboat was taken to Hull to Earle's Shipyard for inspection and repair. Samples of copper, both uncorroded and corroded, were examined and analysed by Hull Chemical Works and it was found that the sheet copper was pure and that the corrosion was "due to some outside action." The packing paper put underneath the copper sheathing was analysed along with all fastening screws. These tests were carried out through October and no cause of corrosion was found. When the lifeboat was inspected and tested for leaks it was discovered that all the discharge pipes showed signs of corrosion and that one of the pipes leaked. Members of the Board of Trinity House were invited to inspect the lifeboat at Earle's Shipyard on Thursday 19th November, after all repairs had been carried out, and the boat was taken back to Spurn on the following day. On November 23rd the City and County Analyst sent his report on the copper and samples of water collected around Spurn. He concluded that there was some action on the copper by the water, but could not account for the strength of the action. In the final sentence of his report it is stated "I am convinced that some action is taking place, the nature of which we are unaware of."

There appears to be no further correspondence on the subject. Did the corrosion recur ? Was the problem solved ? These things are not known. All the time the new lifeboat was unfit for use the men at Spurn had to use the old one which they had condemned as unsafe to use.

The lifeboat was launched on January 22nd 1903 when the watchman reported a vessel aground on the Inner Binks. The vessel was the steam trawler Riversdale, of Grimsby, and did not require any assistance from the lifeboat, only a tug. There was a very different situation early on the morning of Friday 27th February, and a long service, when the French barque Marguerite Molinos, of Havre, broke adrift from the tug whilst being towed into the Humber. The report continues -

"The vessel then had to bring up inside Spurn. It was then blowing a Gale. About 7.0am the ship commenced to drag her anchor and was driven ashore on the Trinity Sand. They at once put up signals of distress. We tried to launch the Tender but we was driven back, on the beach several times. In one attempt one of our men had a very narrow escape of losing his life. He was knocked down by the Tender which drove over him. I just caught him by the hand as the backwash was taking him away. After four hours struggling we succeeded in getting off. Not being able to get to the Life Boat we proceeded with the Tender up the North Channel and crossed the Trinity Sand and succeeded in reaching the vessel. The Captain stated the ship was making no water. By this time the wind had moderated and with the assistance of three tugs we succeeded in getting the vessel off and taking her to a safe anchorage in Grimsby Roads. We arrived back at Spurn about 8.0pm."

The lifeboat was launched at 8.30am on Friday 4th September when there was a strong south east wind and heavy swell. A steamer, name unknown, had stranded on the Binks and when the lifeboat arrived at the vessel Pye "thought it not prudent to go alongside" because of the conditions and the Captain said he did not need any assistance. The lifeboat returned to Spurn at mid-day, the steamer having floated off. There was a similar occurrence on the night of 28th October with the Wilson liner Argo. The Captain said he did not require assistance, but it needed four tugs to pull the vessel off the Inner Binks.

The watchman reported a vessel showing distress signals on the Inner Binks at 2.0am on 28th November 1903. Pye answered the signals with rocket and blue light and saw the vessel float off. The ship went round in a circle and grounded again in almost the same place as before and at 3.0am showed more distress signals. The lifeboat was launched. The report reads -

"On arriving at the vessel she proved to be the ketch Estoile, of Grimsby, bound from London to Grangemouth with a cargo of scrap iron. With the striking on the Binks the ship was leaking very bad. We commenced with the pumps but they choked with the sand which had got into the ship. We stood by her until about 10.0am. We saw no chance of saving the vessel so we landed the crew, four hands all told, arriving at the moorings about 10.30am. At the time the vessel stranded the wind was light and foggy with rather heavy northerly sea. In the afternoon the wind increased to a moderate Gale with a heavy sea. The ship was driven on to the Beach and with the night's tide became a total wreck and is in several pieces between our watch house and the Point."

During 1904 the lifeboat was launched on service only once, to assist the barge Diana, of Rye, which had been damaged in a heavy squall. The lifeboat stood by and then assisted the Diana to Grimsby.

The following year was also quiet, with the lifeboat launching to assist vessels in February and March and then only in December. During that month two trawlers were assisted and the Bull Lightship, which had been badly damaged by a steam trawler. The fishing boat was going out to sea in fine weather when it collided with the lightship and cut through the port bow from the rail to far below the water line and the fore compartment had filled with water. Pye said of the trawler's captain that he "appeared to be the worse for drink."

Pye wrote to Trinity House in July 1905 on behalf of one of the crew members, William Hogg, who had been ill for some time, asking for some light work on land. Hogg had to leave the lifeboat service in September as he was unfit to continue in the crew. Doctors testified that he was suffering from progressive locomotor ataxia, a disease of the nervous system, which they said had been brought on by exposure to wet and cold in the lifeboat. Hogg and his wife moved to Hull and repeatedly asked Trinity House for assistance. Although there was no system of pensions for the lifeboat men Trinity House did grant money from time to time.

Two lives were saved on the night of 20th January 1906 from the sloop British Hero, of Hull, bound for Hull with a cargo of gravel from Orford Ness. The watchman reported distress signals from the Point at 10.35pm and the Tender was launched. The sloop had lost its sails and anchor cable and was in a disabled condition when it ran aground, also being full of water. A strong westerly breeze was blowing at the time and the lifeboat men took off the crew of two men and landed them at Spurn at midnight. Two days later the cargo was thrown overboard, the wreck re-floated and towed to Hull.

One man was rescued on 15th November 1906 when the small fishing boat Columbia, of Grimsby, was returning from the fishing grounds heavily laden with fish. Whilst crossing the Binks the sea broke into the boat and she sank immediately. The lifeboat proceeded as quickly as possible and saved one man, in an exhausted state, floating with the aid of two oars. The other two crew members were drowned.

Through the rest of the year the lifeboat was launched half a dozen times to vessels, but only one Captain accepted the assistance offered.

The first service in 1907 took place on the evening of Wednesday 6th February. two sloops from Hull, the Liberty and the Providence, were loading gravel on the Binks. The heavy flood tide drove the vessels together repeatedly and they signalled for assistance. When the lifeboat reached them the sloops were clashing together so violently that the Liberty sank. The two crew men were saved by the lifeboat. With the help of the tug Pioneer, the Providence was towed to safety in the Humber. On the following day the Spurn men threw out the cargo from the Liberty, pumped out the water and re-floated her. They pulled the vessel off the Binks and sailed her into the Humber, when both sloops then proceeded to Immingham.

Two more men were saved from the Grimsby sloop Chesterfield on 27th February. The vessel loaded gravel from the Binks and then got into difficulties with heavy seas and the strong flood tide and stranded on the Point. The men were rescued by the Tender and landed at Spurn. On the following ebb tide cargo was thrown overboard but the sea was too rough to pull the vessel off. On the following day conditions were still too rough and it was not until 3rd March that it was possible to get the Chesterfield off the Point.

The lifeboat received slight damage as it was being towed out to assist the Norwegian brig Hilding, of Bergen, bound from Bergen to Hull with a cargo of salt. The watchman reported signals of distress from a vessel on the Middle Binks at about 10.0pm on 11th April. The lifeboat was launched and the Captain of the tug Chester agreed to tow out the lifeboat. The report continues

"...we put our warps on board and the anchor was at once got. On the tug turning round she grounded on the Trinity Sand and our boat came under the tug's quarter and bent four of our rowlocks on the port side and our warp got into the propellor and we had to cut it in two places."

By the time the lifeboat reached the Hilding she had floated off and the Captain wanted no assistance, only a pilot. Pye set mast and sail and followed the vessel and advised the Captain to change course or drop anchor or he would quickly be ashore. The vessel drove ashore on the Lincolnshire Main and signalled for assistance. The lifeboat went alongside and with great difficulty Pye and his men took off seven of the crew of the Hilding. The Captain refused to leave the ship although Pye told him it was impossible for the lifeboat to return once it left because of the state of the tide. The Captain remained on board and the seven crew men were landed at Spurn at about 7.30am on the morning of 12th April. The Hilding was last seen by Pye on her beam ends, a total wreck.

When the sailing yacht Ethel, of Hull, grounded on the Inner Binks in a rough sea the two men were taken into the lifeboat. A rope was made fast to the yacht and the lifeboat held her head to the sea for over an hour before succeeding in towing her off. The two men were returned to the yacht and Pye lent them a long oar to steer with to Hull as the tiller had been lost on the Binks.

This was the last effective service in 1907 as on all other launches the Captains told the lifeboat crew that their assistance was not required.

This was also the last effective service of the lifeboat under the control of Trinity House in Hull. During 1907 the Humber Conservancy Act was passed in Parliament. The effect of this Act was to transfer from Trinity House in Hull to the Humber Conservancy Board all responsibilities connected with navigation on the Humber. Along with all this went the lifeboat station at Spurn. After ninety seven years of support and endeavour by Trinity House the Humber Conservancy Board took control of the station on 1st January 1908 .

HUMBER CONSERVANCY BOARD
1st JANUARY 1908 - 1st MAY 1911

When the Humber Conservancy Board took over the lifeboat station at Spurn it became responsible for an experienced Master and crew, their houses, the lifeboat and tender and everything connected with them. This was what Trinity House had undertaken for the preceding ninety seven years.

The lifeboat was still quite new, but morale had suffered because of a change in the gravel business and the cost of crabbing, which reduced the income of the crew. In February 1908 the crew members signed a letter to the Conservancy Board asking for an increase in pay, but more than a year later there had been no award made. Indeed, throughout the three years when the Humber Conservancy Board was responsible for the lifeboat station there was apparently very little correspondence between the two, records of service are very sparse and the Board members appear to have taken little or no interest in the work of the station or the well-being of the crew and families living at Spurn. It is known that during 1908 there were eight service launches and eight lives saved, in 1909 there were four service launches and eight lives saved, but the only information for 1910 is one launch and no lives saved. There is no information of any launches during the first months of 1911.

The Humber Conservancy Act clearly stated that the Board would be responsible for the Spurn lifeboat station, but did not include any statement that there was a legal requirement to continue to maintain and operate the station. From the outset the Board members, and two of them in particular, namely the Chairman of the Board and the Chairman of the Marine and Works Committee, obviously close friends and allies, were determined to pass the responsibility for the station to some other body or close down the station completely and as soon as possible, preferably without being seen to be responsible for the closure.

When the lifeboat crew wrote in February 1908 asking for an increase in pay the Board asked for a statement of earnings for the previous three years for crabbing, gravelling, fishing and salvage money. In 1905 this was six pounds seventeen shillings per man, in 1906 it was six pounds five shillings and only five pounds six shillings in 1907. This was on top of their pay as lifeboatmen, but David Pye, the lifeboat Master, pointed out that "the cost of twine etc. for rigging up of the crab gear every year costs from six to seven pounds per man, and then there is the cost of Boats and the upkeep of the same." The Conservancy Board looked at the income and costs for Trinity House for the lifeboat station for 1907 and found that the total income was from rents and amounted to eighteen pounds nine shillings. Expenditure in the same year was four hundred and eighty pounds, two shillings and elevenpence. Most of this amount was for wages for the crew.

When the Board members realised the cost of running what was described as "entirely a philanthropic matter" and knowing that there was no statutory obligation to maintain the lifeboat station, the decision was taken to hand it over to the RNLI. Mr. Franklin, Secretary to the Conservancy Board, sent a letter to RNLI on 18th May 1908 including a resolution by the Marine and Works Committee, confirmed at a meeting of the Board on 14th May "That the Royal National Lifeboat Institution be asked whether they are prepared to take over the management of the Lifeboat at Spurn, and if so, on what terms."

The letter continues -

"I may say that my Committee feel that however deserving of support the Lifeboat may be from a philanthropic point of view, yet as this Board is practically a commercial body, it scarcely falls within their province to maintain the Lifeboat.

If you would desire to send an Inspector to confer with the officials of this Board on the matter, or to visit Spurn, we shall be glad to arrange to place a steam launch at your disposal for the purpose, by means of which Spurn can easily be visited."

After many letters had passed between RNLI and the Conservancy Board it was finally arranged for Commander Charles E. Cunningham Graham RN, Deputy Chief Inspector of Lifeboats, and Commander Thomas Holmes RN, Eastern District Inspector of Lifeboats, to visit Hull and go to Spurn on 7th July 1908. In the meantime the Conservancy Board had discovered a reserve lifeboat at the Trinity House Buoy Shed in Hull and asked Commander Graham to be prepared to inspect it and assess its suitability for the RNLI. The visit duly took place and the Buoy Yacht "Queen" carried the visitors to Spurn. During the visit, and in subsequent letters, the RNLI asked for more information, some of which had to be obtained from the lifeboat Master, David Pye. RNLI pressed the Board to provide the information immediately, but it was not until July 25th that the facts were supplied to Mr. Franklin, Secretary to the Board, and they were sent as requested. The information included -

"Detailed Statement of Receipts and Expenditure for the years ended September 1905, 1906, 1907.

Statement supplied by the Lifeboat Master of the men's earnings in addition to their wages during the years referred to.

Particulars of the tenure of the school, the public house and the cottages.

Particulars of the services rendered by the Lifeboat crew during the last ten years.

Plans of the Lifeboat."

A copy of the six inch ordnance plan showing the land held at Spurn followed a few days later.

Several letters were sent from the Board asking for the decision by RNLI regarding Spurn, but after a meeting in August the matter was put back to a meeting in November and then again to December 1908. On 10th December 1908 a letter was sent from RNLI to the Board containing the following statements -

"...the Committee of Management would undertake to provide and equip, when necessary, a Life-Boat and boarding boat for Spurn Point; to keep in repair such boats, and to provide them with the gear from time to time on a report being made to the Institution as to such requirements. In addition to this the District Inspector of the Institution would be instructed to make a complimentary visit to the Station at Spurn about twice a year.

It is understood by my Committee that were these arrangements made with the Institution your Commissioners would undertake to provide a competent Crew for the Life-Boat."

This reply was considered at a meeting of the Works and Maritime Committee and a further letter was sent to RNLI asking "whether it is proposed by the Royal National Lifeboat Institution to pay the crew of the lifeboat for launches and practice." A letter written on 15th December made the position very clear -"..the Committee of Management of this Institution does not propose to pay the Crew of the Life-Boat for launches or practice. The proposal does not extend beyond the conditions mentioned in their letter to you of the 10th instant." Following another committee meeting Mr. Franklin wrote to RNLI "...they regret that the proposals made in your letter are such that they do not feel inclined to accept."

Whilst this correspondence was progressing a letter was sent from the Board to Spurn to the Master, David Pye, concerning claims for salvage and the distribution of amounts received. These had been settled by the Master and crew but were now to be arranged only by the Board - "..all occasions on which assistance is rendered by the crew must be reported to me and that in no circumstances must you or any of the crew make any agreement or enter into any negotiations or other transactions with respect to salvage services rendered.

Will you please make this known amongst the crew and give me an acknowledgement of this letter."

This was a return to the conditions during the first thirty years of the lifeboat station, when negotiations were carried out only by Trinity House.

Some five months later on 8th May 1909 the first of many letters was sent from the Board to RNLI asking for an interview for the Board Chairman and Chairman of the Marine Committee with the Chairman of the Committee of Management of RNLI. A date was fixed, then changed, and finally agreed for 3.0pm on 25th May in London. A pencil footnote on one of the letters suggests that the men from Hull were going to put forward the same arguments as previously, as well as discussing the tenure of the lifeboat cottages, and possibly suggesting closing down the station if RNLI could not agree to take it over.

A letter on 17th June from RNLI repeats and confirms the offer made in December "with the addition that my Committee will be prepared to offer the sum of one hundred and fifty pounde per annum as a contribution from the Institution to meet the approximate outlay which would be made by my Committee on Coxswain's salaries etc. and payments for services were the arrangements those of an ordinary Life-Boat Station of the Institution."

This offer was considered by the Maritime Committee and the Board and on 13th September 1909 a letter was sent to RNLI containing the following -

"..a resolution was passed in the following terms:-

'That having regard to the fact that the negotiations with the Royal National Lifeboat Institution relative to their taking over the Lifeboat at Spurn have not resulted in their making any proposal which meets with the approval of the Board, steps be taken to terminate the tenancy of the cottages and dispense with the services of the crew, with the object of disestablishing the Lifeboat Station at the earliest possible date.'"

This prompted an immediate reply from RNLI suggesting that the Board had perhaps not understood clearly that "to take over the Establishment and to pay a permanent Crew for whom they could not find any occupation except on the occasion of a wreck would in fact be ultra vires.

This is a difficulty which apparently does not confront the Humber Conservancy Board."

The Board Chairman sent a private letter to RNLI again repeating the same arguments and saying the Resolution would be implemented, but no immediate action would be taken.

Mr. Pelham, Secretary to the Board of Trade, wrote to the Conservancy Board in October about the lifeboat station at Spurn. He pointed out the value of the station to shipping, the distance to the next nearest lifeboat station at Grimsby, the value of the information from Spurn to the Life Saving Apparatus Team at Easington and of the constant lookout kept by the lifeboatmen. He asked the Conservancy Board to consider reaching some agreement with RNLI. The Chairman answered personally, setting out the Board's case and a much more formal letter was sent from the Board of Trade in reply stating that "the withdrawal of this lifeboat might be a serious matter" for shipping, asking for details of costs, whether or not the Conservancy Board would be prepared to contribute to the costs of the station and again asking for action to be deferred.

This led to private correspondence between the leading members of the Conservancy Board, agreeing that "it is not well that the subject should be made too public at the present time" and deciding to ask for an interview "as I suppose our friend Dibdin has been at them." (Charles Dibdin was Secretary to RNLI) A reply was sent to the Board of Trade re-stating the Conservancy Board's arguments and asking for an interview for the Board Chairman, the Chairman of the Marine Committee and Mr. Franklin. A meeting was arranged but the Board of Trade upset the men from Hull by inviting representatives from RNLI. Another private letter between Conservancy members commented "to appear jointly would, in my view, be like appearing before an Arbitrator, a position which I don't admit, and which I think would tend to strengthen the hands of the Institution." It was resolved to ask for a private, preliminary meeting or to decline to attend. The request for this private meeting was granted and it took place in London on Tuesday 23rd November 1909. On the morning of the meeting the Board of Trade was informed by RNLI that "their representatives did not desire to avail themselves of the opportunity of meeting representatives of the Conservancy Board." The Board Chairman intimated that in those circumstances the only course of action was to disestablish Spurn lifeboat station.

Another letter in mid December from the Board of Trade again asked the Conservancy Board not to take any action and a further one in January 1910 contained the following statements concerning the Humber Conservancy Act of 1907 -

"..this Board did not anticipate that the Humber Conservancy Board would ever contemplate the abandonment of the Life Boat which has been maintained by their predecessors for over one hundred years.

Had this possibility been brought to their notice when that measure was before Parliament the Board would, without doubt, have sought to have a provision inserted in it for the maintenance of the Station."

This letter also referred to the offer by RNLI of one hundred and fifty pounds per annum if the Conservancy Board continued to maintain the station and added that the Board of Trade would pay up to one hundred pounds per annum if the

Conservancy Board accepted the RNLI offer. In Hull it was decided this was too important a matter to put before the Board at short notice and "having regard to the policy which has been adopted of keeping the matter out of the press." A decision was taken to seek another meeting with the Board of Trade and this took place on 23rd February 1910. Unfortunately there is no record of what took place at the meeting, but in March the Board of Trade asked for a statement of the services by the lifeboat during the past ten years and this information was provided in April.

The solicitors for the Chichester Constable family wrote to the Conservancy Board in May 1910 outlining the history of the leases concerning the lifeboat station at Spurn. The letter made it clear that the land was held by Trinity House on a tenancy from year to year subject to a six months notice. It also stated that Trinity House had allowed both Coastguard houses and Lloyds signalling station on land leased at a nominal rent for life saving purposes without informing the owners. It was now felt, in view of the changed circumstances, that notice to quit should be served, effective in one year's time, but that the Conservancy Board could apply for a new lease on new terms if it decided to maintain the station.

This was the opportunity the Humber Conservancy Board had been waiting for and the decision was quickly taken to close the lifeboat station. A letter was sent to the Board of Trade on 3rd June informing them of the decision to close the station in three months time because of the notice to quit. Letters were sent to the Admiralty concerning the coastguards, to Lloyds, to the innkeeper and to the members of the School Board of Managers to terminate the agreements and asking them to apply directly to the Constable family solicitors concerning any proposed renewal. The Admiralty and Lloyds realised that the notice was not effective until May 1911 and asked to be allowed to stay at Spurn until that time and this was agreed. Letters were sent early in June to all members of the crew telling them that notices would be sent out in August to terminate their engagement in September.

Whilst this was happening the Board of Trade asked for further information about lifeboat services and salvage. The information was sent in July with a covering note pointing out that lives could possibly have been saved and salvage operations carried out "by some other means" even if the lifeboat had not existed.

It was impossible to keep the matter out of the press any longer, but the first article found in the Daily News on 20th June appears to be based on a statement by the Conservancy Board. It mentions the notice to quit the land, with the result that "the Board have no alternative but to give the men notice to terminate their engagements." The negotiations with RNLI are referred to "and possibly some action will now be taken to prevent the abandonment of the lifeboat, which has saved life at one time or another and therefore will be held to have justified its existence." The article concludes by pointing out that there are other lifeboat stations at Grimsby, Donna Nook and Withernsea.

This was immediately challenged a few days later in an article drawing attention to the increase in traffic, and especially passenger sailings, on the Humber. The article also highlights the distance of the other stations from the Binks - the nearest one is more than seven miles away - and the time needed to row there in bad conditions. Other letters in the Eastern Morning News and Hull Daily Mail made similar points and criticised the Conservancy Board for trying to save money by "throwing the responsibility for the lifeboat upon public subscriptions" and breaking up "this good old institution to save the paltry sum of about four hundred pounds per annum, and perhaps lose four hundred lives. Are not lives worth more than four hundred pounds? We had no such cheese-paring policy in the days of the Trinity House."

A letter from the British Shipmasters' Association was sent to the Conservancy Board condemning the decision to close the lifeboat station, praising the value of the lifeboat service to the maritime fraternity and appealing for the decision to be re-considered. This letter was written on 13th July but did not reach the Conservancy Board until 18th July, two days after a Board meeting when it could have been read. A private internal letter from the Board Chairman dismissed the writer of the most recent letter in the press by saying "No one treats him seriously or ever replies to his mis-statements." The letter went on to say "There is not the least doubt that the Board's policy of being turned out is a proper one." The final paragraph shows the Chairman's satisfaction at the late arrival of the letter from the Shipmasters' Association. Another internal letter from the Chairman of the Marine Committee states that the solicitors acting for the Constable family "are the proper people to bear the odium of discontinuing the Lifeboat in conjunction with the National Institution." At the beginning of August dismissal notices were sent out to the crew and the Board received letters from the schoolmaster asking for employment when the school closed, and from a lifeboat family asking to be allowed to stay on in the cottage as they could not afford to move elsewhere.

The Board of Trade sent another letter to the Conservancy Board on 10th August stressing the importance of the lifeboat station and asking for the crew to be kept on temporarily beyond the dismissal date of 2nd September to give time for arrangements to be made "for the permanent upkeep of the service." This was agreed to "subject to the fact that the Conservancy will not continue the maintenance of the lifeboat after a period, which gives the Board of Trade a reasonable time to make their arrangements." A member of the Board of Trade made two visits to Hull and Spurn during August to meet the various parties involved

On December 1st the Board of Trade sent another letter asking if the Conservancy Board would be prepared to make an annual contribution of two hundred pounds towards the cost of the lifeboat station, the balance being provided by RNLI and His Majesty's Government. The Marine Committee Chairman wrote an internal letter saying that "we shall be well out of the matter by payment of such a sum. "

In the midst of all this wrangling it must be remembered that the lifeboat crew tried to maintain their service to ships in distress, but on 14th January 1911 the Board wrote to the Master, David Pye, referring to an article in the Hull Daily Mail on Friday, 13 th January 1911. The article reads as follows -

"The schooner Hilda, of Faversham, carrying the Captain and five hands, reached the Humber on Wednesday after experiencing bad weather in the North Sea. She was in a leaky condition and to prevent her sinking the Captain ran her ashore on the Binks, and then exhibited flares. Curious enough, these passed unnoticed, and with the half gale blowing through the night the schooner was blown off the Binks. It was evident she must sink sooner or later unless beached and the Captain next ran her ashore at Clee Ness.

Whilst there this morning the tug Kimberley saw the signals of distress and Captain Ball thereupon went to his assistance and took off the captain and crew and brought them into Grimsby. The Hilda will be salved by tugs and then brought into Grimsby."

The letter asked why the lifeboat had not launched and for Pye's comments on the matter. He replied as follows -

"I do not think the report in the paper is one from the Captain of the 'Hilda', I do not think that any man would try to put a vessel on to the Binks in such weather as we had at the time mentioned. A vessel would not have lasted very long, it would have been a very poor chance for the crew in such a sea. A proper watch was kept throughout the night and none of the men saw a flare. I was on the watch-house myself until very late the same night and no flare was shown, and just about day break on the 12th inst. I noticed the vessel sailing up the Humber at the SW side of the Bull Sand and appeared to be all right. After sailing some distance, the vessel was put round and sailed back towards the Bull Lightship. Whilst coming down on the SW side of the Bull Sand a flag was hoisted to the mast head, and when near the Lightship it was lowered to half mast, and went just to the south east of the Lightship, and then the vessel was put about and sailed back again up the river and stranded on the Clee Ness. I knew it was no use me commencing to sail after her as she was going faster than we could have sailed and was going into smoother water all the time and up the Humber there was tugs and trawlers lying about. I saw the vessel sail onto the Clee Ness, and the tug Kimberley go to the vessel and I saw the crew of the 'Hilda' leave in their own boat and the tug picked them up near to the ship.

I do not believe that the vessel had been on the Binks, if any flares had been shown we should have proceeded to the vessel and rendered what assistance we could as we always have in the past."

This account by Pye was supported by an article in the Eastern Morning News of 13th January 1911 which relates how witnesses on the shore at Grimsby saw exactly what Pye had described.

A letter from the Board of Trade on 28th February informed the Conservancy Board that RNLI had finally agreed to "take over the Spurn Lifeboat Station on the understanding that satisfactory arrangements can be made as regards the tenure of the necessary buildings and the services of the crew, and that your Board will make an annual payment of Two hundred pounds as mentioned above towards the cost of maintenance incurred by the Institution." The necessary assurances were given a week later, but the Admiralty, Lloyds, the School Managers and the innkeeper were all required to reach their own agreements over leases with Major Constable.

Thomas Holmes, Chief Inspector of Lifeboats, visited Spurn on 23rd March and all the crew members agreed to serve under the RNLI from 1st May. Formal notices of termination of contracts were sent out to all the crew members at the end of March, to be effective from the last day of April. Signed and sealed copies of the agreement between RNLI and the Humber Conservancy Board were exchanged on 15th May 1911.

The lifeboat station at Spurn passed into the control of RNLI on 1st May 1911 and so brought to an end some three years of dissimulation and dispute. Pye and his crew were able to settle down in the knowledge that their livelihoods were secure and that the work of assisting vessels in distress and saving lives could continue far into the future.

The existence of the Spurn Lifeboat Station owes a great deal to the vision and generosity of Francis Constable who set the whole train of events in motion. His selection of Trinity House to operate the station was sound and responsible for its success. Having accepted Francis Constable's offer Trinity House spent a lot of time, energy and money on maintaining the station and providing all the necessary equipment. Supplies and equipment for the boat were always the best available at the time. Looking back from the end of the twentieth century it is very easy to be critical of the attitude of Trinity House towards the crew members and their families - reluctance to provide relief when times were very hard, rates of pay once the decision had been taken to pay the crew, lack of pensions after long service or illness or injury. When compared with conditions elsewhere at that time Trinity House is seen to be no worse, and probably much better, than other employers. Certainly it is true that many shipowners and merchants had reason to be grateful for the services provided by the lifeboat, but more importantly hundreds of mariners owed their lives to the skill, determination and courage of the lifeboat crew and without the support of Trinity House none of this could have happened.

APPENDIX

Specification for new lifeboat at Spurn, June 1902.

List of crew members.

Service launches by the lifeboat for which documentary evidence can be found.

Steam assistance for which documentary evidence can be found.

Specification for the Building of a NEW LIFE BOAT to be stationed at Spurn for the CORPORATION OF THE TRINITY HOUSE, HULL.

TRINITY HOUSE, HULL,
JUNE, 1902.

D. CHRISTIE,
SURVEYOR.

DIMENSIONS.—Length 34ft. 6in., beam 9ft. 10in., depth at stem 6ft. 4in.—at stern 6ft.—amidships 4ft. 6in.

MATERIAL.—The whole of the material and workmanship to be the best of their respective kinds and in all respects subject to the approval of the Buoyage and Beaconage Committee. The wood used to be perfectly sound, free from sap, shakes, faults, &c., and in full lengths. The timber to be American Rock Elm, Indian Teak, English Oak of light colour, and Scotch Larch as respectively specified. The timbers where necessary to be through bolted, properly fitted and secured. The whole of the fastenings—unless where specified to be in copper—are to be in yellow metal of best quality and not brittle. The Contractor to supply free of cost samples of any material used. To include generally for all incidental labour or material that may be requisite or necessary, whether or not specially referred to, to complete the boat to the true intent of the drawings and specification. Any parts not fully particularized are to be similar to those of the National Life Boat Institution.

MODEL.—The accepted Contractor will have to supply free of cost a Model to Inch Scale, and also full detail working drawings for approval by the Committee. The details of Construction to be estimated for according to the intent of this Specification, but may be subject to any modifications that may be hereafter decided upon.

FRAMING.—Keel, &c., in Elm; viz. keel, sided 4in. to 3½in., moulded 4½in., hogging piece 5in. by 1½in., keelson 3in. by 3in. To include for lead keel to weigh 15 cwt., cast to shape, and properly secured with gun metal straps and bolts. Stem and stern post in teak and oak—3½in. sided, with aprons, &c., properly butted and scarphed.

The framings to be through bolted, 12in. apart at stem and stern, and 18-in. apart along bottom. To fix galv. iron sheaves in gun metal bearings for anchor chain, and for fixing rudder into position. Timbers of Elm, 1¾in. sided, 2in. to 1½in. moulded, notched and secured to keel—14in. timber and space, also floors of oak in every frame space, sided 3in., moulded 3in. to 1½in. continued in one piece across keel to floor at each side—all through fastened. Shelves and stringers—of Oak, 4in. by 1¾in., ½in. copper bolted to timbers, and with galv. iron breast hooks forward and aft.

Gunwale of Elm, 2¼in. by 2½in. rebated for top strake properly secured, and with breast hooks, &c., complete. Diagonal riders—of Oak, two from each end of keel, 2¼in. sided, 3in. to 1½in. moulded up to thwart stringer, all properly halved over stringers and secured.

PLANKING.—All in Teak—gunwale and bilgestrakes 1in., garboard strakes, 1½in., all others ¾in., all properly fitted, bevelled, lapped 1in. and close copper nailed, properly rooved and clenched.

SHEATHING.—To cover the sides up to the deck level, and including the keel, with pure copper sheets (20 oz.) properly lapped, worked and close copper nailed—including furring out the joggles of the face planking to form a level surface.

DECK.—All in Larch or best Red Wood—beams 3in. by 1½in., 14in. centre to centre, beams for trimming 3in. by 2½in., longitudinal stringers 3in. by 4½in. secured at ends with galv. iron plates. The deck planking to be 4in. by 1⅛in. with rebated joints, and without feather edge ends—yellow metal nailed and caulked—the whole being perfectly water-tight. To include for all notching, framing, trimming, &c., necessary. To provide suitable sockets, &c., for masts, and form water-tight listings, hatch-ways well battened and with fasteners, flush handle rings, &c., listings trimming for pumps, valves, &c., and properly notch out against the side timbers.

THWARTS.—Of Oak, 7½in. by 1½in. and 7½in. to 9in. by 2½in. fitted for masts—with three knee brackets and bolted at each end. To provide suitable iron-work for securing masts. Also provide seat boards, and foot stretchers both sides of each thwart so as to pull ahead or astern.

BOLLARDS.—Oak—one at each of the four corners of the raised casings, each shaped down to 5in. square, brass capped, kneed to the gunwale and through bolted. Also one similar to the above but 6in. square, made portable, well secured and with suitable iron clasps and sockets.

RUDDER AND TILLER.—Oak with gun metal fittings, including braces, telescope socket, 1⅛in, pin, &c., complete, with provision for easily unshipping, &c.

FENDER.—Of best quality solid cork in painted canvas, properly shaped and secured.

CASINGS, &c.—In Larch.—To provide and fix suitable bearers, partitions, upright framings, &c., for the whole of the air tanks, with means of detaching same when required. To form the close boarded boxings, with dove-tailed angles, for the two centre air tanks as shewn. The tanks along the sides and under the fore and aft thwarts to have detachable uprights, &c., for keeping same in position. The side tanks to be covered over with lattice gratings as shewn, suitably secured and supported. The two end framings and lockers to be made perfectly water-tight, and to have screw ventilator gratings. The locker doors, &c., to be properly framed, hung and fitted with brass locks, and the wide thwarts under the same are to be fixed similarly to the other thwarts.

COPPER FITTINGS.---In pure copper, properly brazed, &c.---Ten automatic escape valves, 5½in. diam. (14 B. W. G. copper), flanged ends, properly braced and made water-tight at floor and deck, and with gun metal heads. Two hand pumps 2½in. diam., 1¼in. tail pipe (18 B W G copper) flush with deck, well braced and with gun metal screw caps. Four life rods, ⅝in. diam, copper rod and gun metal studs, viz.: two along the keel and one along each gunwale.

AIR TANKS.---In pure copper (22 B. W. G.), properly brazed, &c., and with straps necessary for fixing. To be shaped as necessary to fill their respective places. There are to be tanks as shewn along the two sides, and under the fore and aft wide thwarts, and also the whole length and width of the space under the deck. The two long centre air tanks to be fitted so as to be easily converted into water ballast tanks, the other tanks under the deck to be fitted so as to be clear of the valve and pump pipes, and none to exceed 2ft. 9in. in length each. Each tank to be tested and to receive two coats of paint before being fixed in position.

CONTINGENCIES.—Include in tender the sum of Eighty Pounds to be afterwards deducted in full for the purchase of sails, masts, and oars, by the Buoyage Committee.

PAINTING.—To stop and prime and give two coats of paint on all parts inside and outside. When completed to have two more finishing coats. To letter on bows "Spurn Lifeboat."

GENERALLY.—All exposed wood-work to be finished smooth. Include generally for any other necessary fittings or construction to render the whole complete, whether or not herein particularized. To also provide and fix suitable fittings as follows, viz: gun-metal row locks, fastenings for masts, sails, and ropes, looped life lines and knotted cords, two life buoys and lines, marine glasses, two axes, two mops, two buckets, bolts, eyes, pins, deck plates, anchor, cable, cable fastening, six cork fenders, &c.

COMPLETION.—At completion the boat to be subjected to such tests as may be ordered by the Committee, and when approved of to be delivered to her station at Spurn.

N.B.—The copy of Plans and Specification to be returned with the tender.

CREW MEMBERS

Before 1845 the record is incomplete. In some cases the starting date for service is simply the earliest date on which a given name appears in the documents. From 1845 onwards the list is thought to be complete and accurate.

John Coulter	14th July 1810 appointed Master, but never served.
Robert Richardson	14th July 1810 appointed Mate; 25th August 1810 Master - November 1841.
Joseph Barron	September 1809 - by April 1819.
Thomas Bird	September 1809 - by April 1819.
Francis Dibney	September 1809 - by April 1819.
William Gray	September 1809 - by October 1822.
George Heath	September 1809 - by April 1819.
William Hodge	September 1809 - by April 1819.
Samuel Hodgson	September 1809 - by October 1822.
Samuel Longhorn	September 1809 - by October 1822.
William Longhorn	September 1809 - dismissed summer 1811.
Richard Shields	September 1809 - by April 1819.
Peter Wilson	September 1809 - by April 1819.
Robert Bird	November 1810 - dismissed summer 1811.
Jonathan Burrell	November 1810 - dismissed summer 1811.
Thomas Carr	November 1810 - dismissed summer 1811.
William Clapham	November 1810 - dismissed summer 1811.
John Cole	November 1810 - by April 1819.
William Hodgson	November 1810 - by April 1819.
William Johnson	November 1810 - dismissed summer 1811.
John Rawson	November 1810 - dismissed summer 1811.
Edward Tennyson	November 1810 - by April 1819.
Edward Wilson	November 1810 - dismissed summer 1811.
William Wilson	November 1810 - dismissed summer 1811.
George Wood	1811 - by April 1819.
Charles Tennison	March 1811 - by April 1819.
F. Wilson	March 1811 - by April 1819.
Thomas Jacobs	1814 - by April 1819.
John Loten	December 1818 - by October 1822.
William Marshall	December 1818 - by October 1822.
Robert Branton	April 1819 - by October 1822.
Thomas Grant	April 1819 - by October 1822.
Robert Johnson	April 1819 - by October 1822.
John Lawty	April 1819 - by October 1822.
Edward Suggett	April 1819 - December 1841.

Thomas Wilson	April 1819 - by October 1822.
James Megginson	April 1819 - December 1841.
William Richardson	April 1819 - discharged September 1842 because of age.
John Harrison	August 1819; Mate by August 1828 - 1837. Died after long illness.
Robert Barker	September 1819; appointed Mate September 1837; was retired January 1842.
James Nixon	November 1820 - by October 1822.
Thomas Lowerey	October 1822; discharged November 1822.
Richard Cook	October 1822; discharged November 1822.
Christopher Thornton	October 1822; discharged November 1822.
John Bradley	October 1822 - 1833.
Theodore Jackson	October 1822; discharged November 1822.
Thomas Megginson	October 1822; discharged April 1844; re-appointed January 1846 - November 1855.
James Christie	November 1822 - by 1831.
Richard Lee	November 1822 - by 1831.
George Robinson	November 1823; was retired December 1841.
George Bradley	November 1823 - 1833.
Francis Reash	November 1823 - drowned March 1833, not on service.
Henry Spendlove	1824; discharged September 1824.
William Watson	1824; discharged September 1824; re-appointed 1842/43 - ?
William Swift	April 1829 - December 1834.
Robert Hunter	September 1832 - January 1842.
Joseph Revel	1832 - 1842
James Bradley	March 1833 - 1834.
William Brown	1835 - March 1836.
Copling	1835 - October 1836.
John Ezard	1835 - was retired 1841.
Summerville	1835 - October 1836.
John Grant	July 1835 - by September 1835.
William Coupland	September 1835; resigned April 1837 because of ill health.
William Laycock	October 1836; was retired December 1841; re-appointed February 1842; Mate 1843; resigned June 1853.
Benjamin Whitehouse	October 1837;was retired December 1841; re-appointed October 1848 - January 1851.
John Myers	December 1841 - March 1842.

Joseph Davey	January 1842 appointed Master; discharged February 1843; re-appointed as crew July 1853; resigned June 1856.
Robert Brown	March 1843 appointed Master; resigned November 1848.
William Watson	November 1843 - October 1844.
John Branton	November 1843; drowned on service October 1850.
Marmaduke Woolas	November 1843 - July 1845.
Joseph Anderson	November 1843 - January 1851.
Robert Ringrose	November 1843 - October 1844.
William Clark	November 1843 - July 1845.
William Hurren	November 1843; was appointed Mate by April 1850; discharged February 1851.
James Bentley	November 1843 - July 1851.
William Wood	April 1844 - July 1855.
Henry Bugg	September 1844 - 1847.
Stephen Wilson	October 1844 - 1847.
John Barnby	January 1845 - February 1857.
John Hardy	January 1845 - by August 1846.
Richard Megginson	1847 - November 1850. (Son of Thomas)
Michael Hansley Welburn	November 1848 appointed Master; died March 1853.
John Welburn	January 1850; appointed Mate by March 1851; resigned March 1852; died March 1852.
James Barnby	October 1850 - July 1857; re-appointed April 1858 - March 1877.
Thomas Morrill	March 1851 - March 1852.
William Maxwell	March 1851; discharged January 1853.
George Goldsack	March 1851 - December 1851.
John Hill	March 1851 - September 1853.
George Scott	January 1852; appointed Mate March 1852; resigned July 1853.
John Coombs	January 1852; discharged January 1853; re-appointed June 1853; drowned on service November 1855.
Joseph Dimmack	May 1852 - November 1853.
John Calvert	May 1853 appointed Master; resigned December 1853.
Richard Parrott	April 1853 - September 1853; appointed Master October 1856; resigned June 1857.
James Taylor	April 1853 - November 1855.
William Thirsk	April 1853 - November 1854.
James Mumby	October 1853 - September 1865.
George Grant	December 1853 appointed Master; resigned August 1856
George Young	November 1854 - April 1857.

Henry Holmes	May 1855; November 1855 drowned on service.
Richard Palmer	October 1855; discharged November 1855.
James Luddington	October 1855; discharged November 1855.
William Long	November 1855; Mate; acting Master August - September 1856; discharged November 1858.
Edward Banham	November 1855 - June 1856.
Charles Ameers	November 1855 - June 1856.
William Watson	November 1855 - June 1856.
William Davy	November 1855 - September 1856.
Henry Smith	November 1855 - June 1856.
Samuel Smith	November 1855 - June 1856; re-appointed August 1857; died April 1858. (Not on service).
Thomas Wallace	November 1855 - June 1856.
George Young	June 1856; discharged April 1857.
James Mearns	June 1856; discharged November 1858.
Robert Rosindale	June 1856 - July 1857.
John Marshall	June 1856 - November 1856; re-appointed August 1857; died July 1865 (Not on service).
George Marshall	June 1856; discharged April 1857.
Francis Wilkinson	September 1856 - November 1856.
Frederick Wilson	September 1856 - November 1856.
George Watson	September 1856 - November 1856.
William Dobson	September 1856 - November 1856.
Josiah Marrat	November 1856 - July 1857.
Francis Gardiner	November 1856 - December 1856.
William Gilbert	November 1856 - January 1858.
Compass Hawksworth	December 1856 - May 1857.
Francis Daltry	January 1857; discharged June 1858.
William Hawksworth	January 1857 - July 1861.
Fewson Hopper	April 1857; Mate by 1864; Master October 1865; resigned December 1877 to become keeper of Saltend Light.
George Agar	May 1857 - December 1857.
William Willis	August 1857 appointed Master; resigned to become lighthouse keeper.
William Todd	January 1858; died June 1858 (Not on service).
Richard Bell	January 1858; discharged June 1858.
Henry Brown	July 1858; discharged November 1859.
Henry Pickering	July 1858 - September 1867.
Robert Tennison	July 1858; discharged November 1879 because of age; died August 1887.
William Stanford	December 1858 - April 1860.
John King	December 1858; Mate; discharged November 1859.

Robert Balfour	November 1859 - May 1865.
John H. Drust	November 1859 - June 1861.
Robert Rounding	July 1861 - February 1864.
John Parrott	July 1861 - February 1867; re-appointed February 1869 - March 1877.
Richard Bland	August 1861 - May 1866.
James Pindar	February 1864 - August 1866; re-appointed February 1891 - October 1893.
John Best	May 1864; Mate 1865; discharged January 1877.
William Ablett	July 1865 - November 1872.
Thomas Winson	December 1865 - February 1869; re-appointed September 1873; Mate March 1877; Master January 1878; resigned March 1894 to become keeper of Thorngumbald lights.
Thomas Hodgson	May 1866 - March 1877.
Edward Wheldrake	August 1866; discharged March 1877;awarded RNLI Silver Medal April 1877 for rescue December 1876.
Robert Hodgson	March 1867 - August 1867.
John Liversedge	August 1867; discharged July 1876; re-appointed, became Mate; discharged July 1893.
John Weatherill	September 1867 - September 1873.
Joseph Wilkinson	September 1872; discharged March 1877.
Thomas Hurren	September 1873
James Hopper	October 1873 - October 1883; re-appointed February 1891 - October 1891.
William Bacchus	March 1877 - October 1883; re-appointed April 1885 - February 1891.
Edward Curtis	March 1877 - December 1892.
Joseph Little	March 1877 - September 1886.
George Fisher	March 1877 - August 1881; re-appointed October 1883 - April 1885.
James Aldridge Bishop	March 1877 - July 1892; re-appointed July 1893 as Mate
Joshua Hudson	January 1878 - October 1883.
William Hopper	May 1879 - October 1883; re-appointed February 1891 - October 1891;re-appointed March 1894; appointed Mate January 1897.
Francis Day	August 1881 - October 1883; re-appointed September 1886 - February 1891.
Joseph Norman	September 1883 - February 1891.

John Spauls	October 1883; discharged August 1889; re-appointed March 1894; discharged February 1896.
Seaman Davinson	October 1883 - October 1890.
Thomas Hodgson Jarratt	October 1883 - February 1891.
Robert Davison	August 1889 - October 1890.
Charles Crask	October 1890 - July 1892; re-appointed December 1892; discharged March 1895; re-appointed November 1895; discharged May 1898.
James Pinder	February 1891 - October 1893.
George William Liversedge	February 1891; Mate 1892; discharged March 1894; re-appointed March 1897 - March 1902
Frederick Hopper	March 1891; January 1892 resigned to become Naval Reserve Man January 1892; re-appointed October 1893;
John Henry Branton	October 1891; discharged March 1894; re-appointed January 1897 - April 1892.
William Chapman	December 1891 - September 1898.
Thomas Charles Winson	January 1892 (son of Master); Mate 1894; resigned January 1897.
Charles Peacock Rispin	July 1892; discharged March 1894.
James Liversedge	September 1892; discharged March 1894.
David Pye	March 1894 appointed Master - July 1912.
Robert George Little	March 1894 - March 1898.
Herbert John Morrill	March 1894 - November 1895. left because of wife's illness.
William Henry Hogg	March 1894 - October 1905. Left because of ill health.
David Henry Craske	March 1896 - October 1902.
Richard Elijah Britton	May 1898 - August 1900.
George Stephenson	September 1898; discharged June 1906.
Richard Major	September 1900 - 1909.
William Curtis	March 1902
Frank Lilford Raspin	April 1902
Robert Cross	October 1902 - 1910.
Benjamin Cross	October 1905 - 1910.
D. Quinton	June 1906 - July 1906.
Thomas Edward Blythe	1909
William Henry Holborn	July 1906
John Thomas Bishop	1910
George Curtis	1910

When the Life Boat Station at Spurn was taken over by the Humber Conservancy Board on January 1st 1908 the Crew Members were

David Pye
Frederick Hopper
William Hopper
Richard Major
William Curtis
Frank Lilford Raspin
Robert Cross
Benjamin Cross
William Henry Holborn
James Aldridge Bishop

Sometime during 1909 Richard Major left the service and was replaced by Thomas Edward Blythe.

Sometime during 1910 Robert Cross and Benjamin Cross left the service and were replaced by John Thomas Bishop and George Curtis.

The Crew when the Spurn Life Boat Station was taken over by RNLI was

David Pye
Frederick Hopper
William Hopper
William Curtis
George Curtis
James Aldridge Bishop
John Thomas Bishop
Frank Lilford Raspin
William Henry Holborn
Thomas Edward Blythe

Masters of Spurn Lifeboat

John Coulter	14th July 1810. Never served.
Robert Richardson	25th August 1810 - 3rd December 1841.
Joseph Davey	4th December 1841 - 13th February 1843.
Robert Brown	14th February 1843 - 31st October 1848.
Michael Hansley Welburn	1st November 1848 - April 1853.
John Calvert	1st May 1853 - 17th December 1853.
George Grant	18th December 1853 - 31st July 1856.
William Long,	Mate acted as Master.
Richard Parrott	1st October 1856 - 30th July 1857.
William Willis	1st August 1857 - 30th September 1865.
Fewson Hopper	1st October 1865 - 31st December 1877.
Thomas Winson	1st January 1878 - 1st March 1894.
David Pye	14th March 1894 - July 1912.

Lifeboat Launches

November	15	1810	John and Charlotte of Newcastle - assisted, towed off and took to Grimsby.
November	21	1810	Young John - sloop - saved three lives.
December	11	1810	Jane - Captain and crew saved - five in all.
October	4	1811	Endeavour - brig - Captain and crew saved - eight in all.
November	15	1811	A sloop from Lincolnshire - assisted.
December	7	1811	A galliot from Hull - assisted.
February	8	1813	William, of Boston - stranded - assisted.
March	21	1813	Elizabeth, brig - assisted.
March	22	1813	Juno of Whitby - assisted.
July	8	1813	William, of Boston - assisted.
October	27	1813	Margaret and Jane, of Sunderland - assisted.
November		1813	Sir Peter - assisted.
November	29	1813	Amity, of Shields - assisted - crew saved in their own boat.
February	15	1814	Amity, of Lynn - assisted crew.
		1815	Spring - assisted.
October	4	1815	Rawcliffe - assisted.
		1815	A Sunderland brig - assisted - saved ten plus one pilot.
November	25	1815	Bell - assistance refused.
November	29	1815	Amity, of Shields - wrecked - crew saved in their own boat.
January	2	1816	Adventure, brig of South Shields - assisted.
January	20	1816	Gambier, brig - assisted.
April	12	1816	Blackbird, brig - assisted.
October	24	1816	Shap Branch - assisted - crew saved.
November	22	1816	Prince of Wales - assisted - saved eleven.
November	25	1816	Ann - assisted.
November	12	1817	John and Elizabeth - assisted.
October	23	1818	Royal Charlotte - brig assisted - crew saved.
October	27	1818	Robert Burn - sloop - assisted.
		1818	Provident - brig - total wreck - saved twelve.
February	21	1819	Isobella - brig - assisted.
February	21	1819	Industry - Captain refused assistance - ship then sank.
		1819	Hero - brig - assisted.
March	1	1819	Little Cherub - assisted.
October	23	1819	Kinlock - sloop - assisted.
		1819	Blayds - brig - assisted.
January	6	1820	Isabella, of Hull - assisted - sixteen men and Captain taken off, later returned.

January	10	1820	John, of London - assisted - crew saved in their own boat.
		1820	Galliot - assisted - crew saved in their own boat.
		1820	Hope, of London - seven men saved by the signals from the Life Boat.
		1820	Amity, of Shields - crew came ashore in their own boat.
		1820	Ocean, of Faversham - crew saved in their own boat.
		1820	Amity - Captain and seven men saved by Life Boat.
January	21	1820	Minerva - wrecked - all crew lost - could not reach her because of sea and tide.
		1820	Friends Adventure - crew drowned.
February	24	1820	Dranbuse - assisted.
		1820	Isabella - crew saved themselves.
March	12	1820	Un-named ship - tried to assist - crew came ashore in their own boat.
		1820	Ewe Bank Pilot - saved by Life Boat.
		1820	Phoebe, sloop - Captain and crew saved .
		1820	Margaret and Jane - Captain and seven men taken out by Life Boat.
October	3	1820	Orwell, of Ipswich - tried to assist - Master refused assistance.
November	30	1820	Truro, of North Shields - saved ten men - crew and Master and much cargo.
March	24	1821	Un-named sloop from Ipswich - assisted but she sank.
June	8	1821	Thomas, transport from London - saved fifty seven including troops, crew, two women and one child.
		1821	Treuza (Preuza ?) - Captain and crew of ten saved.
		1821	Prince of Wales - saved twelve men.
November	8	1821	Tartar, sloop - assisted.
December	7	1821	Better Luck Still, brig - assisted - saved crew of ten plus one pilot.
		1822	Linae - assisted.
February	12	1822	Royal Oak - assisted.
February	12	1822	Rambler - assisted.
February	12	1822	Hazard - assisted.
February	14	1822	Endeavour, sloop - assisted.
November	20	1822	London, of North Shields - assistance refused.
November	27	1822	Thomas, sloop of Sunderland - assisted.
November	27	1822	Lund, brig - assisted.
October	11	1823	Un-named brig - lost with all hands - no Life Boat crew available.
November	22	1823	Mary, brig of Blythe - saved crew of seven and Master.
May	3	1824	Two Brothers, galliot - assisted.

September	25	1824	Alexander, brig of Shields - tried to assist, but failed.
October	10	1824	Marshall Wellington, of London - took off Captain and part of crew - saved eighteen.
November	25	1825	Superb, smack of Leith - saved seventy crew and passengers.
October	29	1826	Squirrel, brig of Sunderland - tried to assist - wind too strong.
November	29	1827	Salacia - assisted.
January	5	1828	George, brig of Newcastle - assisted.
December	19	1828	Pleiades, brig of Sunderland - assisted.
January	5	1829	John Craig, schooner of Sunderland, saved four men.
November	28	1829	Thornton - tried to assist - beaten by weather.
December	25	1829	Thornton, brig of Shields - assisted - saved ten men.
January	31	1830	Sisters, schooner of Perth - assisted.
September	12	1830	Ann, brig of Shields - assisted. First record of Life Boat being towed out by any steam ship - the Prince Frederick.
November	3	1830	Leeds, brig of Newcastle - saved crew, ten men in all.
December	2	1830	Rinswell (Runswick ?) of Hull - assisted.
December	13	1830	Fortitude, ship of London - saved all crew, eighteen men.
August	31	1833	No 1 Pilot Boat of Hull - saved nine pilots.
November	28	1833	Foreign galiot - saved six men.
November		1833	Mary Ann, brig of Gainsborough - saved seven men.
February	23	1835	Un-named schooner - could not assist because Life Boat had broken from her moorings. Mate of schooner drowned.
January		1838	Fame - saved nine men.
February	24	1838	Edgar, brig - crew saved in their own boat. On same occasion two other brigs which Life Boat was unable to reach because of the violence of the weather and sea.
March	20	1838	Un-named sloop - could not assist - crew of three drowned in Humber.
November	26	1838	Catharina, sloop from Altona - assisted.
January	7	1839	Six vessels - unable to assist because Life Boat had broken adrift. Richard Russell - came on shore at Spurn - got crew safe on shore.
December	27	1839	Triphenal, sloop - stood by - no assistance given.
March	18	1840	Mercury, brig of London - assistance refused.
April	10	1842	Rose, sloop of Hull - assisted - crew got ashore in their own boat.

January	10	1843	Rose, sloop of Boston - assisted - Master and Mate taken from rigging then returned to ship later.
February	18	1843	Un-named vessel - went to assist - tide too strong - vessel got off safely.
February	28	1843	Elizabeth, schooner of Hartlepool - burned tar and hoisted signals of distress, but no Life Boat or help.
May	19	1843	Un-named vessel - went to assist - crew taken off by Pilot Boat.
July	12	1843	Rapid, sloop of North Shields grounded on Banks - stood by.
February	22	1844	Express, of Hull - assisted.
March	9	1844	Thomas and Mary, sloop - assisted.
March	10	1844	William, brig of Sunderland - assisted.
February	24	1845	Squirrel, brig of Whitby - assisted off beach.
August	24	1845	Betsey, schooner of Yarmouth) six ships' crews Ark, schooner of Yarmouth:) at Spurn asking Francis, of Ipswich:) Trinity House for Nautilus, of Boston:) blankets but no Providence, of Boston:) reports of rescue Un-named ship:)
March	21	1846	Duchess of Beaufort, of Brixham - went to assist - could find nothing - crew got ashore in their own boat - Master drowned.
April	5	1846	George and Thomas, schooner - saved crew of six.
November	11	1846	Cupid, schooner of Newcastle - assisted.
December	24	1846	Sun Flower, schooner of Harwich - assisted - saved materials.
December	5	1848	Genoa Packet, brig - assisted - crew of five got ashore on their own.
April	17	1849	Enterprize, schooner of Peterfield - assisted - crew abandoned her and got ashore by themselves - two men and one boy.
January	11	1850	Eagle, sloop of Brancaster - tried to assist - beaten by sea - crew landed safely - Life Boat discharged cargo.
April	5	1850	Un-named foreign schooner - tried to assist but Pilot Boat got there first.
October	22	1850	Alert, fishing smack of Hull - saved five of crew
October	25	1850	Cumberland, brig of Newcastle - saved five of crew, but one Life Boatman, John Branton, drowned as Tender overturned - borrowed a fishing smack and saved remainder of crew - nine in all - Master of fishing smack drowned.

January	2	1851	W.W.Gooding, sloop - assisted.
March	21	1851	Celerity, sloop - assisted and saved two hands from the rigging.
March	28	1851	Ann, brig - assisted.
June	13	1851	Michael Hanley Welburn, Master, saved four of the Life Boat Crew when they were overturned when assisting a gravel vessel off the beach.
September	25	1851	Dove, schooner - assisted.
September	26	1851	Ant, schooner.
October	17	1851	G.G., sloop - saved the crew by means of ropes.
November	16	1851	Saved three hands off the Banks.
January	4	1852	Charlie, sloop - wrecked near Kilnsea.
February	4	1852	Coin, schooner - assisted off beach by workmen before Life Boat could arrive.
August	26	1852	Favourite, sloop - assisted.
September	19	1852	Liberty, schooner of Leith - assisted.
October	2	1852	Ann, sloop - saved crew, then discharged her and got her off.
October	26	1852	Schooner and Billy Boy in distress.
November	14	1852	Neptune, steamer - assisted.
November	19	1852	Blessing, Wildblood, Chance, Brunny and un-named brig - assisted.
December	25	1852	Good Intent, schooner - assisted.
January	6	1853	Good Intent, lighter, assisted.
January	10	1853	Ann Moore, brig of Shields - assisted.
February	25	1853	Amazon, ship of Hull - assisted.
May	22	1853	Arendina, Dutch sloop - assisted.
June	12	1853	Three Sisters, sloop of Grimsby - broke up on beach.
August	23	1853	Un-named Dutch galliot - went to assist - not required.
October	10	1853	Ann, brig of South Shields - assisted.
November	5	1853	Nars Nysted, schooner - sunk on Trinity Sand.
November	5	1853	Acorn, brig of Guernsey - assisted.
November	28	1853	Brittania, brig of Hartlepool - assisted.
December	14	1853	Un-named sloop - assisted.
December	30	1853	Medea, H.M.steamer - assisted.
January	4	1854	Un-named schooner foundered - all hands lost.
January	25	1854	Isabella, brig of South Shields - foundered - crew got ashore in their own boat.
February	18	1854	Scandinavia, steamer - went to assist - not required.
			Un-named French lugger - all hands saved by a steamer.
			Dahlia, sloop - assisted - all hands saved.
March	30	1854	A sloop sunk near Clee Ness.
April	21	1854	Greyhound, schooner - went to assist - not required.

June	26	1854	A gravel lighter foundered - all hands saved.
November	2	1854	William Chapman, brig of Hartlepool - went to assist - not required.
December	15	1854	Un-named schooner - assisted.
December	31	1854	Centenary, brig of North Shields - went to assist - assistance refused.
January	22	1855	Tiberius, brig - assisted.
March	22	1855	Un-named schooner - went to assist - schooner got off before Life Boat arrived.
May	29	1855	Un-named fishing smack - assisted.
October	30	1855	Un-named barque - assisted.
November	19	1855	Zabina, schooner of Ipswich - assisted, but two Life Boatmen drowned.
December	6	1855	Dutch galliot - went to assist - assistance refused.
December	28	1855	William and Jane, brig of Sunderland - assisted.
March	2	1856	Mestry, smack - went to assist - assistance refused.
April	27	1856	Water Witch, schooner of London - went to assist - assistance refused.
December	26	1856	Earl of Wemyss, brig - assisted - saved crew of eight men.
January	6	1857	Un-named vessel - assisted.
August	17	1857	A Prussian barque run down by the Scandinavian steamer and sunk.
October	3	1857	Un-named sloop - went to assist - not required.
October	17	1857	Lange Sund, foreign barque - went to assist - not required.
October	23	1857	Un-named sloop - assisted.
October	25	1857	Aegir - assisted - took off crew who were later returned.
March	2	1858	Small foreign vessel wrecked on Inner Binks.
April	1	1858	Tulloch Castle, barque - assisted.
April	2	1858	Stockton Packet, brig of Stockton - assisted - took off crew.
May	27	1858	Saucy Lass, schooner of London - assisted - crew saved in their own boat.
June	3	1858	Elma, schooner of Porsground - assisted.
July	21	1858	Wansbeck, brig of North Shields - assisted.
July	25	1858	William, sloop of Lynn - assisted - crew got ashore themselves.
August	25	1858	Un-named schooner - stood by all night - assistance refused.
November	4	1858	Pegasus, schooner - went to assist - declined assistance.
November	5	1858	Volante, brig of Rochester - assisted her and three other un-named brigs.

November	17	1858	Four Gebroeders, galliot - went to assist - assistance declined.
January	17	1859	Change, schooner of Hull - assisted.
February	9	1859	Miaza, brig of Sunderland - assisted - crew saved in their own boat.
April	30	1859	Glencairn of South Shields, foundered at night - crew saved in their own boat.
November	7	1859	Rebecca and Elizabeth, schooner of Hartlepool - and took off crew.
November	25	1859	St.Hilda, brig of Hartlepool - assisted and took off crew.
December	20	1859	Amalthea, barque of Newcastle - assisted.
January	22	1860	Tranby, brig possibly of Whitby or North Shields had been abandoned - tried to assist but she sank later saved stores.
October	2	1860	Un-named smack - tried to assist but Tender overturned - later smack got off by itself.
November	18	1860	Un-named trawler - sank at night unseen - all hands lost.
January	16	1861	Industry, trawling smack of Hull - took off crew of five - returned later and assisted.
February	9	1861	Active, brig - assisted.
February	18	1861	Un-named schooner - went to assist but she came off before Life Boat arrived.
February	21	1861	Countess of Zetland, brig - went to assist but could not.
March	4	1861	Oak, schooner of London - went to assist - not required.
July	23	1861	Good Intent, ballast lighter of Hull - saved crew by line and assisted.
September	27	1861	Clementina, schooner of Lyme Regis - took off crew and assisted.
November	2	1861	Hotspur, steam tug of Hull - total wreck.
			Captain Cator'sYacht - assisted.
			Endeavour, schooner of Bridlington - assisted.
			Un-named ballast lighter of Hull - assisted.
January	20	1862	Heroine, brig of Shoreham - took off crew - assisted - to no avail.
May	4	1862	Dart, schooner of Sunderland - took off crew - assisted - wreck.
November	19	1862	Thomas and Martha, schooner of Yarmouth - took off crew - assisted - wreck.
November	30	1862	Paulina, brig of Arbroath - wreck - crew abandoned her.
January	5	1863	John and George, sloop of Goole - assisted.
January	27	1863	Un-named brig - on fire and sank - went to assist
August	19	1863	Pamona, sloop of Hull - sank at night unknown.

November	8	1863	Un-named vessel - went to assist.
December	3	1863	Neptune, French sloop - ran ashore abandoned - assisted.
December	3	1863	Levant, Norwegian barque - assisted.
			Several other un-named boats - assisted.
March	6	1864	Rose, schooner of Grangemouth - assisted - took off two men.
September	14	1864	Mary Ann, sloop - assisted.
October	2	1864	Allison, smack of Hull - took off crew and assisted.
October	24	1864	Un-named vessel - went to assist - not required.
December	20	1864	Reclaim, galliot of Schleswig Holstein - assisted.
October	28	1865	Superior, schooner of Navrin, N.Wales - rescued five men and one boy.
November	9	1865	Frolic, smack of Grimsby - assisted.
December	9	1865	Alabama, barque - assisted.
January	2	1866	Wave, schooner of Lowestoft - took off crew.
			Pearl, schooner of Honfleur - saved three men, one woman and three children - assisted.
January	22	1866	Hopewell, schooner - assisted.
June	4	1866	Dispatch, steamer of Hull - went to assist - not required.
June	28	1866	Pilot Cutter No.9 - went to assist - not required.
December	7	1866	Nelson, brig - assisted.
			Rising Sun, brigantine - assisted.
			Mary Ann, schooner - took off crew.
December	12	1866	Un-named smack - went to assist - assistance refused.
January	6	1867	Un-named vessel - possibly the Alkali of galliot of Goole - went to assist - unable to do so - already sunk with all hands.
January	10	1867	Un-named brig - went to assist - assistance refused.
January	16	1867	Un-named vessel - went to assist - unable to do so because of sea and weather.
February	21	1867	Sarah, brig of Whitby - assisted.
May	27	1867	Killarney, steamer - went to assist - assistance refused.
November	30	1867	Baltic, sloop of Grimsby - assisted.
December	2	1867	Fidelity, schooner - assisted.
January	19	1868	Newcastle, vessel of Newcastle - went to assist - assistance refused.
January	31	1868	Echo, barque - assisted - crew taken off by tug.
February	1	1868	Henry, schooner of Goole - assisted.
			Kyanite, barque - assisted.
July	24	1868	Fredrica, brigantine of Danzig - stood by and assisted - took off crew of six - later returned.

November	10	1868	Jason, smack of Hull - saved five - stood by - Master drowned.
January	2	1869	Cautious, vessel of Whitstable - assisted.
January	29	1869	Betsey, keel - assisted by putting out fire in cargo of coal.
February	8	1869	Eliza, brig of Shoreham - assisted.
March	19	1869	Minnie, smack - assisted.
March	20	1869	Un-named brig - went to assist - assistance refused.
March	21	1869	Nelly, of South Shields - assisted crew who landed in their own boat.
August	19	1869	Plummet, smack of Hull - went to assist - not required.
September	5	1869	James Clay, smack of Brixham - took off crew - returned next day.
October	20	1869	Alert, of Arbroath - went to assist - not required.
November	13	1869	De Salabey, barque - went to assist - assistance refused.
February	14	1870	Bause, brig of Sunderland - went to assist - not required.
March	3	1870	Josephine, schooner of Malden - assisted - took off crew - crew returned later.
January	16	1871	Traveller, sloop - saved crew of three.
February	10	1871	Fortune Teller, schooner of Fowey - saved crew of six.
March	26	1871	Jane Bonfore, schooner - went to assist - assistance refused.
August	8	1871	Echo, fishing yacht of Lowestoft - went to assist - not required.
February	12	1872	Myrtle, schooner of Chichester - lost with all hands - could not assist.
February	14	1872	Frances, steamship of London - crew saved in their own boat or a fishing smack - could not assist.
April	25	1872	Fido, steamer of Hull - went to assist -assistance refused.
July	14	1872	Un-named schooner - went to assist - assistance refused.
September	25	1872	Ariel, schooner - assisted.
September	27	1872	Henry, schooner - assisted.
November	11	1872	Maria, schooner - assisted and took off the crew.
November	23	1872	Elizabeth, schooner of Teignmouth - saved crew of six and assisted.
January	19	1873	John Read - went to assist - not required.
March	16	1873	Aberdeenshire, steamer of Hull - saved ten of crew - three men refused to leave and were drowned - assisted.
September	29	1873	Swanwich, fishing smack of Grimsby - went to assist - not required.
November	23	1873	Commodore, schooner of Jersey - went to assist - not required.

December	28	1873	Onward, brigantine of Plymouth - went to assist - assistance refused.
February	11	1874	Shamrock, steamer of Hull - went to assist - not required.
March	16	1874	Artos, steamer of Hull - stood by.
March	21	1874	Altofts, steamer of Hull - stood by.
June	10	1874	Good Desire, of Colchester - ship lost - crew landed in own boat.
June	19	1874	Victory, smack of Hull - assisted.
December	7	1874	Harriet, smack of Grimsby - assisted - crew saved in their own boat.
August	31	1875	Un-named steamer - went to assist - assistance refused along with name of ship.
November	13	1875	Elizabeth and Susan, of Yarmouth - saved crew of four men.
November	14	1875	Martin - crew saved in their own boat - vessel sank. Un-named vessel - assisted - pumped out and towed to Grimsby.
November	19	1875	Joanne, fishing smack of Grimsby - assisted.
December	15	1875	Golden Horn, steamer of Newcastle - assisted.
February	4	1876	Undaunted, smack of Grimsby - saved crew of six.
April	13	1876	Un-named vessel - went to assist - beaten by wind and sea - vessel sank before Life Boat arrived.
August	17	1876	Constantia, Norwegian barque - assisted.
December	8	1876	Haze, smack of Hull - assisted.
December	9	1876	Hannah, fishing smack of Grimsby - assisted.
December	14	1876	Un-named steamer - went to assist but she had got off the bank.
December	25	1876	Grace Darling, sloop of Goole - saved three men - Edward Weldrake was awarded RNLI silver medal for his bravery.
January	20	1877	Queen Adelaide, brigantine of Lynn - took off the crew.
February	7	1877	Verona, barque - went to assist - not required.
April	19	1877	Start, smack of Grimsby - assisted.
June	13	1877	William Varney, schooner - went to assist - not required.
October	15	1877	Un-named brigantine - went to assist - steam tug arrived first.
December	14	1877	Autumnia, schooner of Exeter - assisted.
December	29	1877	Bertie, schooner of Bristol - went to assist - not required.
February	3	1878	Went to investigate flaring lights - found nothing.
February	12	1878	United, steam tug - went to assist - not required.

April	8	1878	Earnest, fishing smack of Hull - assisted and took off crew.
			Freedom, schooner of Fowey - saved crew.
September	1	1878	Myrtle, steam pleasure yacht of Hull - assisted.
September	25	1878	Three Sisters, lugger of Lowestoft - stood by.
			Florence Nightingale, lugger of Lowestoft - stood by.
November	1	1878	Neptune, brigantine of Sunderland - assisted.
November	8	1878	Un-named brig - went to assist - found her to be abandoned.
			Triumph, schooner of Liverpool - went to assist - assistance refused.
November	16	1878	Un-named brigantine on fire - went to assist - found her to be abandoned.
November	16	1878	Marie, German brig of Barth - assisted.
			Agricola, brig of Aberdeen - assisted.
November	18	1878	Un-named barque sunk in collision. (Deerfoot ?)
January	8	1879	Billow, trawling smack of Grimsby - went to assist - assistance refused.
March	13	1879	Wanderer, trawling smack of Grimsby - crew saved in their own boat - could not assist - became total wreck.
March	18	1879	Sarah King, brigantine of Portsmouth - went to assist - not required.
March	22	1879	Reliance, cod fishing smack of Grimsby - saved crew of eleven - became total wreck.
April	27	1879	Diamanten, Norwegian brig of Arendal - assisted.
April	28	1879	Oliver Cromwell, fishing smack of Grimsby - went to assist - not required.
May	5	1879	New Hope, sloop of Hull - assisted.
August	23	1879	Un-named steam boat - went to assist - not required.
September	6	1879	Un-named small yacht - assisted.
September	10	1879	Ulysses, iron fishing smack of Hull - assisted.
October	16	1879	Ann Sins, fishing smack of Hull - assisted.
November	24	1879	Patience, Billy Boy schooner of Goole - assisted.
February	20	1880	Rose and Polly, fishing smack of Grimsby - assisted.
March	1	1880	Albion, Billy Boy schooner of Barton - assisted.
May	12	1880	Annie, Billy Boy schooner of Grimsby - went to assist - not required.
June	26	1880	Johanne-Marie, Norwegian sloop - assisted.
August	9	1880	Bull Light Ship - assisted after a fishing smack collided.
October	21	1880	Loch Tyne, fishing smack of Hull - assisted.
October	29	1880	Oimara, trawling smack of Grimsby - assisted.

January	17	1881	Un-named fishing smack - warned off with rockets.
February	7	1881	Loyal, fishing smack of Hull - saved crew of four and assisted.
February	10	1881	Premier, smack of Hull - assisted - crew saved in their own boat.
February	14	1881	Lord Exmouth, brigantine of Lowestoft - saved crew of four and assisted.
March	5	1881	Linden, steamer of London - went to assist - not required.
May	21	1881	Sarah, sloop of Hull - assisted and took off crew of five.
June	11	1881	Ben Ledi, fishing smack of Grimsby - assisted and took off crew of five.
August	12	1881	Celerity, steam cutter of Grimsby - went to assist - not required.
October	5	1881	Star of Peace, trawling smack of Hull - stood by.
October	16	1881	Dare, brigantine of Sunderland - assisted and took off crew of six.
October	19	1881	Henrich and Emil, brig of Rostock - went to assist - could not.
October	20	1881	Agile, fishing smack of Grimsby - took off crew of five - stood by.
October	22	1881	Mary Jenny, fishing smack of Grimsby - went to assist - not required.
October	27	1881	Emerald, fishing smack of Hull - went to assist - not required.
November	4	1881	Mary, smack of Grimsby - assisted.
December	6	1881	Collina, brigantine of Faversham - assisted.
December	11	1881	George Avery, fishing smack of Hull - saved crew of six - assisted - later returned crew.
February	11	1882	Caterina Schiaffina, Italian barque - assisted.
August	26	1882	Vulcan, brigantine of Hull - went to assist - not required.
October	25	1882	Silver Cloud, whelk smack of Grimsby - assisted.
November	3	1882	Nicholas Smith, brig of Hartlepool - saved crew of six - assisted.
November	7	1882	Irene, schooner of Hull - took off crew of five - assisted - later returned crew.
November	9	1882	Madoria, smack of Cleethorpes - wreckage washed up.
November	21	1882	Ocean Monarch, smack of Lowestoft - lay by and assisted.
November	21	1882	Un-named smack of Hull - went to assist - not required.
December	2	1882	Forester, smack of Grimsby - went to assist - unable to do so - crew saved in their own boat.

December	7	1882	James Southern, steamer of London - lay by.
December	18	1882	Mary Anne, cod smack of Grimsby - saved crew of twelve.
January	28	1883	Medea, brig of Poole - assisted.
February	15	1883	Enchanter, barque of Grimsby - lay by and assisted.
March	6	1883	Young Mechanic, trawling smack of Grimsby - saved crew of five and assisted.
May	28	1883	Dew Drop, ketch of Guernsey - went to assist - not required.
October	4	1883	Foriningen, Barque of Lyschil - saved crew of nine and assisted.
October	6	1883	Empress,steamer of Hull, on fire - assisted - crew saved in their own boats and tugs.
October	16	1883	Samland, steamer of Konigsburg - went to assist - not required because steam tugs arrived first.
December	1	1883	Un-named Scottish fishing smack - went to assist - not required.
December	7	1883	Un-named vessel - went to assist - beaten back by tide and wind - vessel later towed in by tug.
December	15	1883	Margaret, schooner of Caernarvon - assisted into Grimsby.
December	18	1883	C.M.Norwood, of Hull - stood by with Tender - vessel broke up and all hands (five) lost because Life Boat was still missing.
January	22	1884	Cicerone, schooner of Falmouth - saved crew of six and assisted.
September	13	1884	Joseph and Francis, smack of Hull - went to assist - not required.
November	12	1884	Specimen, smack of Hull - lay by and assisted.
November	15	1884	Chesterfield, sloop of Lynn - tried to save vessel but failed - crew saved in their own boat.
December	1	1884	Virgin, schooner of Caernarvon - took off three men - lay by and assisted.
December	21	1884	Muriel, smack of Hull - assisted.
December	24	1884	Athenian, barque of Grimsby - lay by vessel.
December	25	1884	Hesleyside, steamer of Newcastle - lay by vessel.
January	19	1885	Gladstone, smack of Grimsby - assisted.
July	17	1885	Sedgemoor, steamer - went to assist - not required.
August	30	1885	Waverley, steamer of Liverpool - went to assist - not required.
September	28	1885	Amity, cod smack of Grimsby - went to assist - not required.

October	16	1885	Nordstjensen, Norwegian brig - saved crew of eight and assisted.
November	26	1885	Star of Peace, smack of Hull - went to assist - not required.
November	26	1885	Alma, cod smack of Grimsby - went to assist - not required.
December	8	1885	Un-named vessel - went to assist - not required.
December	22	1885	Abuklea, small steamer of Blakeney - assisted off the Binks.
January	14	1886	Pansy, smack of Grimsby - saved crew of five and assisted.
January	18	1886	Albert, fishing smack of Hull - went to assist - assistance refused.
January	18	1886	Szapary, steamer - lay by vessel.
January	22	1886	Marie, German barque of Rostock - saved crew of eleven and assisted.
February	10	1886	Climat, smack of Grimsby - assisted.
February	15	1886	Ryemerchant, schooner of Rye - could not assist - already sunk.
March	2	1886	Southern Belle, barge of London - assisted.
March	6	1886	Humber, smack of Grimsby - saved crew of five.
October	26	1886	Leo, fish cutter of Grimsby - went to assist - not required.
December	14	1886	Yorkshire Lass, trawling smack of Hull - went to assist - lay by vessel.
December	20	1886	Gertrude, steamer of Middlesbrough - lay by vessel.
January	27	1887	Carl Christoph, brigantine of Russia - went to assist - not required.
February	28	1887	Ariel, HMS Gunboat - went to assist - not required.
March	10	1887	Thomas and Charlotte, smack of Grimsby - went to assist - not required.
			Othello, smack of Hull - went to assist - not required.
May	13	1887	Hanna, barquentine of Arendal, Norway - saved crew of nine and one Humber Pilot.
September	10	1887	Guide, schooner of Weymouth - went to assist - not required.
September	20	1887	Mona, pilot cutter No 7 - went to assist - not required.
November	2	1887	Conquest, smack of Grimsby - went to assist - not required.
January	12	1888	Good and Blanchard, smack of Hull - assisted - crew had already abandoned.
January	26	1888	Bull Light Ship - broke from moorings - assisted.

January	29	1888	Lawrina, smack of Hull - saved crew of five.
February	14	1888	Winifred, schooner of London - saved crew of five
June	17	1888	Argo, smack of Grimsby - went to assist - not required.
September	8	1888	Perfect, smack of Grimsby - lay by vessel.
			Buttercup, herring lugger of Lowestoft - lay by vessel.
October	5	1888	Un-named smack - went to assist - not required.
November	3	1888	Swift, brig of Shoreham - saved crew of eight.
November	14	1888	Un-named smack - went to assist - not required.
December	15	1888	L'Avenir, smack of Grimsby - went to assist - not required.
February	9	1889	Arthur, keel of Hull - rescued crew of three and assisted.
March	22	1889	Siloam, brigantine of Faversham - lay by vessel.
April	14	1889	Un-named smack - went to assist - not required.
August	20	1889	Star of the East, coaster of Sunderland - saved crew of two by heaving line.
October	21	1889	Mary and Maria, ketch of Beverley - saved crew of three and assisted.
January	26	1890	Launceston, schooner of Bideford - pumped and assisted.
February	12	1890	Jane, sloop of Lynn - assisted.
February	15	1890	Smelt, cod smack of Grimsby - saved crew of six and assisted.
April	18	1890	Mermaid, whelk smack of Grimsby - saved crew of four and assisted.
April	26	1890	Confidence, trawl smack of Grimsby - went to assist - not required.
November	2	1890	Un-named steam boat - unable to assist.
November	7	1890	Vacuna, ketch of Bideford - saved crew of three.
December	12	1890	Answered signal gun and rocket - found nothing.
February	20	1891	Henry Freeman, smack of Grimsby - went to assist - not required.
			The Brothers, yawl of Filey - went to assist - not required.
February	27	1891	Alert, steam boat of Hull - went to assist - not required.
October	13	1891	Petrel, trawling smack of Grimsby - saved crew of six.
November	11	1891	Caroline, schooner of London - saved crew of four and assisted.
November	28	1891	John Fildes, cod smack of Grimsby - saved crew of seven and assisted.
January	17	1892	Pride of Essex, smack of Harwich - assisted - crew of ten saved by Bull Light Ship and then put on Life Boat.

January	19	1892	Florence Laurina, of Grimsby - went to assist but vessel had got off.
January	23	1892	Agra, trawl smack of Grimsby - assisted.
January	29	1892	Two Friends, brigantine of Guernsey - assisted.
April	18	1892	Esmaralda, smack of Grimsby - went to assist - unable to do so.
August	17	1892	Vindomora, steamer of London - went to assist - not required.
October	14	1892	Albert, barque of Finland - went to assist - ship already wrecked and crew safe.
November	12	1892	Boldero, smack of Grimsby - went to assist - not required.
			Tommy Cambell, smack of Grimsby - went to assist - not required.
November	14	1892	Caroline, steamer of London - went to assist - not required.
January	13	1893	Specimen, trawl smack of Grimsby - assisted - crew had already abandoned.
February	8	1893	Try-on, Billy Boy schooner of Goole - went to assist - not required - chose tug instead.
March	4	1893	Laura Ann, schooner of Yarmouth - assisted.
April	10	1893	Thornback, smack of Hull - assisted.
November	20	1893	Un-named ship - went to assist - ship had floated before Life Boat arrived.
December	20	1893	Mary Louise, schooner of Brixham - saved crew of six - became a wreck.
January	15	1894	Harrold, smack of Hull - went to assist - not required.
February	23	1894	Bull Light Ship had been hit in collision - assisted.
March	29	1894	Invicta, fishing smack of Hull - assisted.
March	30	1894	Chaster, steamer of Grimsby - went to assist - not required.
May	15	1894	Albina, schooner of Goole - went to assist - not required.
August	16	1894	Result, herring lugger of Lowestoft - took off part of crew and assisted.
			Valkyrie, herring lugger of Lowestoft - saved crew of nine.
August	17	1894	Fern Brook, steamer of Middlesbrough - went to assist - not required.
November	4	1894	Jane Knox, schooner of Goole - went to assist - assistance refused.
March	24	1895	Eagle, brigantine of Yarmouth - assisted.
December	17	1895	Un-named steamer - went to assist - not required.

January	16	1896	Achievement, trawl smack of Grimsby - saved crew of five and assisted.
January	27	1896	Demaris, schooner of Teignmouth - went to assist - not required.
February	14	1896	Francis Ann, sloop of Goole - assisted.
November	17	1896	Alfred and Henry, oyster dredger of Grimsby - saved crew of six and assisted.
January	9	1897	Chanticleer, trawl smack of Grimsby - went to assist - vessel had sunk and crew left.
January	22	1897	Moonlight, steam barge of Hull - saved crew of three and assisted.
March	3	1897	Amy, barge of Harwich - saved three of crew and assisted.
March	20	1897	Bull Light Ship - assisted to restore it to position.
June	18	1897	Zingara, trawl smack of Grimsby - went to assist - assistance refused.
January	3	1898	Un-named smack - went to assist - not required - tug arrived first.
January	4	1898	City of Glasgow, steam trawler of Hull - assisted
February	12	1898	Promise, sloop of Hull - assisted.
April	6	1898	Un-named steam trawler - went to assist - not required.
September	6	1898	Fannia, steamer of Russia - went to assist - vessel towed off before Life Boat arrived.
October	17	1898	Bull Light Ship - assisted in returning it to station, having broken loose.
January	12	1899	Jane, sloop of Lynn - assisted.
January	14	1899	Amy, steam fishing boat of Grimsby - assisted off the beach.
September	29	1899	Atlantic, steam trawler of Hull - went to assist - not required - later assisted off beach and to Hull.
October	5	1899	Promise, sloop - assisted.
November	5	1899	Un-named vessel - went to assist - not required - vessel floated off.
December	5	1899	Francis Ann, sloop of Goole - assisted.
			Horncastle, sloop of Hull - saved crew of two and assisted.
January	1	1900	Eddystone, steam trawler of Hull - assisted.
January	7	1900	Demaris, schooner of Goole - saved crew of five and assisted.
			Experiment, lighter - saved crew of four and assisted.

September	17	1900	Retriever, steam trawler of Hull - went to assist not required.
			Danube, steam trawler of Hull - went to assist - not required.
November	7	1900	SS Salmo, of Hull - went to assist - not required.
December	20	1900	Lord Kitchener, steam trawler of Hull - saved crew of three and assisted.
March	19	1901	Un-named vessel - went to assist - could not find vessel - assumed proceeded.
October	26	1901	Excelsior, steam trawler of Hull - assisted.
October	30	1901	Hercules, steam trawler of Grimsby - went to assist - vessel floated off before Life Boat arrived.
November	22	1901	Sultan, ketch of Yarmouth - went to assist - arrived too late.
November	23	1901	Bull Light Ship (collided -Calcutta - steam trawler of Hull) assisted.
November	24	1901	Celerity, steam ship of London (Middle Light Ship) collided - went to assist - not required.
November	26	1901	Bull Light Ship) - collided - went to assist - Un-named lighter) not required.
December	5	1901	Bull Light Ship - assisted with the moorings and mooring Light Ship.
March	26	1902	Mosquito, steam trawler of Hull - went to assist - not required.
April	5	1902	Un-named steam trawler - went to assist - arrived too late.
September	22	1902	Doris, steam drifter of Lowestoft Venus, lugger of Yarmouth Both collided -went to assist - not required.
September	22	1902	Rugby, steam trawler of Grimsby Lady Primrose, herring lugger of Banff Both collided went to assist - not required.
September	28	1902	Aquila, schooner of Goole - saved crew of three - vessel sank.
November	21	1902	Olympia, barge of Faversham - assisted.
November	26	1902	Yorkshire, steam trawler of Hull - assisted.
January	21	1903	Riversdale, steam trawler of Grimsby - went to assist - not required.
February	27	1903	Marguerite Molinos, barque of Le Havre - assisted after difficulties and accident.
May	23	1903	Saved two seamen, drunk, from drowning off beach.
September	4	1903	Un-named steam ship - went to assist - not required.

October	28	1903	Argo, steam liner of Hull - went to assist - not required.
November	28	1903	Estoile, ketch of Grimsby - saved crew of four - vessel wrecked.
April	6	1904	Diana, barge of Rye - assisted.
December	30	1904	Olive Branch, sailing smack of Grimsby - assisted.
January	28	1905	Un-named steamer - went to assist - boat got off before Life Boat arrived.
February	1	1905	SS Player, of Teignmouth - went to assist - not required.
February	21	1905	Bull Light Ship - went to assist - not required.
March	23	1905	Enterprise, sloop of Hull - assisted.
December	1	1905	Bloodhound, steam trawler of Hull - assisted.
December	1	1905	Italy, steam trawler of Grimsby - went to assist - not required.
December	9	1905	Knot, steam trawler of Hull (Bull Light Ship) collided - assisted Light Ship - trawler required no assistance.
December	29	1905	Orlando, steamer of Sweden - went to assist - not required.
January	20	1906	British Hero, sloop of Hull - saved crew of two and assisted.
January	27	1906	Lord Alcester, barge of London - went to assist - not required.
April	6	1906	Joseph Rickett, steam ship of London - went to assist - not required.
April	12	1906	Temple, steam ship of London - went to assist - not required.
September	17	1906	Un-named vessel - went to assist - not required.
October	18	1906	Bull Light Ship - assisted.
November	15	1906	Columbia, fishing boat of Grimsby - saved one of crew.
December	8	1906	Quail, steam trawler of Hull - assisted.
December	12	1906	Dagmar, brigantine of Faversham - went to assist - not required.
February	6	1907	Providence, sloop of Hull (Liberty, sloop of Hull) collided - saved.crew of two of Liberty and assisted.
February	24	1907	Young Tom, ketch of London - went to assist - needed doctor.
February	27	1907	Chesterfield, sloop of Grimsby - saved crew of two and assisted.
April	11	1907	Hilding, brig of Bergen - saved seven of crew and assisted.
June	1	1907	Admiral, crabbing boat of Grimsby - assisted.

July	19	1907	Ethel, sailing yacht of Hull - saved crew of two and assisted.
July	30	1907	Woodlark, sloop of Grimsby - went to assist - not required.
September	12	1907	Africa, steam ship of Goole - went to assist - assistance refused.
September	12	1907	Early Morn, steam herring drifter of Lowestoft - went to assist - assistance not required.
September	10	1908	Bull Light Ship - assisted.
March	23	1909	SS Nidaros. of Esbjerg - outward bound from Grimsby - stranded on Point - proceeded with Tender - floated off without assistance.
October	31	1909	Bull Light Ship drifting up river after being collided with by"Orinoco" - assisted to get Light Ship anchor down.
December	22	1909	SS John bound from Middlesbrough - cargo of chemical salts - stranded off Dimlington - eight lives saved - vessel sunk.
December	2	1910	Un-named vessel - went to assist - not required as Donna Nook Life Boat arrived on scene.

Whilst remembering that the documentary evidence is far from complete and that there must have been many services for which no records now exist, the following can be authenticated.

Number of service launches	540
Number of times an entire crew was saved, without starting the number of people involved	30
Number of other lives saved	760

STEAM ASSISTANCE

September	14	1830	Steamer Prince Frederick towed out Life Boat to Ann, of Shields.
September	19	1852	Tug Peep a Day Boy assisted Life Boat by towing schooner Liberty, of Leith, off the Banks.
July	22	1858	Steamer assisted Life Boat by towing brig Wansbeck to Grimsby.
November	7	1859	Tug engaged to tow schooner Rebecca and Elizabeth to Grimsby.
February	18	1861	Tug James Watt came to tow schooner - schooner got off before tug arrived.
November	2	1861	Tug Hotspur, of Hull, came ashore and completely smashed in gale.
January	29	1862	Un-named steamer towed wreck of brig, Heroine, to Grimsby.
December	9	1863	Tug towed sloop, Neptune, to Hull.
December	26	1863	Tug Pilot towed the dismasted ship Levant to Grimsby.
March	6	1864	Tug from Hull assisted and later towed schooner, Rose, to Grimsby.
November	30	1867	Tug towed the sloop, Baltic, into Grimsby for the Life Boat.
January	31	1868	Tug took the crew of the barque, Echo, to Grimsby for the Life Boat.
June	19	1874	Tug Charm towed out the Life Boat to the brig Victory, of Hull, and towed the brig to Hull.
December	7	1874	Tug assisted Life Boat and towed the smack Harriett to Grimsby.
November	14	1875	Tug towed un-named ship to Grimsby for Life Boat.
December	15	1875	Two tugs towed the large steamer, Golden Horn, off the Binks.
February	4	1876	Tug took crew of smack, Undaunted, to Grimsby.
April	13	1876	Tug Victor towed out Life Boat to a ship - ship sank before Life Boat arrived.
August	17	1876	Two tugs assisted Life Boat to tow off Norwegian barque, Constantia, near Kilnsea.
April	8	1878	Tug Goole No 3 towed smack, Earnest, to Hull and assisted Life Boat.
November	1	1878	Tug Wilberforce towed brigantine, Neptune, to Grimsby.
April	27	1879	Three tugs towed Norwegian brig, Diamantia, off the beach after the Life Boat could not do so.

March	1	1880	Tug Samson towed billy boy schooner, Albion, to Grimsby for Life Boat.
May	12	1880	Tug Spurn towed billy boy schooner, Annie, to Grimsby.
October	21	1880	Tug James Watt assisted Life Boat to float Loch Tyne, of Hull.
October	29	1880	Steam Boat Charm assisted Life Boat and towed fishing smack, Oimara, to Grimsby.
February	7	1881	Tugs Samson and Garibaldi assisted Life Boat and towed smack, Loyal, to Grimsby.
February	10	1881	Tugs Charm and Garibaldi assisted Life Boat to pull the smack, Premier, off the beach near Kilnsea Beacon.
March	5	1881	Tug Victor, of Grimsby, towed out Life Boat to steamer, Linden, and assisted.
June	11	1881	Tug assisted Life Boat with fishing smack, Ben Ledi, of Grimsby, and later towed her to Grimsby.
November	4	1881	Tug Champion assisted Life Boat to tow smack Mary of Grimsby, off the beach and to Grimsby.
December	6	1881	Tug assisted Life Boat to pull brigantine, Collina, off the Inner Binks and tow her to Grimsby.
February	11	1882	Tug Humber assisted Life Boat and towed Italian barque, Caterina Schiaffina, into Grimsby.
November	4	1882	Tug Humber assisted Life Boat to tow brig, Nicholas Smith, to Grimsby.
December	19	1882	Steam Boat Lorne, of Hull, towed Life Boat out of Humber to go to help cod smack, Mary Ann, of Grimsby and save crew.
January	28	1883	Tug Humber assisted Life Boat with brig, Medea, and helped to tow her to Grimsby.
February	15	1883	Tug Liverpool assisted Life Boat to tow barque, Enchanter, off the Inner Binks and then to Hull.
March	6	1883	Tug Samson assisted Life Boat to pull Grimsby smack, Young Mechanic, off the beach and helped to tow her to Grimsby.
October	5	1883	Tug Champion assisted Life Boat to tow barque Foringen, to Grimsby after rescue.
October	8	1883	Tug Flying Scud assisted Life Boat with steamer, Empress of Hull, on fire, and took some passengers to Hull.
December	18	1883	Tug May assisted Life Boat Tender with disabled vessel, C.M.Norwood, of Hull, but in vain.
December	23	1884	Steamer Active, of Hull, assisted Life Boat and towed smack, Muriel, to Hull.

December	24	1884	Three tugs assisted Life Boat with barque, Athenian, of Grimsby, and towed her off Inner Binks.
January	20	1885	Tug United assisted Life Boat by towing smack, Gladstone, onto Binks to prevent sinking and later towed her to Grimsby.
October	21	1885	Tugs Champion and Victor assisted Life Boat to pull Norwegian brig, Nordstjernen, off Inner Binks and then took her to Hull.
November	26	1885	Tug Ayr, of Newcastle, towed out Life Boat to assist Hull smack, Star of Peace.
January	19	1886	Tugs Champion and Victor assisted Life Boat and towed off steamer, Szapary, and then towed her to Grimsby.
January	23	1886	Tugs Liverpool and May assisted Life Boat with German barque, Marie, - towed her to Grimsby and then Liverpool towed Life Boat back to Spurn.
May	13	1887	Tug Conqueror assisted Life Boat when she transferred crew of Norwegian barquentine, Hanna, as Life Boat was over-loaded and took them to Spurn
November	2	1887	Tug Humber assisted Life Boat and towed off trawl smack, Conquest, of Grimsby from Bull Sand and towed her to Grimsby.
January	13	1888	Tug Humber assisted Life Boat to pull smack, Good and Blanchard, from beach and then took her to Grimsby.
January	26	1888	Tug Champion towed and assisted Life Boat when Bull Light Ship was driven from her station.
February	15	1888	Tug may assisted Life Boat by towing schooner, Winifred, to Grimsby.
November	3	1888	Tug Gipsy King assisted Life Boat with the brig, Swift, of Shoreham, and then towed her to Grimsby.
December	29	1888	Tug Champion assisted Life Boat and towed off Grimsby smack, Accord, and then towed her to Grimsby.
February	9	1889	Tug Humber assisted Life Boat and towed the keel, Arthur, of Hull into the Humber and sank her on Trinity Sand.
January	26	1890	Tug 'Steam Boat' assisted Life Boat by taking schooner Launceston, of Bideford, to Grimsby after rescue and pumping.
November	12	1891	Tug Humber assisted Life Boat with schooner Caroline, of London, towed her off Trinity Sand and to Grimsby. Mr.Twiner owns tug.

January	19	1892	Tug Lady Bute towed out Life Boat to smack Florence Lauria.
January	30	1892	Tug Humber assisted Life Boat to get brigantine Two Friends off beach and to Grimsby.
April	19	1892	Tug Humber towed Life Boat to smack Esmaralda.
October	14	1892	Tug Champion - owner Mr.Oates of Grimsby - towed Life Boat to a reported barque on Haile Sand - nothing found.
February	8	1893	Tug Humber assisted Life Boat to tow off Billy Boy schooner Try-on from Trinity Sand.
March	4	1893	Tug Lady Bute towed out Life Boat to Binks to schooner Laura Ann and assisted Life Boat to get schooner to Grimsby.
March	30	1894	Tug Marple, of Grimsby, towed steamer Chester from the Binks after Life Boat assistance had been declined.
November	4	1894	Tugs towed Jane Knox from the Binks after Life Boat assistance had been refused.
March	24	1895	Tug Champion assisted Life Boat to take brigantine Eagle off the mud to Grimsby Roads after Life Boat had pumped her dry.
January	27	1896	Tug Gipsy King towed off schooner Demaris from Binks after Life Boat assistance not required.
January	31	1896	Tug Champion, of Grimsby, towed smack Achievement off the Point after Life Boat had assisted.
February	14	1896	Tug Gipsy King, of Grimsby, towed gravel sloop Francis Ann from the Binks.
January	23	1897	Tug Pendragon, of Grimsby, towed steam barge Moonlight, of Hull, to Grimsby after Life Boat had saved crew.
March	5	1897	Tug Pole Star, of Grimsby, towed barge Amy, of Harwich, to Grimsby after Life Boat had taken off crew and pumped vessel dry.
June	19	1897	Tug Alice, of Grimsby, towed off trawl smack Zingara, of Grimsby, after it went aground on Trinity Sand and refused Life Boat assistance.
January	4	1898	Tug Champion towed a smack off the Inner Binks just as Life Boat arrived.
January	6	1898	Tugs Humber and William towed the steam trawler City of Glasgow to Hull after Life Boat got her off the beach at Kilnsea.

September	6	1898	Steam trawler and two tugs, all of Grimsby, towed the Russian steamer Finnia off the beach North of Spurn as Life Boat arrived. Life Boat salvaged deck cargo which had been thrown overboard.
January	14	1899	Sloop Jane, of Lynn, was pulled off the beach inside Spurn by Life Boat, was pumped out, then towed to Grimsby by Tug Humber.
September	30	1899	Tug Frenchman, of Hull, towed Life Boat to steam trawler Atlantic stranded on beach North of Spurn - crew landed by coastguards.
October	2	1899	Life Boat and tugs Scotchman and Frenchman towed trawler Atlantic off the beach and took her to Hull.
December	6	1899	Sloops Horncastle and Francis Ann both in difficulty on the Binks after loading gravel - Life Boat assisted and engaged tugs to tow them into the Humber.
January	6	1900	Tug Solway towed the lighter Experiment from the Inner Binks into the Humber after lifeboat had taken off the crew.
October	30	1901	Tug Chester towed lifeboat to steam trawler Hercules, of Grimsby, stranded on Inner Binks. Vessel floated off as lifeboat arrived.
October	29	1902	Lifeboat and tug Humber, of Grimsby, assisted barquentine WW Lloyd, of Guernsey, off the beach at Kilnsea.
November	22	1902	Tug Humber assisted lifeboat to take barge Olympia of Faversham, to Grimsby after lifeboat crew had put out fire in cargo of coal and then pumped her dry.
November	27	1902	Lifeboat assisted by tugs got the steam trawler Yorkshire, of Hull, off the beach at Kilnsea and assisted her to Hull.
January	22	1903	Tug towed steam trawler Riversdale, of Grimsby, off the Binks after lifeboat assistance was not required.
February	27	1903	French barque Marguerite Molines pulled off Trinity Sand by three tugs and lifeboat, after lifeboat assisted vessel, and taken to safe anchorage in Grimsby Roads.
October	31	1903	Wilson Line Argo towed off Inner Binks by four tugs after lifeboat assistance declined.
April	2	1904	Lifeboat and tug Solway pulled barge Diana, of Rye, off the Inner Binks and assisted her to Grimsby.

May	14	1904	Sailing yacht towed off Inner Binks by tug Humber of Grimsby.
December	7	1904	Steam trawler towed off Inner Binks by tug after lifeboat assistance not required.
January	6	1905	Sailing smack Olive Branch, of Grimsby, towed off beach at Spurn by tug after stranding on December 30th 1904.
December	1	1905	Tug JW Jewitt, of Grimsby, assisted lifeboat to pull steam trawler Bloodhound, of Hull, off the Inner Binks after lifeboat assisted.
January	23	1906	Tug Solway, of Grimsby, assisted lifeboat to refloat sloop British Hero, of Hull, and tow her to Hull after she stranded on the Point and was assisted by lifeboat on the previous day.
September	17	1906	Tug Englishman towed lifeboat to a vessel ashore on Lincolnshire Main.
September	21	1906	SS Pine Branch towed lifeboat off beach at Kilnsea Warren after stranding the previous day.
December	10	1906	Tug Humber towed steam trawler Quail, of Hull, off Inner Binks and to Hull after lifeboat had assisted.
December	12	1906	Tug JW Jewitt, of Grimsby, towed the brigantine Dagmar, of Faversham, off the Trinity Sand after refusing lifeboat assistance.
February	6	1907	Tug Pioneer, of Hull, assisted lifeboat to tow sloop Providence, of Hull, off the Binks and to safety in the Humber.
February	24	1907	Lifeboat assisted ketch Young Tom, of London, then tug JW Jewitt, of Grimsby, towed the ketch to Grimsby as the Mate required medical attention.
April	13	1907	Tug Chester towed out lifeboat to assist Brig Hilding, of Bergen, aground on the Middle Binks.
September	12	1907	SS Africa stranded on beach near lighthouse - refused all assistance - owners sent tugs from Goole to pull her off.
January	11	1908	Tug Winchester and Humber Conservancy Yacht towed Bull Lightship to station after lifeboat rescued her.
December	2	1910	Tug Solway, of Grimsby, towed lifeboat back to Spurn after lifeboat had gone to assistance of un-named ship near Tetney.